Successful Projects

DEDICATION

To dear Geetika

who arrived in this world just as we put the finishing touches to this book

who is too young to realise what it is all about and so smiles at the world as if it is her oyster

who, more than anybody else, does not understand why grandparents can have anything else to do

who is too young to realise what this is all about, but may cherish it in due course.

THE AUTHORS

After three decades in teaching and industry in the USA, the UK and India **Dr O P Kharbanda** now runs his own consultancy advising clients in many parts of the world and across a wide range of industries. He is a Fellow of the Institution of Chemical Engineers, a Visiting Professor, and regular leader of seminars on corporate planning, cost estimating, project management and communication skills. Dr Kharbanda has published or contributed to eight books and more than 150 papers in scientific and technical journals.

Ernest A Stallworthy has for many years been a management consultant with his own company, Dolphin Project Management Services. He was previously a manager responsible for the cost control of large-scale projects in the petrochemical industry. He is a Fellow of the Association of Cost Engineers and a member of the American Association of Cost Engineers. Mr Stallworthy is co-author (with O P Kharbanda and L F Williams) of *Project Cost Control in Action* and (with Dr Kharbanda) of *How to learn from Project Disasters, Total Project Management, International Construction* and *Management Disasters* – all published by Gower.

Successful Projects

with a moral for management

O. P. Kharbanda
E. A. Stallworthy

Gower

© O. P. Kharbanda and E. A. Stallworthy, 1986

All rights reserved. No part of this publication may be reproduced, stored in a retrieval system, or transmitted in any form or by any means, electronic, mechanical, photocopying, recording, or otherwise without the prior permission of Gower Publishing Company Limited.

Published by Gower Publishing Company Limited,
Gower House, Croft Road, Aldershot,
Hants GU11 3HR, England

British Library Cataloguing in Publication Data

Kharbanda, O. P.
  Successful projects: with a moral for management
  1. Industrial project management – Case studies
  I. Title   II. Stallworthy, E. A.
  658.4′04′0722   HD69.P75

ISBN 0-566-02651-1

Printed in Great Britain at the
University Press, Cambridge

Contents

	Page
List of illustrations	xi
Preface	xiii
Acknowledgements	xvii

PART ONE   SETTING THE SCENE
1 There must be a plan	**3**
Corporate planning	3
Project definition	4
The project plan	8
Project organisation	11
The managing contractor	12
The 'top ten'	13
The planning constraints	16
Summary	17
References	18
2 Project cost control	**19**
Project control	20
Effective project cost control	20
The role of the capital cost estimate	21
The use of contingency	23
Escalation and the impact of inflation	24
Cost coding as a management tool	25
Administrative procedures	26
Commitment control	27
Value of work done	28
Cost control and planning	30

Type of contract	33
The irrelevance of the expenditure record	34
Summary	34
References	35

3 Prediction – perhaps!	**36**
The failing company	36
Projects and project management	38
The road to success	39
Early warning signals	42
The pre-emptive audit	43
Success – by design!	44
Summary	48
References	48

4 Management determines success	**49**
Construction management	50
What is success?	52
The elements of success	54
The role of communications	56
References	58

PART TWO   THERE IS STRENGTH IN COOPERATION

5 Motivate and succeed	**61**
Nationwide cooperation	62
Now the robot	63
The factory of the future	66
Let's get back to basics	67
Summary	69
References	69

6 Success – through international cooperation	**71**
The Sasol projects	72
Engineering in South Africa	74
Initiating the project	76
The process complexities	77
Project execution	78
Project cost control	79
The lessons	82
Summary	83
References	83

7 Cancel and succeed!	**85**
The 'point of no return'	86

The feasibility study	87
On budget, on schedule	88
Project financing	89
Now we go cross country	90
Problems met and overcome	92
Project management *is* cost control	93
Summary	93
References	94

PART THREE THE DEVELOPED COUNTRIES LEAD THE WAY

8 A team can work wonders!	**97**
The historical background	97
Efficient communication works wonders	99
The measure of success	100
The project team concept	101
Little by little	102
Summary	103
References	103
9 Success – even with nuclear plants!	**105**
A sorry story	106
Man bites dog	107
The road to success	108
But success brings its problems!	109
Management the crux	109
References	110
10 Listen to learn	**112**
The background	112
The project centre concept	114
The strength of the team	115
The *Fiero* project	117
Intrapreneurship	118
Back to the *Fiero*	119
Independence is the answer	120
Summary	123
References	124
11 Striving for perfection	**125**
A quiet giant	126
Schlumberger	127
The managerial and entrepreneurial spirit	128
Successful motivation	129

The approach to perfection	130
The impact of diversification	131
The secret of success	133
Summary	134
References	135

PART FOUR THE DEVELOPING COUNTRIES FOLLOW

12 A successful project, but . . .	**139**
A project in prospect	139
Advance planning	140
Work starts in earnest	142
Problems galore	143
The finale	144
The aftermath	147
Summary	148
References	148
13 Technology transfer is not easy	**150**
Technology transfer in action	151
It works!	152
Cooperation continues	153
The Asahan project	153
The financial agreement	155
The benefits	158
Summary	159
References	160
14 Joint ventures in China	**161**
China is changing	162
Growing cooperation	163
China takes time and patience	164
The move to joint ventures	166
The social scene	168
Summary	170
References	170

PART FIVE CONQUERING REMOTE AREAS

15 Transport the key to success	**175**
Nothing stays the same	175
Live site working	178
Innovation everywhere	180
Superlatives all the way	183
Looking after the workers	184
The 'sky hook'	184

Summary	186
References	186

16 Coping with the environment 187
Finn-Stroi Limited	187
Kostomuksha	189
A dairy on the permafrost	190
Now we go to the Antarctic	191
The logistics	193
The entrepreneurial spirit	194
Now to the Equator	195
Ok Tedi	196
Moving mountains	198
The innovative spirit	198
A sting in the tail	200
Summary	201
References	202

17 The offshore challenge 203
The role of the North Sea	203
Continuing development	207
Now we go to Norway	208
The emplacement	210
Summary	211
References	213

PART SIX WORKING FOR SUCCESS

18 Management remains the crux 217
Coping with crisis	217
Dreadful news!	218
The chairman becomes project manager	218
Resolving the crisis	219
Success the result	220
Making joint ventures work	221
Bridging the cultural gap	223
The role of the expatriate	223
A word of advice	227
References	227

19 The project team must team up 229
The project manager	230
The client-contractor relationship	232
Project team organisation	233
Keep it simple	235

Getting the best out of people	236
The principle of delegation	237
When is a team really a team?	238
Management information and reports	239
The spirit of cooperation	240
A case in point	241
Summary	243
References	243
20 Prevention is better than cure	**245**
The road to success	246
Continuing innovation	248
Take the time	249
Scope changes	252
The human condition	252
Ever learning	253
References	256
Index	**257**

Illustrations

Figure		Page
1.1	Manpower versus time	6
1.2	Progress per project phase	7
1.3	Construction manpower	9
1.4	The basic relationship	10
1.5	Annual turnover	14
1.6	Internal organisation chart	16
2.1	The cost of accuracy	22
2.2	Capital cost estimates – trend	23
2.3	Value of work done versus expenditure	29
2.4	A data access system	31
2.5	Which type of contract?	33
3.1	Cost control potential	41
3.2	Project development	47
4.1	The tug-of-war	53
6.1	Sasol Two in operation	73
6.2	Engineering contractors on Sasol Two	73
6.3	Gasification section – synfuels production	74
6.4	Organigram – Richards Bay Minerals Project	78
6.5	Bid analysis form	80
7.1	Nigeria	91
7.2	Project management on the gas pipeline	92
8.1	IBM and the competition	99
9.1	Regulations	106
10.1	The *Fiero* at speed	121
12.1	The Kudremukh Iron Ore Project	146
13.1	Project locations – Indonesia	154
13.2	Investment in the Asahan Project	157
14.1	Ammonia and urea plants in China	165
14.2	A typical installation	169
15.1	Specification – the *Happy Buccaneer*	177

ILLUSTRATIONS

15.2 The *Happy Buccaneer*	178
15.3 The latest modular transporter	179
15.4 A vacuum column on the road	181
15.5 Derrick Barge 102	183
15.6 Bechtel's heavy-lift crane in action	185
16.1 Kostomuksha	188
16.2 The Falkland Islands	192
16.3 The jettyhead at East Cove	194
16.4 Papua New Guinea	196
16.5 The Fly River	197
17.1 Typical offshore development elements	206
17.2 Towout of the Statfjord 'B' GBS	211
17.3 Statfjord 'B' after deckmating	212
18.1 Fertiliser plant at Qatar	224
19.1 Typical construction site organisation	234
20.1 Consumption of primary fuels in the UK	245
20.2 UK offshore oil production	247
20.3 Concrete innovation	250
20.4 A design detail	251
20.5 A diagram to think about	254

Preface

Project management and particularly its most vital element, project cost control, has been a theme of ours for many years. We learn by experience and we learn most from our own mistakes. It is a trite saying indeed, that the person who never made a mistake never made anything. If we learn not only from our own mistakes but from the mistakes of others, and so avoid some of these, then we are wise indeed.

In demonstrating the mistakes made in project management we have always taken specific projects as case studies and analysed them. Till now, the great majority of our case studies, though by no means all, have been project disasters, where the mistakes that have been made are very apparent – at least in retrospect. This enables us to learn from the mistakes that others have made.

The tendency is to avoid discussion of one's failures and it is true that 'failed', 'bankrupt', 'broke' and 'bust' are not pleasant words. Yet they are a reality in the corporate world and the number of company failures worldwide has been increasing so fast as to justify its being called a growth industry. For these reasons we have written not only about the art of project management but also at length and in detail about project and management disasters and corporate failure.* We have done this with a view to learning how such tragedies can be prevented – and that is the first step on the road to success.

However, the majority of projects are completed *reasonably* successfully and some *very* successfully. Yet, whilst one would have thought that such a subject would be an attractive one to study, we are not aware of any book that has made a serious

---

How to learn from Project Disasters and *Management Disasters* (both published by Gower) and *Corporate Failure* (published by McGraw-Hill).

analysis of a series of successful *projects* in order to learn the lessons, establishing just how it was done. Much has been written about success in management – excellence is a word often used in this context – but managing a project is very different from managing a company, although there are of course some parallels. Just to give a little indication as to the extent of the explosion in books relating to this subject, the latest edition of the annual *Cumulative Book Index*, which lists all books published in the English language worldwide during a year, lists over a hundred titles relating to success and associated topics – but only ten relating to failure. Yet not one of these is confined to projects, successful or otherwise. Such is the lack of coverage of the subject we have singled out here for study in the hope that we may learn to manage projects ever better.

The project manager develops and grows in experience as he moves from project to project, learning from both his mistakes *and* his successes, so we thought the time had come to analyse a series of outstandingly successful projects, to see if we could discern some of the major elements of success in that particular field. We are also keen to correct any impression that may come as a result of a perusal of our previous work in this area, that we are experts only in 'failure' or 'disaster'.

In selecting the projects for study we have cast our net far and wide. We have sought examples in both the developed and the developing world and for projects of varying size, type and complexity. We have taken our illustrations from industries as different as transport, robotics, computers, energy, mining, automobiles and fertiliser plants. We have also sought to identify the key to success in each case that we study and then by comparison establish common features that can be applied to any and every project. Therein lies the moral for management. Success in project management is *not* a matter of luck or good fortune, although this may help. Success is largely the result of the careful application of the basic rules of project management. If in our earlier works the emphasis was on *how not to do it*, in order to avoid disaster, in this present work we stress *how to do it* to achieve success.

This book is not about the administrative procedures and the practical techniques involved in project management, which we have covered at length elsewhere.* However, since a successful project is the direct result of the successful application of management skills, it is very necessary that we devote some attention to

---

*Project Cost Control in Action and *Total Project Management*, both published by Gower.

the fundamentals of project management. Thus we begin with a section on the basic principles of project management, in Part 1. Then, having taken and analysed a range of successful projects (Parts 2–5), we return to that subject in Part 6 ('Working for Success'), illustrating the lessons that, if learnt, will lead to success. We come to realise that whilst sound management remains crucial, even more crucial is the character and the attributes of the members of the project team. Involve the wrong people in a project and disaster can be at the door.

Having looked at successful projects *worldwide*, it is interesting to see that wherever we go, whatever the culture, traditions or language, the right people are *there*, waiting to be used. This means that in relation to *your* projects the right people are there, waiting to be used. So look for them. A significant part of the art of successful project management, and hence successful projects, lies in choosing the right people for the project you have in mind. It is our hope that this study of the way in which others have been successful will make a real contribution to *your* success.

We have sought to bring a light-handed, if not a light-hearted approach to what is, after all, a very serious subject. Success is enjoyable when it comes, though at times we wonder about that, but we do hope that you will enjoy reading about it.

O.P. KHARBANDA E.A. STALLWORTHY
Bombay Coventry
India United Kingdom

Acknowledgements

We have much pleasure in acknowledging our continuing debt to the multitude of technical writers whose books, papers, articles and the like are published or referred to in the technical journals and the transactions of the various professional bodies, national and international. These have been of great help to us and we have referred to their work wherever possible in the *References* that are listed at the end of each chapter.

We are also indebted to a number of construction companies and industrial firms who have supplied us with data and illustrations, which are acknowledged where they are used. Whilst we have throughout discussed real projects, real owners and real contractors, even venturing to describe the projects upon which they were engaged as 'successes', most of the time, that choice has been purely arbitrary. They may well be typical but they are not representative. Our objective has been to highlight some of the lessons that are to be learned from the experiences of others, and that can only be done effectively using real-life situations. For the same reason we have supported the text with a number of photographs. That, we believe, is the next best thing to visiting the site and seeing such projects in progress.

Our families and particularly our wives, Dorothy and Sudershan, have been pillars of strength, especially when things have been getting difficult – as they do! We all have to realise that success cannot be achieved without meeting problems on the way.

OPK
EAS

Part One
SETTING THE SCENE

1 There must be a plan

We have seen hundreds of projects come and go and that thought brings us straight away to one fundamental truth in relation to any and every project: it has both a beginning *and* an end. It comes, but it also goes. So project management is concerned not merely with starting up a project and getting it going, but also with bringing that project to a successful conclusion. The *end*, as well as the beginning and the duration of a project has to be properly planned. In this there is a marked and essential difference between company management and project management.

Good company management calls for planning, and in that context it is usual to speak of the corporate plan. Since company managers and project managers often have to work together and even exchange roles on occasion, it is useful to examine in some detail the manner and role of corporate planning, so that we can contrast it with project planning.

Corporate planning

The term 'corporate planning' is some twenty years old now, yet there is still considerable confusion as to its real meaning. Whilst it may well involve the assessment of products, markets, production, finance and personnel, it is essentially directed to an assessment of the company, and should be quite simple, consisting of two parts:

> Corporate objectives
> Corporate strategies designed to achieve those objectives

The latter is sometimes called strategic planning and then tends to be confused with corporate planning, but strategic planning is only a part of the whole. There are now some hundreds of books written on the subject, of which those by Argenti and Hussey are typical.(1,2) Despite the time and the resources spent on strategic planning in the USA, the competitive position of a great many companies there has been declining. It is suggested that one reason for this is that strategic planning has become an end in itself, whereas it should only be the *way* and the *means* to an end.(3) The development of a corporate plan, whilst it should be a simple, straightforward exercise, is by no means easy, because:

> The future is unpredictable
> Predictions are subject to large errors
> The decisions reached will be subjective

We wish to highlight the essential differences between corporate planning and project planning and perhaps a simple way to do that is to look briefly at the Argenti System of corporate planning.(4) This is a step-by-step system designed to show the top managers of the smaller and medium-sized companies how to prepare their own corporate plans. They are advised thus:

> To decide your strategies – and these are difficult decisions of enormous importance to the long term health of your company – The Argenti System requires your Planning Team to devote two hours a week (average) for approximately six months: companies employing say 50-200 people should take less: 2000-5000 employees much more, but at the end a set of strategies should be determined and then, except for 'monitoring', no further planning is normally needed for several years.

This approach is vastly different to project planning, because plans are being laid for a long-term, continuing future. By way of contrast, a project is normally short-term (say six months to three years) and is thus of an *ad hoc* nature. We wish to look at the project plan and at the same time compare it with the corporate plan, but first we ought to define what we mean when we speak of a project.

Project definition

The projects we are going to survey are all the same in that they concern the construction of buildings, factories or structures such as bridges and harbours. With some of our case studies we may concentrate our attention more on the product, such as a car or a camera, than the facility that is built to make it, since product development should be a project in itself. We said that all projects had both a beginning and an end – but perhaps these need some elaboration. The phases of a typical project have been said to be, in the order in which they arise:(5)

Conception
Initiation
Study and evaluation
Design development
Detailed design
Contracts and procurement
Manufacture and construction
Commissioning
Operation and maintenance

Whether we are dealing with a factory or a bridge the phase described as 'operation and maintenance' relates to the use of the facility, so that the project is completed once it is commissioned. That is the 'end' so far as we are concerned. But where do we begin? A project is conceived, then studied and evaluated. Study and evaluation will result in estimates of time and cost. It is these estimates of time and cost that give 'shape' to the project and are the basis of a decision to proceed with the project. Of course time and cost are not the only factors leading to the decision to proceed: sometimes they are not even the most important factors. In the private sector the profit motive usually prevails, but in the public sector many, if not most projects are conceived for social-economic reasons rather than just to make a profit. Hence the cost may well be of secondary importance whilst a decision is being reached. Once, however, the decision has been taken, cost may then become of primary importance, inasmuch as a budget sum has to be allocated, which thereafter must not be exceeded.

A project is defined, then, by estimates of time and cost and will begin following a decision to proceed. As that decision is implemented, the project begins to take shape. This can be illustrated graphically, as in Figure 1.1. Here the manpower involved in the project is plotted against time. Whilst the data presented in Figure 1.1 relates to a process plant, very similar plots would result if the data related to a factory production unit, buildings or any other type of project. The relationships would vary, but the shape of the various curves would be much the same.

If the data presented in Figure 1.1 is related to the project

6 SETTING THE SCENE

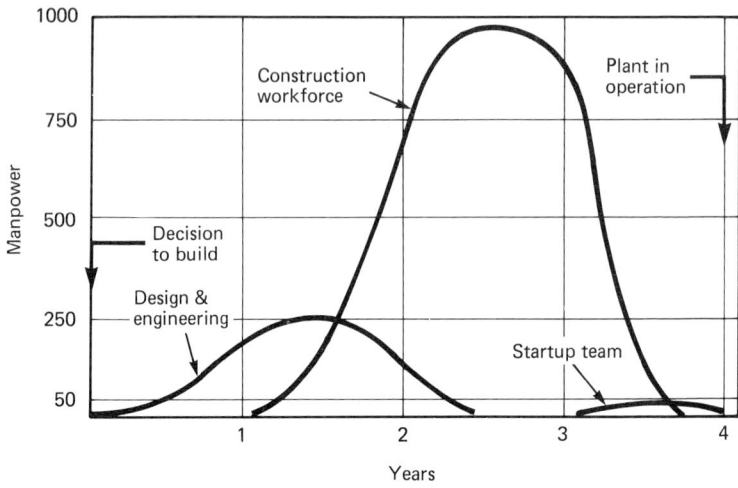

Years

Figure 1.1 Manpower versus time
With effective planning, design and engineering should be well in hand when work starts in the field. These figures relate to a project of the order of £100 million (1985 prices).

phases given above, it will be appreciated that a major area of effort has not been delineated. This is described as 'procurement and manufacture' if we assume that the term 'contracts' applies to the construction work, with 'orders' being placed for materials and equipment manufactured off site and later delivered to site. The term 'construction' is then confined to the work done on site. We have now divided the project into three major groups – design, procurement and construction – which project subdivision can also be represented graphically, as in Figure 1.2. Once again, these curves are quite typical, but since the vertical cost parameters are expressed as a percentage, the relationship between them in terms of cost is not apparent. However, we can say that for a wide range of projects that relationship will be roughly as follows:

Design, engineering, project management
and site supervision: 25%
Procurement of equipment and materials
(as defined above): 40%
Site contracts (for construction): 35%

As discussed elsewhere, there is a continuing trend towards manufacture off site, in particular by the use of module techniques,(6) so there is nothing special or sacrosanct about the

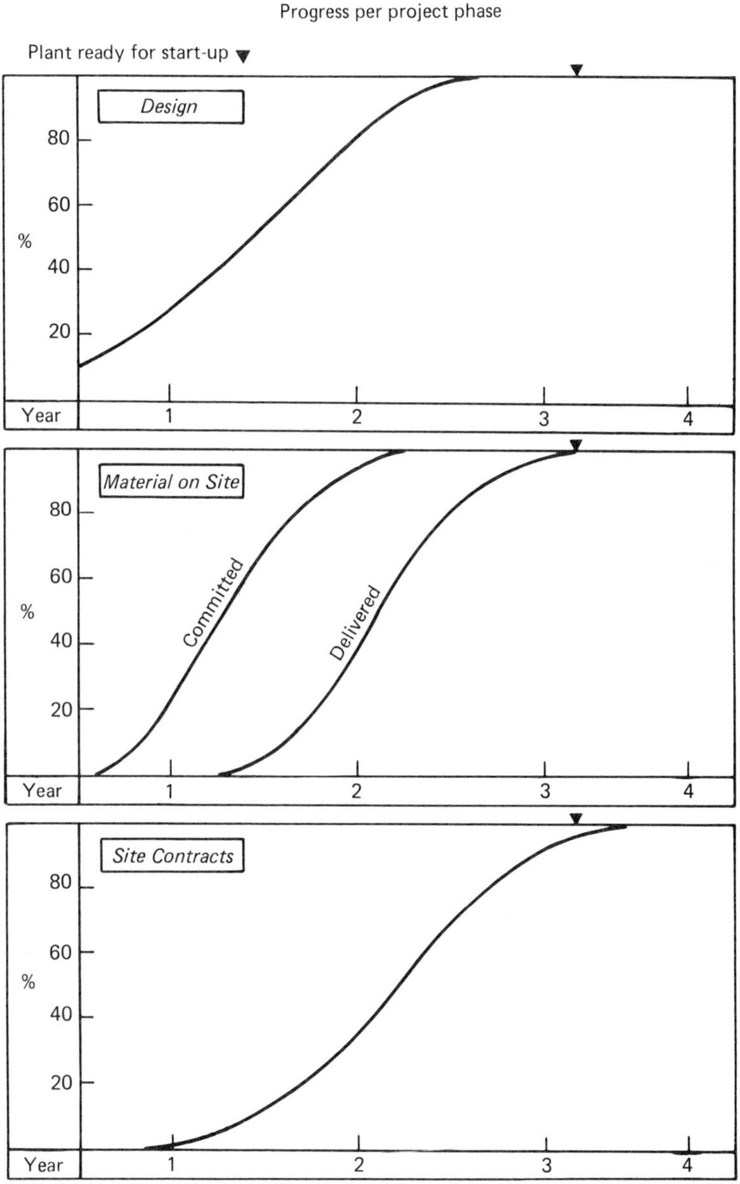

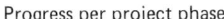

Figure 1.2 Progress per project phase
Typical progress in terms of value of work done on the project for the three basic phases into which every project can and should be divided.

above relationship. Indeed, the procurement element may well grow to 60 per cent with some projects, but we doubt whether it will ever get much above this.

The project plan

Now that we have some concept of what is involved in a project and its shape let us see what this means in terms of project planning. There are various techniques used for project planning, of which the two most common are bar or Gantt charts and network analysis methods, which are used under various names, such as CPM, PERT and precedence networks. A project planning system, it is said, must 'be able to formally schedule all the necessary activities on the project in a manner which will permit the evaluation of actual progress against plan, and which will identify the interdependencies between activities'.(7) The language is far removed from what one meets when discussing a corporate plan. The corporate plan is concerned with company policy, the company accounts, potential profit and is ongoing. With a project we are concerned with 'activities' over the limited duration of *that* project. We do not propose to enter into the details of project planning. Harrison, whom we have just quoted, devotes three chapters in his book on project management to the subject, climaxing in a chapter titled 'Modern project planning methods'. Let us consider, rather, the outcome of the project plan, as earlier depicted graphically in Figure 1.1.

In Figure 1.3 we present an actual plot of the construction curve for two different projects. Curve A depicts the progress achieved on site during the construction of a major process plant project. Curve B shows what happened when a much smaller, but similar project was built a few years later on the same site. Project B was poorly planned, with the result that work was started on site too early. The error was compounded when plant and equipment were delivered late, resulting in the initial 'tail' and the 'slump' in the curve that can be seen as civil work tailed off, but mechanical construction was only slowly building up. But the results of poor planning did not stop there: it influenced project completion as well. That also dragged on, giving a second 'tail' at the end of the project. All this takes time, costs money, thus adding to the overrun in both time and cost – something that should not happen on a successful project.

Figure 1.1 and Curve A in Figure 1.3 represent the result of a well planned project, with a proper flow of materials to the site,

THERE MUST BE A PLAN

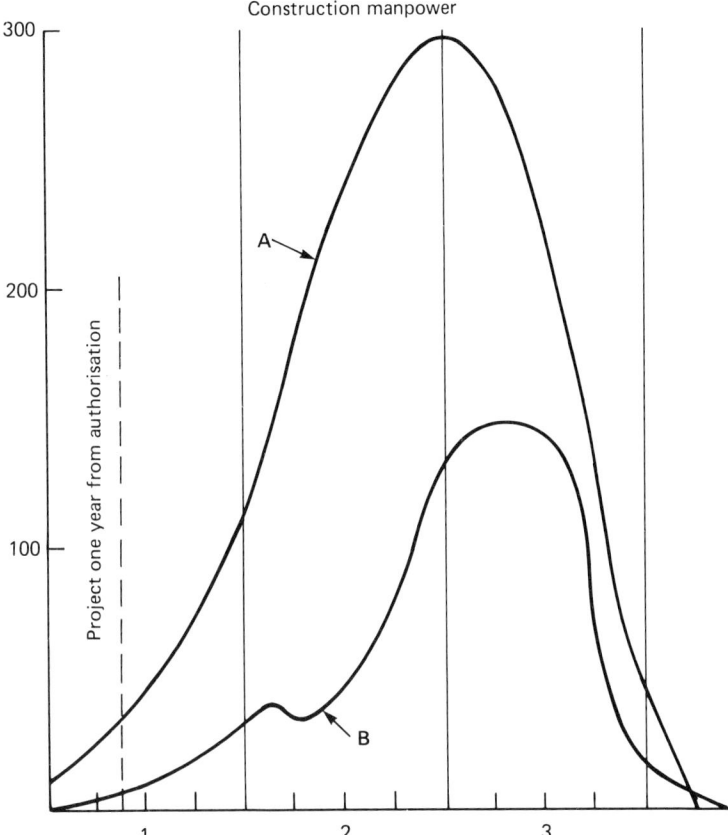

Figure 1.3 Construction manpower
Here the overall manning on two different projects on the same site is compared.

where the construction force builds up to a peak and then finally falls sharply away as the project is completed and turned over to the startup team. Notice the steep upward climb and then the sharp fall. These are most desirable characteristics for a properly managed, cost effective and thus successful project. If a project develops 'tails' or 'slumps', as is seen in Curve B, then the project is going wrong.

Project planning has to be concerned not only with building effort up to the appropriate peak, but also in ensuring that as completion approaches, effort is scaled down efficiently. Once again, we have a sharp contrast with corporate planning, where

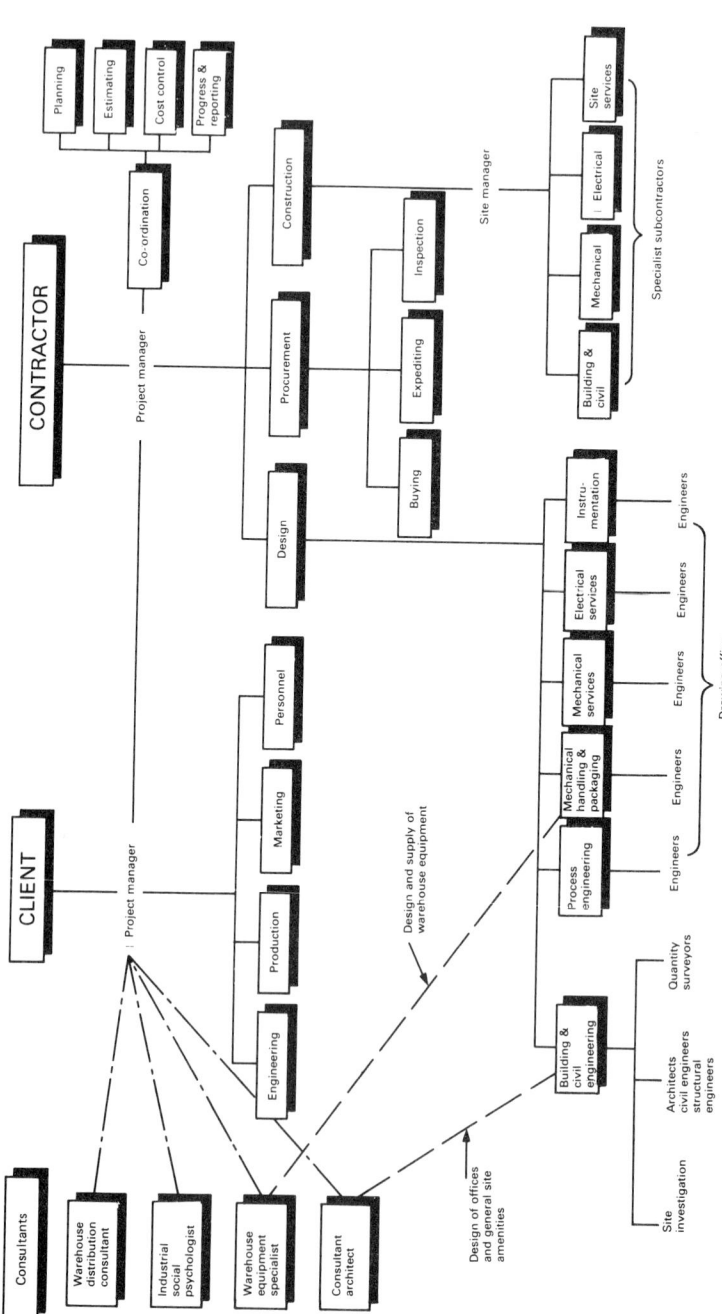

Figure 1.4 The basic relationship
Here we see the relationships that are established between the main parties normally involved in a project as it develops.

there is normally no question of bringing the corporate effort to an end.

Project organisation

A project plan implies the existence of the 'planner' and a related organisation. There will be those who require the project and those who implement the project and both may be involved in the planning and subsequent control of the project. It is our view that the control of any project must rest, first and foremost, with the 'promoter' of the project and the effectiveness of that control will depend on the decisions taken by the promoter. The term 'promoter' describes the owner, client, sponsor, or user. He may approach the implementation of his project in a variety of ways, the 'variety' depending largely upon the degree to which he utilises outside help. That in turn depends largely on the extent of the in-house resources that are available. But whichever way a project is handled, there must always be the formation of a project team, headed by a project manager, that carries out the function of project management. We propose to concentrate our attention on project management, so that, of the wide range of alternatives that can be practised with respect to project organisation, we shall only consider two: one where the project management is carried out by the promoter and the other where the promoter shares the project management with a contractor. We shall refer to such a contractor as the 'managing contractor'. There is a third alternative: the 'turnkey contract', but here the promoter plays a minor role.

Since control of the project should rest primarily with the promoter of the project and he should have a project team to ensure that his objectives are secured, the appointment of a managing contractor will result in there being two project teams, as illustrated diagrammatically in Figure 1.4. This diagram introduces a third party to notice, the consultant. The three separate roles illustrated in Figure 1.4 can be described as follows:

1 *The promoter* (owner, client): oversees and pays
2 *The consultant*: advises the promoter
3 *The managing contractor*: gets the job done

The managing contractor may well employ a large number of suppliers and contractors (reserving the latter term for companies that carry out work on the site) in order to get the job done and often the promoter will enter this field as well, placing orders and contracts directly, rather than through his managing contractor. The various case studies to which we shall turn in due course will provide practical examples of all these various alternative approaches to project organisation and we hope to demonstrate their relative effectiveness. For the moment, however, let us look a little more closely at the managing contractor.

The managing contractor

Whilst we are concerned with project management rather than with company management, we should take some interest in the management of those companies whose basic business is project management. They form part of what is described as the 'construction industry'. Practically all the companies involved in the construction industry are continuously involved in projects and project management. To illustrate the scope of interest, the Associated General Contractors of America keeps its members in touch with one another through the *Constructor* magazine, which has a circulation of some 40 000. Using this as a yardstick, there is every likelihood that the number of companies States-wide large enough to need some form of project organisation and administration could well exceed 100 000, and worldwide there could well be more than a million. In this assessment we are seeking to exclude what we might term the 'one man business', where the project management would never be formalised.

Amongst this vast number of firms involved in project management we hear only of a few, but the many have the same problems as the few. Construction companies have certain characteristics which differentiate them quite sharply from the rest, characteristics with which the company management has to cope to survive. For instance, the construction industry is labour-intensive and its turnover/capital ratio is very high. With a small capital base in relation to turnover, the construction company is always vulnerable. Even a relatively small loss on one contract – small, that is, in relation to the turnover on that contract – can land a construction contractor in deep trouble and even bring him to bankruptcy, as we have demonstrated elsewhere.(8) Another problem is the wide oscillations that can occur in workload. Work from one year to the next can be halved or doubled. This brings staffing problems. Experienced staff are lost when work falls away and are difficult to find when the need returns – and the smaller the company the greater the problem. To quote:(9)

> Sometimes we get confused with the notion that the Bechtels, Fluors and the MWKs etc., are the only people in the construction industry.

The firms named are major construction companies with staffs of many thousands and an annual turnover of many billions of dollars, but it is the special problems of the smaller company that the writer highlights. The point is made that the cyclical nature of the construction business means that with the smaller firms only a minimum of staff survive the low point in such cycles. This has the result that such firms do not have the staff or the experience immediately available, when work builds up, to cope with the developing situation. But the problem is still there however large the company.

The 'top ten'

The three companies mentioned above all appear among the 'top ten' in the listing of the *Top 400 Contractors* published annually by the US magazine *Engineering News Record*. The listing relates to US contractors only, and the place in the list is determined by the volume of business done. This is most difficult to assess in the construction industry, because large contracts are often undertaken on a 'fee' basis and this is especially true of management contracts. The contractor receives a fee for his own work and services, usually limited to design, procurement, and site supervision. The cost of the works is then 'reimbursable' but whilst those costs can go through his books and become part of his business turnover, this is not necessarily so. With many such contracts the vendors and subcontractors are paid directly by the owner, after the contractor has checked and certified the invoices for payment. So turnover is no guide to the real volume of work being handled.

This same journal, *ENR*, also publishes a survey of design firms. When studied, we see that this illustrates the changing emphasis in the work undertaken by construction contractors in the USA – and it is true worldwide. We see a steady movement from 'construction' to 'design-construct', then to 'construction management'. But size is not the only criterion for success. A record of steady growth is also a sound indicator. It is a basic management philosophy of

14 SETTING THE SCENE

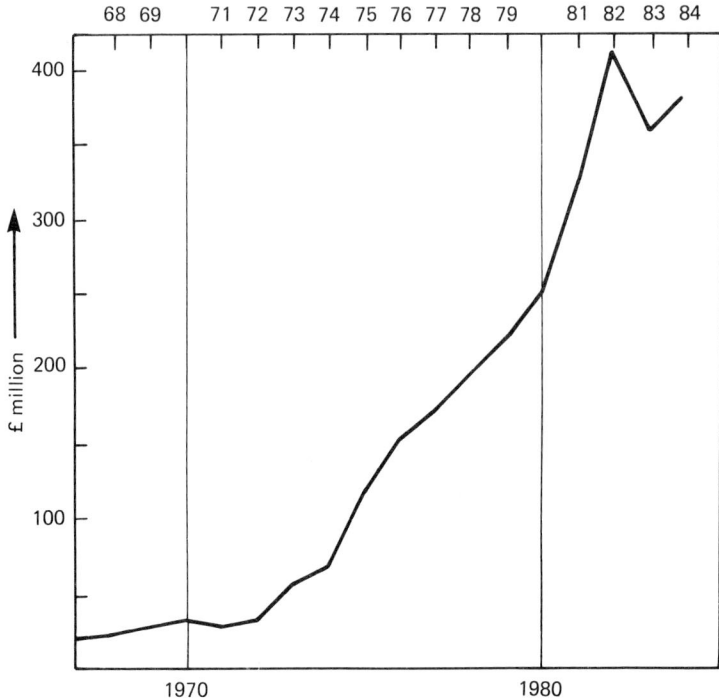

Figure 1.5 Annual turnover
These figures for turnover, abstracted from the Annual Accounts, illustrate steady growth. *Source: Group Financial Record, Matthew Hall PLC.*

ours that one should learn from experience – that is why we shall be bringing you a series of case studies – so that you may learn from the experience of others, as well as your own. Our present series of case studies are success stories, but we have seen successful contractors emerge from disaster with renewed strength. One such was Davy McKee. Back in 1966 Power Gas, a member of the then Davy-Ashmore Group, a major British engineering group, secured a contract for the design and construction of the Conoco Humber Refinery. Two years later the chairman of the company reported in the Annual Accounts:(8)

> Our entire situation is coloured by the contract for the Humber Refinery. The order is for £25 million, we are one

year late, the overrun may reach £12 million. There is the problem of liquidity.

Yet a year later the chairman could report that they had 'come out of an exceptionally difficult year with our contract obligations honoured, our debts paid and our resources substantially restored'. From then on the group went on from strength to strength. Company structure and organisation developed and changed to adjust to growth and the mergers that were taking place, culminating in the merger with McKee, a US-based company, in 1978. Sales and profits showed rapid growth for some ten years. The company demonstrated that it *could* learn from experience.

But perhaps even better is the company that avoids disaster and continues to grow even in a time of depression, such as most of the world, and Britain in particular, has been going through recently. Matthew Hall plc is one such company. We have plotted their turnover since 1967 in Figure 1.5 because we find a graph is much more expressive than a table of figures. It is interesting to note that over the years the turnover has been roughly ten times the total assets employed, a specific illustration of the fact that such companies have a very high turnover/capital ratio. With manufacturing companies, by contrast, the ratio may be 1:1 rather than 10:1. The true ratio for Matthew Hall could be even higher: that would depend upon the number of contracts they handled where procurement was handled by the client, thus not passing through their books.

The turnover of Matthew Hall, £383 million in 1984 (Figure 1.5) brings it nowhere near the 'top ten' with whom we started this section, since the business volume of the tenth in the list exceeds US$2 billion, nearly four times that. However, size is not in itself a sign of success. We shall be looking for aspects of success that both *can* be imitated and are worthy of imitation. Some of the companies in the 'top ten', whilst they have survived, have come through difficult times and in some cases their size is due in part to mergers with other companies in the field designed to cut overheads and thus increase their efficiency. However, it should not be forgotten that too large a company may become unmanageable, especially if it is over-centralised.

The business of all these companies is projects, and they will have many projects, large and small, in hand at any time. This demands that the company set up an organisation that can handle all these projects, each of which in turn will need a project manager and a project team.

16 SETTING THE SCENE

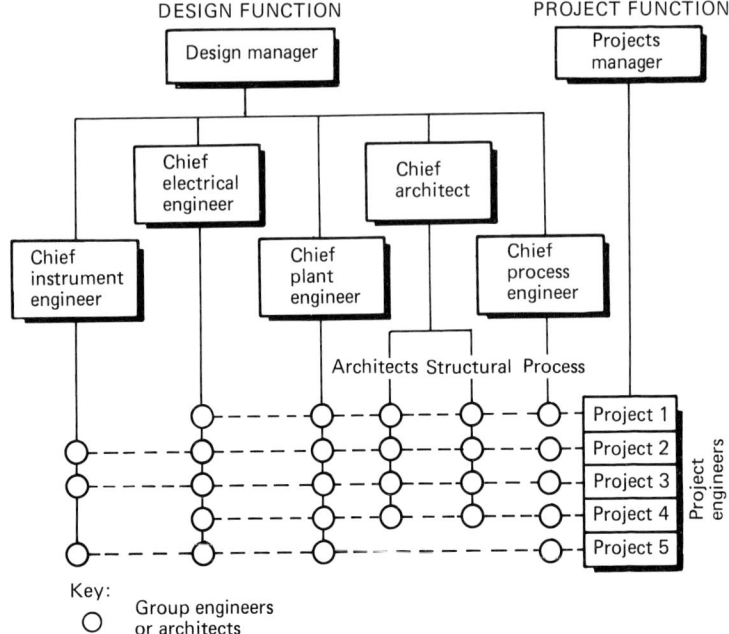

Figure 1.6 Internal organisation chart
This chart demonstrates the manner in which the design department, grouped under section leaders, integrates with the project management function. Whilst the design department is necessarily internally streamed and managed in accordance with the several disciplines involved, the service offered is on a project basis.

The planning constraints

Within the organisation of the managing contractor there will usually be a *design* function and a *project* function. The projects director will be responsible for a number of projects, each in charge of a project manager at site, assisted by a construction manager. The design manager provides the various design services, usually at the home office. There will be a procurement manager providing procurement services and probably a legal advisor providing legal services, also at the home office. We could go on and on in this vein. The length of the list depends to some extent on the size of the project and of the company. To simplify the matter, let us just consider the relationship between the projects manager and the design manager – diagrammatically illustrated in Figure 1.6. This type of design organisation relates to a contractor involved, for instance, in the oil, gas and chemical sectors of industry, which call for design services such as have been designated in the diagram. It is, of course, very much simplified, showing only five projects.

The point we wish to make is that within the organisation we now have conflicting interests, which have to be reconciled. It is their reconciliation that will impose constraints. A project team has to be formed for each project as a contract is received. Each project will make different demands upon the design resource, since each project is different both in nature and size. This type of variation has been indicated in Figure 1.6. For instance project 1 does not require any instrumentation, whilst project 5 has no building works: some other contractor has been given that work.

Ideally, the resources of the design department would be such that they match the requirements of the project group, with a slight reserve of capacity, but that just never happens. The design resources will always be limited somewhere and this leads to competition for those resources as between the various projects. Each project will have its own plan and its own programme, but now we see a further need: there must be planning of the resources of the company to cope with the work as it comes in. And do not forget, that workload can fluctuate widely. So here is another aspect of planning. The available resources must be assessed and suitably deployed.

The assessment of the available resources is a matter, in the first instance, for the promoter of the project. If he turns to a managing contractor, he will make enquiries and choose a managing contractor who has the resources needed to implement his particular project, but the matter of resources does not end there. Demands are going to be made far beyond these two key groups – the promoter and the managing contractor – and restraints may be found on those areas as well. With a major project, manufacturing resources may well be called upon worldwide, whilst with a development project calls may be made for items that have even to be invented if the project is to be brought to a successful conclusion. It will be appreciated that it is not so much the size of a project but its *nature* that is all-important in this context. That is why we believe that the satisfactory completion of a development project is indeed a success and deserves to go on record as such.

Summary

Having looked at planning in relation to projects and companies we have demonstrated that the project plan is very different from the corporate plan. When we turn to companies engaged on projects as their business, such as the construction contractors, we see that those companies will not only have to plan each project, but plan the entire work of their company to cope with the projects they take on. Then, over and above all that, will be the corporate plan directed at the continuing prosperity of the company as a whole. It is indeed true, as we proclaimed in our title, that 'there must be a plan' – indeed, many plans – for a project to be brought to a successful conclusion.

References

1 Argenti, J., *Practical Corporate Planning*, Allen & Unwin, 1980.
2 Hussey, D.E., *Corporate Planning – Theory and Practice*, 2nd edn, Pergamon, 1984.
3 Hayes, R.H., 'Strategic planning – forward in reverse?', *Harvard Business Review*, **63**, Nov./Dec. 1985, pp.111-119.
4 Brochure: 'The Argenti system of corporate planning', published by Argenti Systems Limited, 12 Lower Brook Street, Ipswich, IP4 1AT, UK.
5 Corrie, R.K. and P.D. Hudson, 'The consultants' role in the international contract scene'. Paper presented at a one-day Symposium on 'Contracts, claims and costs', held in London 20 June 1980, *The Cost Engineer*, 19, issues, 4,5,6, 1981.
6 Stallworthy, E.A. and Kharbanda, O.P., *International Construction and the Role of Project Management*, Gower, Aldershot, 1985, 301 pp.
7 Harrison, F.L., *Advanced Project Management*, Gower, Aldershot, 1981, 332 pp.
8 Kharbanda, O.P. and Stallworthy, E.A., *How to Learn from Project Disasters*, Gower, Aldershot, 1983, 274 pp.
9 Thomas, K.O., 'Cost control and the small construction company', *Cost Engineering*, 25/6a, November 1983.

2 Project cost control

Having realised that any and every project must be planned, we were led to the further fact that we must have a project organisation. We saw too that the necessary project organisation could well have two parallel streams and two parallel project teams, when the promoter of the project felt the need to call in a managing contractor to handle the project for him. (Refer back to Figure 1.4.) Not all the case studies to which we shall give our attention will have this particular type of project organisation, since we shall look not only at civil engineering and engineering construction projects, where work is carried out both in design offices and on a construction site, but also at projects involving the establishment of a new item of equipment, such as robots, a new car, or the latest in heavy transport facilities. Here our attention will be focused on the efforts and objectives of the project team or the company, rather than the detailed implementation of the facility where these things are to be made or used, when the detailed project organisation we have already began to outline would play a role. Nevertheless, whatever the project, planning is essential. Similarly, whatever the project, project cost control is essential. Indeed, it is the crux!

Of the various types of project which we have chosen to study, that involving civil and mechanical engineering, with a construction site, is probably the most complex in terms of project organisation. We shall therefore have that type of project in the background as we turn to consider the importance of project cost control, but we do not propose to enter into the details of the project organisation relevant to such complex projects: we have done that elsewhere.(1)

Project control

Without entering into detail, let us then just recognise that a project organisation that is established for the administration of such complex projects – and we have some amongst our case studies – is set up by promoter of the project, usually the owner. The purpose is to give him real and effective *control* of the project. To achieve this, he must:

1. Give the project manager *total* responsibility for the entire project: design, engineering, procurement and construction. That manager should produce a monthly project cost control report.
2. Provide a cost engineering function to operate first at the design offices and then at the construction site, responsible to the project manager and headed by a senior project cost control engineer.
3. Ensure that the finance department works in close liaison with the cost engineering function, whilst maintaining their own normal expenditure records and a cumulative commitment record.

The primary control in such a context is essentially financial, though within that financial control there will be control of many other aspects of the project, such as quality and time. The duty of the cost engineering function will be to establish the exact position of the project at all times in terms of cost, comparing actual progress with target progress. With that background let us now look in some detail at project cost control.

Effective project cost control

Effective project cost control is, in our judgment, the key to successful project management and hence an essential element in every successful project. Yet, despite its importance, it is still a very neglected subject, preached far more often than it is practised. Project cost can get out of hand very easily indeed. No great effort is needed for that! Cost overruns, arising from time overruns, and other lapses, are commonplace. The hallmark of the successful project is without doubt completion on time and within budget. On the other hand, a project which is put in hand with an incorrect estimate of either time (project duration) or money (project cost) is doomed. Bad estimating in these areas will negate the most painstaking efforts at cost control during design and construction. Attempts to save money on the estimating and cost control effort at the drawing board stage of a project will only give renewed force to the old adage: 'Penny wise, pound foolish'.

A sound estimate of the capital cost of a project is an essential basis for effective project cost control. Whilst the original capital cost estimate for a project may not necessarily be prepared by those later involved in implementing a project, both its content and its format will play a significant role in relation to project cost control. The economic viability of the project is going to be assessed and reassessed at intervals throughout its development, both before and after the project has been approved. At each reassessment an estimate of the capital cost will be prepared. It is on the basis of one such estimate that the money required will have been voted or budgeted. That creates a commitment for those later involved in project implementation, since they then have to keep costs within that amount. A low estimate, therefore, could bring them a lot of trouble. But a high estimate, whilst making it easy for those building the project, is also undesirable, since it leads to a waste of money. Parkinson's Law operates and expenditure rises to meet the budget.

The role of the capital cost estimate

There is a lot of debate about the role played by the capital cost estimate. The first question is: How accurate ought it to be? During feasibility studies an accuracy between -10 and $+25$ per cent is considered to be reasonable, since the decisions being taken are not likely to be affected with such a margin of error. The ability to prepare an accurate estimate depends upon the amount of information available. As a project develops, the amount of information grows steadily until of course, at the end the final truth is known: the actual cost. It also costs money to prepare an estimate and the greater the degree of detail entered into, the greater the cost of preparation of the estimate. This is illustrated graphically in Figure 2.1.(2) It is recommended that the estimate used as a basis for the authorisation of the money required, that thus becomes the target for cost control, should have an accuracy of the order of $+/-$ 10 per cent. This is before contingency. If a contingency of 10 per cent is then added, the presumption is that the money voted should not be exceeded. The initial target for the purposes of project cost control will then be the net estimate, exclusive of contingency.

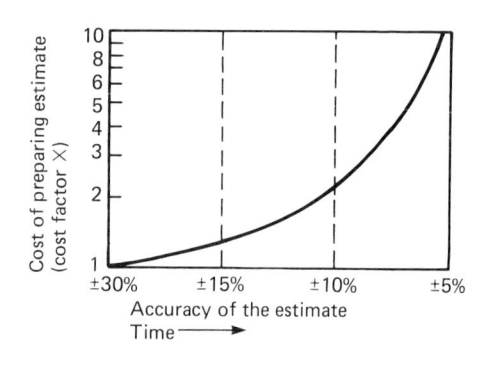

BASIC PROCESS DATA	AVAILABILITY OF DATA		
Plant type and size	x x x	x x x	x x x
Outline flowsheet	x x	x x x	x x x
Heat and energy balance	x	x x x	x x x
Equipment and instrument list		x x x	x x x
Equipment data sheets		x x x	x x x
Details of plant location			x x x
Details on utilities			x x x
ENGINEERING DESIGN DATA			
Equipment sketches		x x x	x x x
Plant layout with elevation		x x x	x x x
Layout of off-sites		x x	x x x
Schedule of piping			x x x
Piping layout			x x x
Electrical oneline diagram			x x x
Piping isometrics			x x
Instrument loop sheets			x x
Electrical control drawings			x
Foundations, detail drawings			x
Buildings, outline drawings			x
Suppliers' quotations, equipment			x

Figure 2.1 The cost of accuracy
The cost of preparing an estimate depends on the data involved and used. The more data available, the greater the possible accuracy.

In practice, as design and construction proceed, the final cost of the project is continuously reappraised and revised estimates are established, usually from month to month. It is a matter of experience that during the early stages of a project the estimate of final cost falls, as compared to the amount authorised, only at the last to come back to and more often than not exceed that amount. The reason for this is that the early estimates make provision – and sometimes excessive provision – for the 'unknowns'. At a later stage in the project, it is believed that all the 'unknowns' are

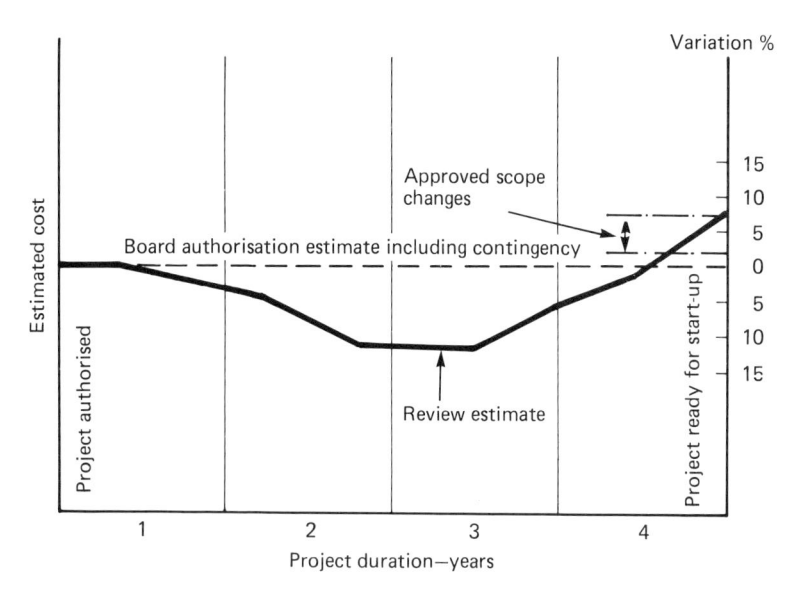

Figure 2.2 Capital cost estimates – trend
Experience shows that this graph is completely characteristic: therefore the initial saving, when anticipated, should be ignored.

known, when sadly this never is the case. This cycle of events is depicted graphically in Figure 2.2. Scope changes usually play a significant role in this final surge upwards in cost, but they must be seen as specific additions to the original estimate.

The use of contingency

The purpose of contingency should be clearly defined and its use limited to the purpose as defined. The purpose of contingency is to allow for unforeseen increases in cost that are statistically likely to occur. It should exclude escalation, which should be separately assessed. Then contingency is designed to cover the errors and omissions of both the estimator and the engineers who provided the data from which the estimate was developed. But all this relates to a scope of work as defined. Contingency should *never* be provided for or assumed to cover potential changes in scope. These changes, it is true, are also likely to occur and are probably inevitable. Changes in scope, however, should always be treated as variations to the original scheme, separately assessed and measured, and added or deleted as the case may be from the original scope as approved and the related estimate of cost. A change in scope can never be defined until it is proposed. It is therefore impossible for contingency to cover a change in scope and it should never be assumed that it does.

Each estimate that is prepared for cost control purposes will have a provision for contingency, which will get smaller as time passes, until it disappears altogether. Whilst contingency is not used directly, since the cost control techniques ignore it, it is always necessary to add contingency in order that comparison may be made with the amount voted and a realistic appraisal made of the final cost of the project. It is desirable to estimate contingency on some consistent basis throughout the life of the project. One approach is to divide the review estimate into three cost groups: materials and work uncommitted, committed (that is, on order), and value of work already done. There is no contingency required on work already done, whilst commitments will require less contingency than that which is not yet committed. Thus, if the original contingency provision was 10 per cent, this could still be applied to that which was uncommitted and say 5 per cent to commitments not yet delivered. Such a consistent approach to the evaluation of contingency would result in its progressive reduction to nil by the time the project was complete.

Escalation and the impact of inflation

An estimate, as first prepared, should always be an assessment of the cost at the time of preparation. Then consideration should be given to the time the project will take to design and construct, and the possible rate of inflation over that period assessed. From this data a provision of cost escalation can be estimated and added to the estimate. This provision then becomes an integral part of the estimate and part of the cost control target. Inflation is the word applied here to the price movement over time of commodities, salaries and the like. The word 'escalation' will be reserved for the movement in cost of an installation which is the combination of supplied equipment, materials and labour, constructed over a period of time. Escalation therefore reflects and includes inflation, but the movement in escalation is not necessarily parallel to the movement in inflation. Escalation can move faster or slower than inflation, according to circumstances. For instance, when times are hard, a manufacturer will hold or even reduce his prices despite being faced with inflationary increases in the cost of his raw materials or his labour. Or he may be able to hold his prices in the face of inflation because of technological improvements or better productivity.

In order to make provision for escalation, it is necessary to estimate the future trend and relate that to the way in which it is expected that the project will develop in terms of the commitments placed and the work done. It is not proposed to enlarge on this process here, since no general data can be provided. Each project has to be studied individually and there are various books, including *Project Cost Control in Action* which give details of the various techniques.(3) For now, the point must be made that escalation should be monitored as part of the cost control function, and the provision for escalation will obviously get smaller as the project progresses.

Cost coding as a management tool

The ideal system of cost coding will be that which it is possible to use at all stages in the development of the project. Such a system would first be adopted in the preparation of the estimate – that is why it is mentioned in this section – then used for the identification of equipment in the relevant equipment schedules and on the drawings. The requisitions and related purchase orders would also use the code as part of their numbering system, this ensuring that the same number would appear on the vendor's invoice. Thus at all stages, from design through the steps of commitment, delivery and payment, a common system of cost allocation is being used. The integration of the coding system adopted in the estimate at the beginning into all the administrative procedures through to the final accounting is not merely an estimating tool: it is also a basic system for the provision of information to management and fundamental to effective project cost control.

A variety of systems can be adopted to achieve this end and most contractors have their own coding system. Typical cost codes (or code of accounts) are also published, as for instance in the book *Project Cost Control in Action* referred to above. It is important to realise that such a system of cost analysis should only be followed to the extent necessary for the objective in view. Care must be exercised if the system is not to negate its usefulness by its very complexity.

In addition, the detail in the coding system should be realistic. For instance, if insulation is purchased at rates which include both materials and labour, there is no merit in separating the materials and the labour by the use of different cost codes. Another aspect of the coding system which is very important is that each code requires clear and careful definition of its content. This ensures consistency in the allocation of costs throughout the life of the project, allows both estimate and cost to be compared on a 'like with like' basis, whilst the collected costs, analysed across known and specific codes, will provide a sound foundation for estimating data in relation to future projects.

Administrative procedures

As we have already seen, project cost control must be an integral part of a project organisation. It is, however, within that framework a service, directly related to three other key disciplines:

> Engineering
> Accounting
> Material control

Material control covers not only purchasing, expediting and inspection but also material storage and handling at the worksite. Each project is unique, and this means that all these various disciplines have to be 'tailored' to the specific requirements of the project.

However, there are certain basic guidelines and underlying principles which should always be followed. When a project is initiated the first step must always be to take stock of the human resources that *are* available and plan for their optimum utilisation, supplementing them by outside resources as then seen to be necessary by the use of consultants or contractors, or both. The functions *directly* involved in a project are:

> Project management
> Design
> Procurement
> Construction

The functions *indirectly* involved are:

> Planning
> Estimating
> Cost control
> Finance and accounts

It is the responsibility of one person, normally designated the project manager, to coordinate all the various activities and to arrange outside help as necessary to the extent that it is not available to him internally, as outlined above. Each of the functions mentioned is specialised and their scope and duties are dealt with in a wide range of books and other works of reference so we do not need to enter into detail here.

It is useful to liken the role of the project manager to that of the conductor of an orchestra. The members of the 'orchestra' are the various members of the project team, each a specialist in one or other of the functions mentioned above, who each have to respond immediately to the conductor's 'baton' and work in harmony with all the other members of the team. This picture emphasises the need for continuous, comprehensive and rapid communication between all the members of the project team. The objective: completion of the project on time and within budget.

Commitment control

The first major purchasing exercise, once a project moves into detailed design, is the writing of the requisitions and the placing on order of all the major plant and equipment. This should proceed fairly rapidly and all the equipment is usually on order by the time the project is 30 per cent complete in terms of the estimated project duration. It is crucial to commitment control that the following rule be written down and obeyed:

> No commitment may be entered into with an outside company without prior *written* authorisation

The mechanics of commitment control can be simplified by the use of the appropriate forms. With such forms, much of the work becomes a routine, but the final implication of the rule just cited must also be appreciated and followed:

> No invoice is to be paid unless it is covered by a written order or an amendment thereto.

If these rules are obeyed then one would expect the cumulative commitment record to provide the total cost of the project and that well before project completion, since costs cannot exceed the commitment. But it is still possible for costs to be incurred which are not treated as a commitment, so great care has to be taken to ensure that such costs are both recorded and monitored. Typical of these are in-house costs, such as design and project supervision and on-costs, such as insurance and freight charges. These *can* be significant and can easily be overlooked. The in-house costs are often called 'implied commitments', and if they are to be set against the project then a projection should be made of the possible final cost. Another example of an implied commitment is a contract with an outside party to do work or services on a continuing basis. Here estimates *must* be made of the extent to which such services will be required for the project in hand, and the commitment recorded and then reassessed as necessary as work proceeds. A realistic commitment record is vital to success in terms of project cost control and it will be the responsibility of the various members of the project team to ensure that the record is sound. This also demands close liaison with the accounts department, who will be keeping the cost records.

Where a contractor is employed, whilst one might expect that commitments will be properly supervised and controlled, there is no guarantee of this, and the procedures being used by the contractor should be reviewed to ensure that they are adequate.

Value of work done

The assessment and precise recording of 'value of work done' is also crucial to project cost control, since it is the key to successful forecasting of the final cost of a project. The commitment record makes some contribution to forecasting, as already indicated above, but the continuous assessment of value of work done constitutes the major tool for forecasting – and accurate forecasts are essential if management are not to be taken unawares by demands for more finance at a late stage, a disaster on any project.

Value of work done is *not* and must never be, expenditure as such, although it finally equals expenditure. It is described by the accountant as 'work in progress' and it is, for most of the time, greater than expenditure as recorded by him. Figure 2.3 illustrates the relationship between *value of work done* and *expenditure* as recorded over the life of an average project. Value of work done can be briefly summarised as: design and such other costs as incurred, whether they are incurred within the owner's own organisation or by a contractor; the value of materials only as and when they are delivered to the job site or the related warehouse; and the value of work as it is done on site against site contracts.

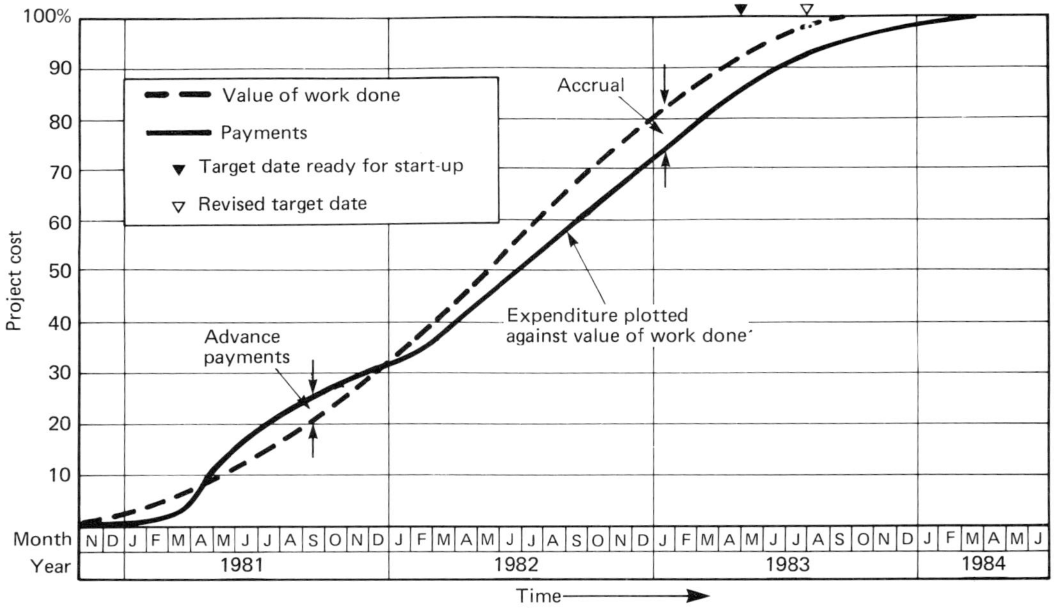

Figure 2.3 Value of work done versus expenditure
In the early stages, down payments and progress payments made before equipment and materials arrive on site may cause expenditure to run ahead of value of work done, but most of the time it will lag some two months.

This means that payments made in advance of delivery are not counted as value of work done, although that is of course expenditure. The finance department should separately record and control such advance payments, in order to facilitate the work of cost control. Value of work done is largely an estimate. It is therefore an approximation, but an approximation advised today is far more useful in this context – project cost control – than a more precise figure advised some three to five weeks later, when the invoice comes in. It should be assessed once a month, and there are three main areas of interest:

1 Home office effort (off site)
2 Materials delivered to site (on site)
3 Site contracts (work done on site)

We do not propose to enter into the details of the assessment of these various cost areas, since it is sufficient for our purpose here to illustrate the need. Indeed, these days all this is likely to be accomplished via a computer, using the relevant programs. The computer is a wonderful tool and it can facilitate the performance of repetitive work quickly and cheaply. But whilst it is a time saver it is not a miracle worker and its limitations need to be recognised. Indeed, whilst it is common for the various programs, including programs used for project cost control, to be made interactive, this is not necessarily the best approach for project cost control purposes. It is usually better to transfer data from other programs (such as that available via the finance or planning departments) into the cost control program manually. This concept is illustrated diagrammatically in Figure 2.4. Then the available data can be surveyed via a VDU and a selection made which can be manually transferred to the cost control data bank. That program will then print or display the relevant reports as needed, when called for.

This is not the place to discuss the relative merits of the various programs that are available, but the growing availability of the microcomputer, or 'desktop' computer and the related programs must increase both the availability and ease of handling of cost control data. However, care must be taken to ensure that this does not lead to the input and processing of largely irrelevant material.

Cost control and planning

We have devoted a whole chapter to the necessity of planning and its role in effective project management. When it comes to

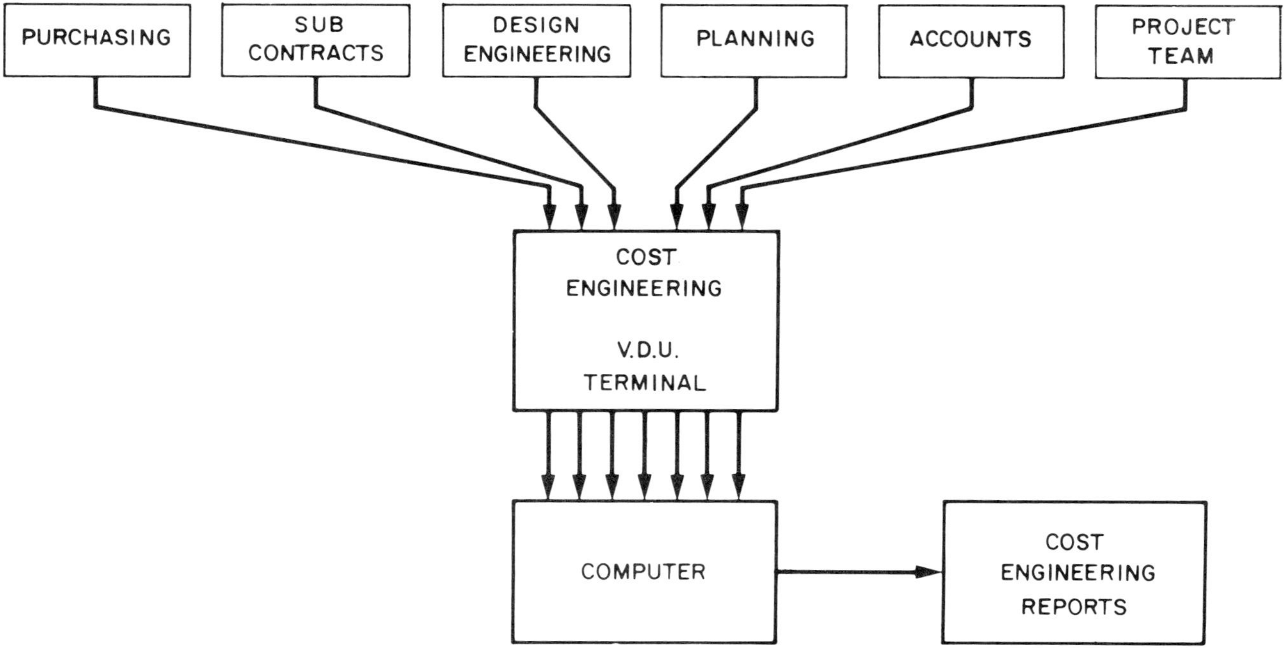

Figure 2.4 A data access system
Information can be made available to the cost control engineer via a VDU. He takes the data relevant to his program, and then processes it.

establishing proper targets for cost control purposes the two skills of planning and cost control go hand in hand. There are always two basic targets: *time* and *money*. Initially such targets are estimates, but their validity (or otherwise) will be demonstrated as the project proceeds, especially if the appropriate cost control techniques are used. Obviously the truth will be known when the project is complete, but the fundamental objective is to know whether the targets are valid and to correct them if they are not, *as early as possible*. Project cost control might be better described as project cost monitoring, in that the control has to be exercised by the project manager and others, using the information provided by the cost control function. When an appraisal of the project indicates a cost or time overrun, there is time to do something about it if that is indicated early: even to abandon the project if the finance is not available or the project no longer profitable because of the increased cost or loss of time. The interrelationship between the two targets of time and money must also be recognised. A low cost estimate almost invariably leads to an under-estimate of the time required to complete the project, which in itself will bring additional costs. Again, the impact of quality requirements on cost should never be forgotten.

Earlier (see Figure 2.2) mention has been made of the general trend in the estimate of total project cost. This experience – the initial optimism, followed by final overrun – is so universal that it has become the subject of caustic comment: surely we should know better by now. But we never do. This arises because whilst there are a number of pitfalls ahead, they cannot be seen or assessed before they arrive. They include:

1 Inadequacy of scope definition
2 Changes made in the scope of the project
3 Influence of external conditions

Inadequacy in scope definition results in under-estimation, or allows work to be done on the project that was not in the 'real' scope. Formal changes in scope are more manageable, in the sense that they can be evaluated, approved and specifically controlled. Unfortunately, all the changes made, whether formal or not, will have the same end result: the cost of the project will go up. They will be carried out because they are supposed to be essential for the safety or proper operation of the plant. So they remain an inevitable and unavoidable increase in cost as compared with the original estimate. It is most important, therefore, to assess such changes as soon as they are brought to notice and incorporate them in the target estimates of cost and time.

Type of contract

Another aspect of significance in relation to project cost control is the type of contract that is entered into between the various parties. There will be a contract between the promoter of the project and his managing contractor, if he employs one, and there will be contracts (often called subcontracts) between those running the project and the various contractors they engage to do the work. It is these last that are of particular interest in the context of project cost control, since they can range all the way from a 'cost plus' contract to a 'fixed price' contract.

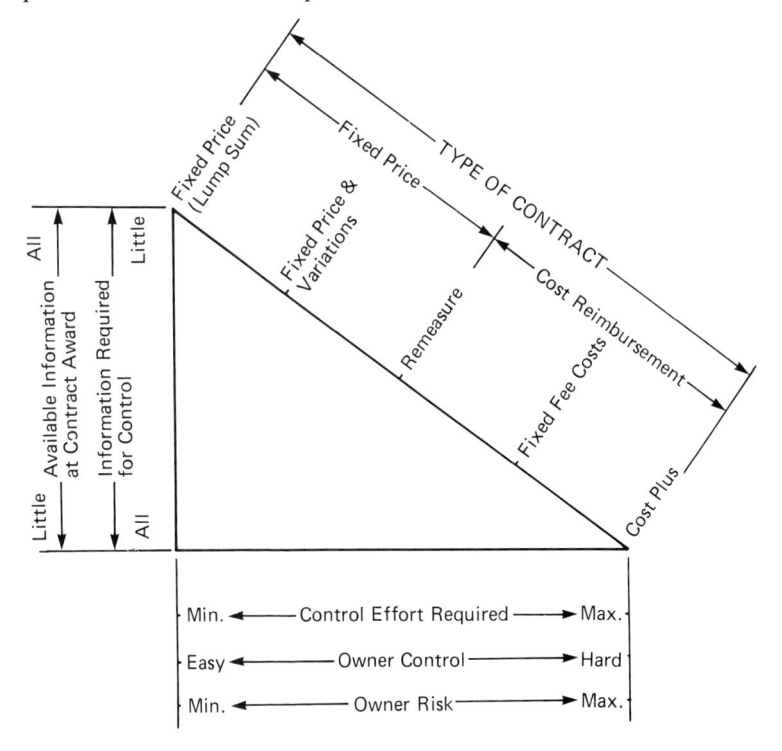

Figure 2.5 Which type of contract?
This diagram illustrates the relationship between the type of contract that can be employed and the control effort then required, the choice of contract usually being governed by the amount of data available. (See Ref.4.)

The relationship between these several forms of contract and the effort required for their control is well illustrated by Figure 2.5. The diagram is simple enough, yet the manner of presentation means that the implications of change in the form of contract can be clearly seen, together with the demand then made on detail.(4) It should be realised that this variety of choice does not affect the need for cost control: only that, as the triangle is climbed, the work of cost control is made easier. It therefore becomes important to assess the potential number and size of what are called 'cost reimbursement' contracts, since these demand the most effort in terms of control, so that the staff made available can cope. Many of these contracts are handled, costwise, by quantity surveyors in the UK.

The irrelevance of the expenditure record

To describe the expenditure (payments) record on a project as irrelevant is of course not true, but it must be recognised that from the point of view of project cost control it offers no real help. Of course the expenditure being incurred is crucial, in that it becomes the actual cost of the project and the rate at which it is being incurred is also important, because the money has to be found as it is required, but if that data is used for project cost control it can be very misleading.

The relationship between expenditure and the value of work done over time has already been presented graphically earlier – see Figure 2.3. Of course, expenditure is indeed the 'end of the line'. At project close-out, commitments will equal expenditure and value of work done will also equal expenditure, as the graph shows. Whilst the expenditure record will be the responsibility of the finance function, the value of work done record will be the responsibility of the project management team. They should watch the expenditure record and its relationship to value of work done, since that can help in cost control, but it should never be directly used for the assessment of project progress.

Summary

We have taken a broad look at the function of project cost control, set within the framework of a project organisation, chiefly to establish its vital importance to the success of any project. We have seen that whilst vital, it cannot stand alone and that, above all, project cost control still lies with the project manager. It is he who has to implement the actions that need to be taken, as indicated by the cost control function, if cost is to be contained.

Whilst we have examined the project cost control function within the framework of a major construction project, many of the principles seen to be crucial to success will apply to any and every project. For the project manager to be effective, however, he *must* receive early warning as to the way things are going. It is that aspect that we take up in detail in the next chapter.

References

1 Lock, D., ed., *Project Management Handbook*, Gower, Aldershot, 1986, ab. 400 pp. Chapter 3, 'Establishing a project organisation', by Kharbanda, O.P. and Stallworthy, E.A., deals with the subject in detail.
2 Stallworthy, E.A., *Control of Investment in New Manufacturing Facilities*, Gower, 1973, 287 pp.
3 Kharbanda, O.P., Stallworthy, E.A., and Williams, L.F., *Project Cost Control in Action,* Gower, Aldershot, 1980, 273 pp.
4 Internet (International Management Systems Association) 'Cost control in project management', a paper in the proceedings of the 4th International Expert Seminar, 13-17 October 1975.

3 Prediction – perhaps!

Our subject is the project and we now want to see if it is possible to predict whether a project will succeed or fail before we begin, or whilst it is in progress. Prediction is a form of forecasting and we have cautioned in the past that all forecasting is suspect. The longer the period for which the forecast is made, the more suspect it must be. Nevertheless, plans have to be made, as we have already seen. However, the plans first laid may well be subject to change as the situation develops. We are saying that despite all, prediction is possible: prediction of what? It seems that it is possible to predict failure before it comes and that both highlights what is going wrong and thus points to the steps that could be taken to avert that failure. If the management is sound – we are back to good management once again – then it is very possible that failure *can* be averted and a successful outcome the result. Whilst we are looking primarily at the individual project, it is helpful to look as well at the company, since management is involved in both cases and there are some lessons in company management that can be successfully applied to project management. So we will look first of all at prediction in relation to companies.

The failing company

An earlier work of ours has dealt at length with corporate failure and the subtitle, *prediction, panacea and prevention*, outlines the several phases of the subject.(1) Prediction is the necessary prelude to either a panacea or prevention. Until you know what is happening it is hardly possible to take steps to prevent it. In that earlier work we devoted four full chapters to the theme of prediction – the chapter titles are of interest in that they convey the approach we made to the subject. They were:

Where it all began
Knowledge grows, but problems grow faster
Small is *not* beautiful
We recommend

Prediction of company failure has quite a long history, having its beginnings in the assessment of credit worthiness, but we only propose at this point to consider the recommendations to which we were led by our survey of the available knowledge on the subject, seeking to apply them not only to the company but also to the individual project.

One very interesting fact disclosed by our research was that, as one of the chapter titles quoted above declared, 'small is *not* beautiful'. The failure rate for small companies, as a percentage of the total number of such small companies, is much higher than the average and this was true worldwide. What, then, is the position with respect to projects? Do many small projects fail? There is no data whatever available, as there is for companies, but we strongly suspect that this is indeed the case. We suspect that a great many of the smaller projects are *not* successfully completed, although of course we never hear about them. They never make the headlines, as a major project is liable to do. Nevertheless, for those involved in them, the consequences can be equally disastrous. The basic reason for failure will also be the same: mismanagement. Good managers are a relatively scarce commodity, so that the smaller projects are more likely to be mismanaged: the risks being smaller, less effort is likely to be put into ensuring that such projects have good project managers. Cost will also play a role: it may well be felt that the degree of management seen to be desirable cannot be afforded and risks are therefore taken in that area.

The various methods that have been published for the prediction of company failure fall broadly into two classes – the quantitative and the qualitative. The first type is seen to be what might be called objective, whilst the second is most certainly subjective. The quantitative approach to prediction takes the published accounts of a company, develops financial ratios and derives factors which are said to indicate the 'health' of the company and hence its potential for failure. Whilst seeming to be an exact, scientific approach to the problem, it has severe limitations, since published accounts often present misleading data. On the other hand, the qualitative approach, which assesses the quality of the company management, demands an intimate knowledge of that management, something not readily acquired from outside. Whilst it is a subjective approach, demanding personal assessment, it is undoubtedly the best approach, and it can obviously be readily applied by the company management itself, if it will but choose to do so.

So far as companies are concerned, it seems to us that a combination of the two approaches to assessment just outlined will lead to a sound answer as to whether a company is at risk of failure and we expect the future trend in failure (bankruptcy) prediction for companies to follow this course. Indeed, the trend is already being established, for we have seen a brochure on the subject which declares: 'The assessment of risk critically depends upon the accurate measurement of a customer's financial health *coupled with a personal judgement* of the ability to make repayment'.(2) It seems the experts, such as bankers, are steadily coming to this view. A survey amongst nearly a hundred of the largest banks in the USA pointed to the conclusion that whilst predictive financial models (the quantitative approach) can help in deciding the grant of a commercial loan, the bank should simultaneously use an alternative approach, that of personal judgment.

When it comes to projects, however, we suggest that the subjective approach, the assessment of the type, style and quality of the project management, should dominate when judgments are being made as to the future prospects of a project. The life of the average project is too short, when compared with that of a company, to allow the financial trends to give much forewarning of potential disaster.

Projects and project management

If failure can be predicted, then so can success, for the one is the converse of the other. Of course, if analysis of the project allows one to assert that failure is *not* in prospect, that does not mean that success will inevitably follow, but it does tell us that the project has a good chance of being successfully completed. We can at least say that all that could be done *has* been done. Then, when situations arise that could lead to disaster, it is to be expected that those situations will be dealt with in such a way that disaster is avoided. We shall see many such incidents successfully coped with when we come to our case studies. But it all comes back to management.

When we look at management in relation to a project, we see the management of a project vested in a project team, led by a project manager. The constitution of the project team is of great importance, but the qualities inherent in the project manager are of supreme importance in relation to the success of the project.

When it comes to companies the same is true: the chief executive makes all the difference. In that field personalities often reach the headlines: individuals such as Harold Geneen of ITT, Lee Iacocca of Chrysler, Armand Hammer of Occidental Petroleum and G.D. Birla of the Birla Group in India became legends in their own lifetime. Autobiographies of the first two just named were actually featured in the list of 'best sellers' for months on end. Just as the chief executive is the 'hero' in relation to his company if it is successful, the project manager is the 'hero' in relation to the successful project, but he almost never reaches the headlines.

We have attempted to portray this 'hero': the successful project manager.(3) That book devoted four full chapters to that one man and the chapter titles should give you some feel as to his function and his importance to the project. These are:

> The project manager – man or superman?
> The project manager and his team
> The project manager must really listen
> The total project manager

What does all this mean? It means that in assessing whether a project is going to be successful or not, the first thing to be looked at is the qualities and attributes of the project manager. A good project manager is the best possible insurance for success. But, of course, he does not stand alone. The nature, quality and attributes of his project team are also of great importance – and if he is a good project manager, he will have chosen them correctly.

Similarly, when it comes to assessing the potential for failure in a company, the subjective approach, such as that proposed by Argenti, requires us to evaluate the management. The approach enumerates and assesses defects. It asks whether the chief executive is an autocrat, whether he has a passive board, whether that board is unbalanced and so on. Very similar questions can be asked and answered in relation to the project manager and his project team. Just as a poor score would lead to the conclusion that disaster could be around the corner, so a good score must be a good omen for the eventual success of the project. The project manager makes or mars the project. He is all-important. But the composition of the project team and *its* quality are also vital to success.

The road to success

We have just asserted that the first of the many criteria for a successful project is the project manager, the second, his project team. It is a patent over-simplification to say that an effective project team will ensure success. Nothing can *ensure* success. But the probability of success is now high. Success, however, does not just happen. It has to be designed: it has to be worked for. This involves meticulous planning. Just as a company encounters problems on its way, so does a project. Nothing in this world ever goes smoothly from start to finish. In our book *Project Cost Control in Action* we equated project management and cost control, saying:(4)

> Project cost can get out of hand very easily indeed. No great effort is needed for that! Cost overruns arising from time overruns and other lapses are commonplace. The overrun can be so serious as to prove fatal not only to the project, but also to the contractor or owner involved.

It is very true. The crash of giants such as Lockheed and Rolls Royce in 1971 can be traced quite simply to a poor cost estimate on a *single* project and even poorer or perhaps more properly, *no* cost control. This resulted in quite fantastic overruns. Thus we see that project failure can lead to company failure, where the project is major in relation to the activities of the company.

The only way to avoid such disaster is by careful costing and planning – the two are very closely interwoven and can never be separated. This must take place right at the beginning of the project, during conception. The decisions made at this point in time go a long way towards determining the final cost of the project, although it may be several years before that final cost is known. The early decisions are crucial and no amount of effort thereafter is likely to have significant effect, provided that the scope of the project is maintained. It is always possible, of course, to cut cost and reduce time by curtailing a project, but that is to change its original scope significantly. Intensive effort on the part of project management can only contain the cost within the figure predetermined by those early decisions. Lack of effort, of course, will allow costs to run rampant. This fact of life in relation to any and every project is well illustrated by the diagram presented as Figure 3.1: a diagram we continually repeat because it carries an abiding lesson.

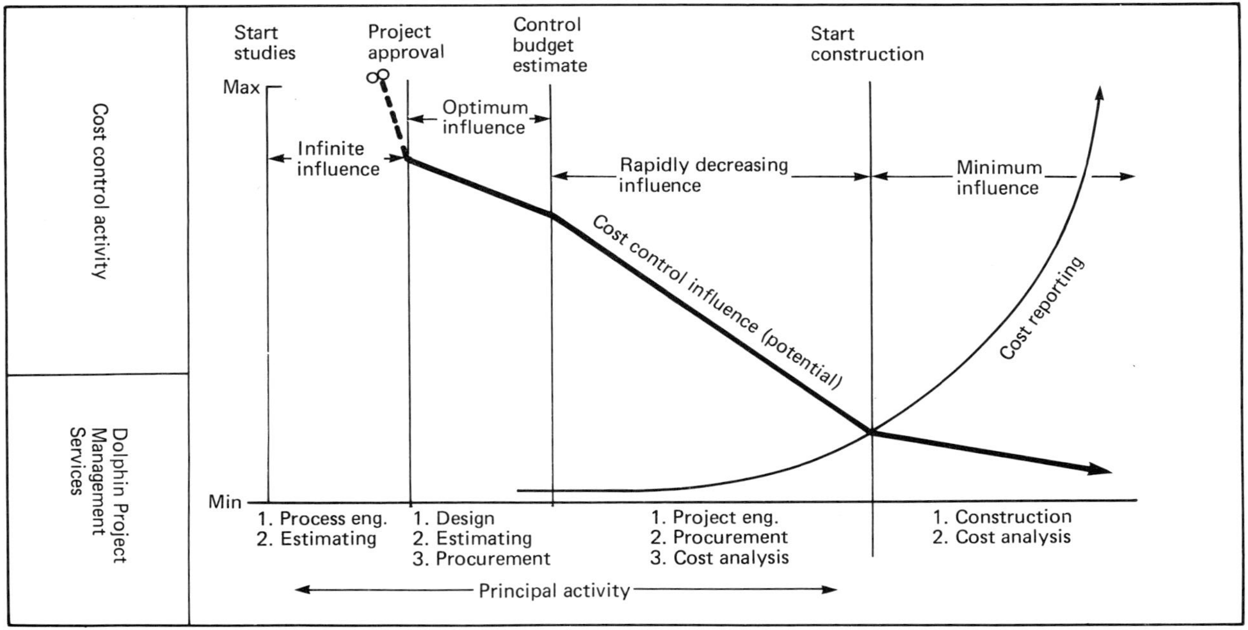

Figure 3.1 Cost control potential
This curve represents an axiom that must never be forgotten. (Originally attributed to Mr. G. Azud, this diagram first appeared in his paper 'Owner *can* control costs', included in the 1969 Transactions of the American Association of Cost Engineers.)

Early warning signals

Whilst project scope and effective project management are leading to what seems to be a predetermined end, about which very little can be done, management, nevertheless, likes to know what that end is going to be – and as early as possible. To quote:(5)

> Great is the grief of one who is deeply entrenched in a capital spending programme and *suddenly learns* [our emphasis] that the cost will exceed expectations.

No management likes to learn suddenly, without warning, that its budget is going to be exceeded. Much, much better to know well in advance, before it happens, so that something can be done about it before it is too late. Management techniques that contribute to an early assessment of the cost trend are therefore very valuable indeed, since they thereby provide an early warning system in relation to both cost and time. Such techniques are based upon the constant monitoring of the actual cost and progress during project execution and then comparing it with the estimates that have been made earlier. Such comparison provides evidence of a trend. When the trend is adverse, then it may be necessary to do more than attempt to correct the trend. It may be the time to decide whether the scope of the project should be curtailed, should it be imperative to contain costs within budget. Much, of course, depends upon the type of project at this point. Some projects are of such a nature that they cannot be limited or curtailed: they have to be either proceeded with in their entirety or abandoned.

This is not the place to enter into the details of project management systems that provide early warning: that has been done elsewhere.(4) What we do wish to emphasise is that good management will ensure that early warning *is* provided before it is too late. Figure 3.2 presents a typical sequence for project development, and it will be noticed that there is a 'point of no return'. This is the point in time when it becomes more expensive to cancel the project than to complete it. Thus it must be possible to ascertain where the project is going before that point is reached and it is no longer possible to do anything effective. Some companies have cost control procedures that demand a detailed project review *before* that point is reached, where the cost of cancellation is seriously assessed. This review allows the right decision to be made: all a part of effective project management, leading to a successful project rather than to a disaster.

The pre-emptive audit

The trends to which we have referred above, which provide the project team with early warning signals are mainly qualitative, and are assessed by the engineers in the team. But in or close to the project team there will be a financial man, responsible to the management and reporting project cost. He wishes to have the trends precisely evaluated in financial terms. Can that be done? We suggest that it can. In the past the prime function of the cost accountant has been to *record* costs, but it seems that at last they are beginning to take an interest in *controlling* costs. Till now, cost control has been largely the domain of the engineer, the attempts by the accountant to see what is coming being restricted to the assessment of commitments. Recording costs and commitments is of course vital to cost control, but it is only a part of the whole. It has to be done correctly, but if that is all that is being done, then the project team are blind and helpless, despite the cost information made available to them.

The interest of accountants in cost control is of comparatively recent origin, starting perhaps with the historic words of Elmer Staats, former Comptroller General of the United States:(6)

> Traditionally, auditors like to look at records of transactions that occurred weeks or months ago and check on the way they were handled, to reach a conclusion as to whether such transactions were proper, economical and so on. The days in which such auditing can be done are numbered. In the systems of the future . . .

The revolutionary concept being propounded was brought to a practical issue when a sum of US$800 million for the Arkansas Power & Light Company was approved on the basis of the 'appointment of independent public accountants' who would:(7)

1 Monitor the construction of the plant
2 Review all contracts
3 Submit semi-annual reports identifying deviations from budgetted construction expenditures

This was quite a step forward from the normal auditing role, but the additional features to be audited were still to be audited *after* the event. The auditing accountant is therefore only controlling to the extent that those doing the work know that he will scrutinise what they have done, and may therefore exercise more restraint and more care than they otherwise would have done. But if they are indeed inefficient, that will only be exposed too late for anything to be done in relation to the project in hand.

This weakness has since led to the concept of the 'pre-emptive audit' whereby the auditor goes further outside his basic function to become a concerned 'listener'. He takes note of the words and actions of the project manager and his team, *not* with a view to making *ex post facto* comments, but with the intention of making a positive contribution to what is going on. It is interesting to note that one of the meanings given in the dictionary for 'auditor' is 'listener', but what the auditor should now do is not merely listen, but immediately comment and act upon what he hears.

Though still in its infancy, pre-emptive audit has already proved its worth. Broadly speaking, the pre-emptive audit consists of two phases:

>The planning phase
>The compliance phase

The benefits of the pre-emptive audit is that it monitors project performance in terms of budget, schedule and targets, whilst providing much improved relationships with any regulatory bodies that may be involved in the financing of the project. Savings have been seen in both time and cost when the principles of the pre-emptive audit have been applied.

Whilst the concept is still novel it is already apparent that it can be a most valuable tool for project administration and control. In due course one would expect it to become a most valuable tool, serving not only the project manager but those who fund him and the contractors whom he has to pay. The first and at present the only book on the subject, *Managing Capital Budget Projects*, by Felix Pomeranz, explains in detail how to use the system of pre-emptive audit in order to control construction cost and thereby effect substantial savings in project cost.

Success – by design!

Whilst failure often appears to be quite sudden, it never really is. The warning signs are always there to be looked for. The same is true of success. The signs of success are also there, if they are looked for. And of course, one should go a step further. If the signs of success are not seen – perhaps even some signs of potential failure – then the appropriate steps should be taken in an endeavour to ensure success. This means that success can be planned for. The planning has to be designed for success. Planning alone is not of course sufficient. It must be associated with hard work and discipline. There are, we believe, three key factors that will help to ensure success: *planning*, which we have just mentioned, *teamwork* and what we call *layered management*.

We have already looked at planning in some detail (Chapter 1): let us now look at those other two factors, teamwork and layered management. Time and again we have emphasised the importance of the project team working in unison and in harmony, as does an orchestra. All members of the team must be fully aware of the objectives and requirements of the team leader (conductor), the project manager. Team development, once an art exercised by the good manager, seems now to have become a science.(8) The characteristics of a successful team have been found to be:

    Consistent and appropriate leadership
    Well qualified, diverse team members
    Clear and well ordered objectives
    Integrated personal and team goals
    Fair and consistent rules

Within a productive, successful team the several individuals often experience deep feelings of attraction one for the other, enjoying both their work and the comradeship it brings. We have already demonstrated the key importance of the project manager, or team leader, and he must ensure that this spirit of comradeship and partnership is there. Much will depend, of course, on the constitution of the team, which takes us back to the selection of individual team members. The selection of the team members is usually one of the most difficult decisions that have to be made in respect of a project, but it deserves the most careful attention. Peter Drucker, a world-renowned management 'guru', tells us that there is no magic solution to this problem.(9) What is required is hard work and disciplined thought. It is the age-old question of matching the job with the person and not putting 'a square peg in a round hole'. This demands an appreciation of the requirements of the given job (we recommend a written job description) with the strengths and weaknesses of prospective candidates. Techniques for personnel selection are being constantly refined, with well designed application forms, psychological tests and carefully rehearsed personnel interviews. A recent and novel addition to the battery of tests is the analysis of handwriting, much more of an art than a science at the moment and very much in the hands of the experts. This technique, called graphoanalysis, has been used extensively, but perhaps at a not too technical level, as a help in personnel selection in West Germany, France and Switzerland for the past forty years.(10) Many firms in the UK still insist on handwritten, rather than typewritten, applications for jobs. In the USA it seems that interest in this approach to personnel selection is now growing. For instance, an applicant for a job at Crown Office Products in Chicago was hired solely on the basis of an analysis of his handwriting, and despite poor oral skills and an inadequate appearance. He proved to be one of their best employees and rose to become the company's general manager. Aristotle expressed it thus: 'Handwriting is a symbol of speech and speech a symbol of mental experience'.

Coming back to the UK, the oil company Petrofina conducted an experiment where twelve members of their senior staff volunteered for graphoanalysis. The results showed that in 80 per cent of the cases it was 80 per cent accurate. Indeed, the technique has been found to be highly objective and many cynics and sceptics have become ardent converts once they have seen the system in operation.(10) Its objectivity is assured since the graphologist will not normally meet the applicant. We would not suggest that the project manager place his whole trust in a scrutiny of his team members' handwriting, but it is a factor he should not ignore. We personally have always felt that untidy writing is a sign of an untidy mind.

Now we come to our third key factor in the development of a successful project – layered management. This is inherent in the 'task force' concept, which must be implicit in any and every project. Every project, whatever its context, must have a project manager and a project team – a task force – and the creation of the task force is the first step in project implementation. Whilst this may seem a violation of the old adage 'don't put the cart before the horse', it must be done.(10) Whilst a project proceeds in phases, as illustrated in Figure 3.2, these phases do not need to be taken in strict sequence and there can always be substantial overlapping, as is indeed indicated in the diagram. Much time can be saved by the overlapping of the several project phases and this should normally be done. If we analyse the execution phase in a little more detail we have a standard breakdown: design, procurement and construction. Whilst in the broadest sense design *must* precede procurement, yet it is usually good project management practice to order long-delivery items almost as soon as design gets under way. Similarly, it is very possible to start in the field with initial construction works long before design is complete. This 'layering' of the various phases of project effort is another essential ingredient in the successful project.

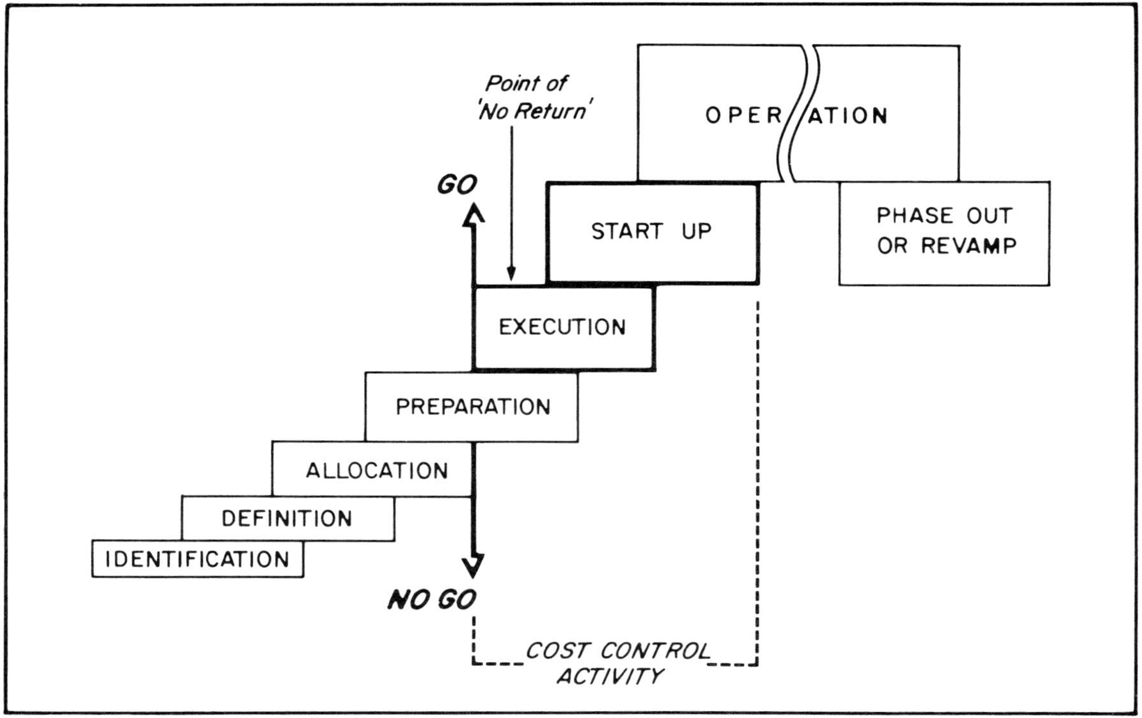

Figure 3.2 Project development
This diagram highlights the basic steps in project development. As time passes the commitment grows, and once the point of no return has been reached it costs more to cancel than to complete.

Summary

We began with the concept that prediction of the final outcome of a project is indeed possible during its early stages, if the project is properly managed, and its administration results in the development of the appropriate early warning signals. This means that success can be planned for, although of course it can never be assured. However, the appropriate management systems will contribute to keeping a project on course to success, of which one of the most recent, the pre-emptive audit, holds much promise.

We have also seen that the project manager and his project team – more particularly, the constitution of his project team – are crucial to success. This implies that the team members have to be carefully selected, which demands the use of the best available techniques.

References

1. Kharbanda, O.P. and Stallworthy, E.A. *Corporate Failure – Prediction, Panacea and Prevention*, McGraw-Hill, Maidenhead, UK, 1985, 212 pp.
2. *PAS and the Credit Manager – a Logical Partnership*, Performance Analysis Services Ltd, London.
3. Stallworthy, E.A. and Kharbanda, O.P., *Total Project Management*, Gower, 1983, 329 pp.
4. Kharbanda, O.P., Stallworthy E.A. and Williams, L.F., *Project Cost Control in Action*, Gower, 1980, 273 pp.
5. Miller, W.B., 'Fundamentals of project management', *Journal of Systems Management*, 29, November 1978, pp.22-29.
6. Staats, E.B., 'The increasing importance of internal auditors in today's world', *GAO Review*, Fall 1977, pp.1-8.
7. Pomeranz, F., *Managing Capital Budget Projects*, Wiley, New York, 1984, 258 pp.
8. Berger, M.A. 'The technical approach to teamwork', *Training and Development Journal*, 39, March 1985, pp.52-5.
9. Drucker, P.E., 'Getting things done – how to make people's decisions', *Harvard Business Review*, July/August 1985, p.22+ (4 pp.).
10. Lynch, B. 'Graphology – towards a hand-picked workforce', *Personnel Management*, March 1985, pp.14-17.
11. Abbott, K.W., 'Construction driven project management', *Hydrocarbon Processing*, March 1985, p.85+ (4 pp.).

4 Management determines success

Having looked at what we consider to be key aspects of project management: the planning, cost control and sound monitoring of progress, we now wish to take a look at the context of it all. It is the construction industry that plays the dominant role in relation to projects: its life is made up of one project after another. Whilst manufacturing industry is no stranger to projects as we define them – a team effort that has both a beginning *and* an end – and we shall take some examples from the world of manufacturing to illustrate some aspects of project management that contribute towards success, it is the construction industry that must remain our major interest.

The modern construction industry, in the form we know it today, started at the end of World War II. Until then construction activity was almost entirely localised. Construction companies rarely operated outside their own country. However, the massive destruction caused by that war, both in Europe and the Far East, called for quick and extensive reconstruction. This work stimulated a very rapid growth of that industry both in the United States and Europe. Once the reconstruction work in Japan had been completed, Japanese construction contractors, armed with the experience that they had gained at home under the supervision of their American colleagues, ventured abroad: first to the Middle East and then to Africa. Then came the mega-project, where the cost of each project, still under the supervision of one contractor or consortium, ran into several billions of dollars, although it is now suggested that such projects are becoming few and far between, following the general turn-down in the economy.

The latest entrants into the construction industry on an international scale are the Korean, Turkish and Mexican construction contractors, who moved from national to international projects because they had the advantage of a highly skilled workforce, low wages and high productivity, relative to their competitors elsewhere in the world. And once again they had been taught how to go on by the American contractors who had come and built major projects in their own country with their assistance. But the scene is still changing, for both India and China, with their enormous resources of skilled manpower, are learning both to build successfully in their own country and also to take their skills abroad on an ever-increasing scale. All in all, the construction industry is rapidly changing and highly competitive: an industry where the law of the 'survival of the fittest' undoubtedly prevails.

Construction management

We live in an age of technological revolution and some of the case studies that we shall be looking at make that very plain. Computerised process plants and robotised manufacturing plants are now the order of the day and we see that the type and content of the projects being handled is changing and this brings with it changes in project management as that adapts to the changing situation. Dingle, for instance, has pointed out that most large scale projects now coming forward are going to be built in remote areas, with but little available in terms of industrial infrastructure, but much in the way of complexity, such as construction consortiums, multiple ownership, elaborate financial provisions and all the complications of political ideology.(1) Project management has to cope with this changing need, and we see a new breed of project manager now coming to the fore, who is both businessman and technician. Dingle, noting this, believes that the business role is assuming ever-increasing importance. Mr E.T. Ireland, in his presidential address to the Institution of Professional Engineers, New Zealand, made the point even more forcefully by saying: 'Money is an engineering material'.(2) In pointing out that without money at his command an engineer has very little and that money is not an end in itself, but a means, he may well be felt to be stating the obvious, but nevertheless the point needs to be made. If there is no effective management of money then all involved in the project will suffer and the project can never be a success.

Project management is only indirectly concerned with the financing of a project: where the money is to come from and the terms upon which it is secured. But once the money is made available, it should be *very* concerned with the way in which that money is handled and disposed of between the various parties involved in the project, primarily the owner, his managing contractor (if he has one), the vendors and subcontractors. A key aspect in all this, as we have already seen, is a sound and satisfactory estimate of the amount of money that is going to be required to complete the project, which in its turn is related to and to some extent dependent upon the time that the project is going to take.

The more difficult the project in terms of access and location, the more difficult it becomes to make a precise assessment of the amount of money that will be required. Another factor that makes a cost assessment difficult is the degree of design and engineering development involved in a project. Whilst it is possible to make estimates of cost to a degree of accuracy that is adequate for project funding, the uncertainties, particularly those of location and design development, may well make it impossible for the contractors to tender for the works on a lump sum basis. Obviously, as time passes and more and more information becomes available, the accuracy of the estimate can be improved. But what is to be done meanwhile, because the two major uncertainties we have mentioned can only be resolved by actually building the project? The information that will answer the questions only becomes available as the project is put in hand.

This constantly recurring problem of money management has led to a very specific method of project management, born out of the risks inherent in situations where the scope of the work cannot be precisely defined before the contract is let, whilst the volume of that work may well run into billions of dollars. In such circumstances a lump sum bid is just not feasible, yet what is known as the 'cost plus' contract puts the owner at a severe disadvantage. This aspect has already been discussed in Chapter 2 (see, in particular, Figure 2.5). There we illustrate the relationship between the several basic forms of contract that are available and the effort required for their control. It is the lump sum contract which demands the maximum detail in terms of information and is also the easiest type of contract to administer. It is therefore highly desirable, but it has to wait on the detail. This has led to what is commonly known as the 'fixed fee plus reimbursable cost' type of contract, with the contractor being called a 'managing contractor' and receiving a fixed fee for his own work and services, the actual cost of the project being reimbursed to him by the owner at cost. Thus the risk taken by the contractor is limited to his fee and the managing contractor becomes a specialist in 'construction management'.

Construction management became widespread with the construction boom in the Middle East in the 1970s, and was in effect a 'marriage' between the owner, the contractor and the designer.(3) The function of the project manager is then to reconcile the diverse objectives of these three disparate groups in order to serve the best interests of the owner. Leading construction companies such as Bechtel pioneered this concept, particularly in the Middle East. Judging by results it has been very successful and is here to stay.

What is success?

Having laid such emphasis on the importance of completing a project to budget and on time, is that to be considered success? Hardly, because the project must also fulfil the function for which it was built. That introduces us to the concept of quality. Is the completed project the *best* answer, or is it merely an adequate answer, in terms of fulfilling the objective or dealing with the need the project is required to meet? The impact of quality is wide-ranging. With a manufacturing plant, we can consider the quality of the product, but we can also consider the quality of the plant that makes that product. Is it safe to operate? Is it a pleasant plant in which to work? Is the cost of maintenance minimal? Have we the best solution? One should not stop even there, because the impact of the plant on its environment is also worthy of study.

It is generally recognised that quality can be enhanced at the expense of cost or time, or both, as illustrated in Figure 4.1. There is continual conflict between these three basic elements and the successful project must be one that allows none of the three to dominate. The optimum should be the objective: a project built in reasonable time, economic in terms of cost and adequate so far as product and plant are concerned. In looking for a successful project we are not necessarily looking for excellence. What we are really looking for, we suggest, is competence. The book *In Search of Excellence*, whilst drawing lessons from a number of the best-run companies in the United States, did not suggest that those studied were the *only* companies that were well-run.(4) There were many, many more. Similarly, the projects that we have taken as case studies are only a few from a great multitude that have been brought to a successful conclusion. We, however, have not been in search of excellence and the choice of project has been determined more for the lessons that it has to offer than anything else.

That is not to say that those involved in projects and project management should not themselves be striving after excellence –

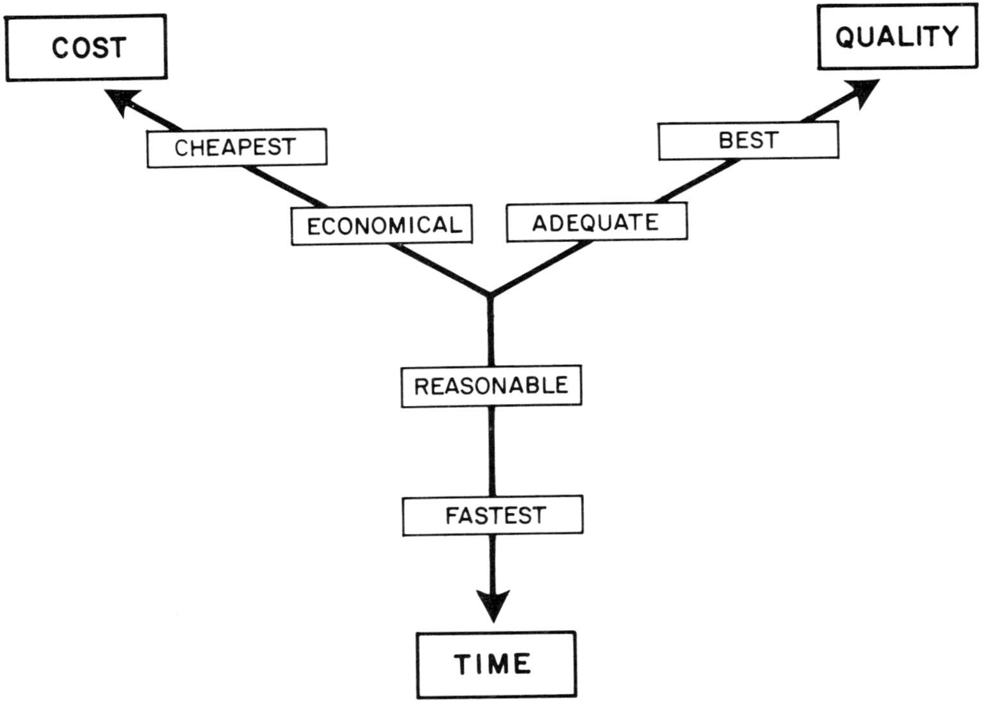

Figure 4.1 The tug-of-war
Cost, quality and time are essentially incompatible. The art in project management is to maintain a proper balance between the three. (With acknowledgements to M. Snowdon, author of *Management of Engineering Projects*, Butterworth, 1977.)

or even perfection. It is always possible to do better and every good project manager realises this: he would never 'rest on his laurels' as the saying goes. Once a project manager and his team cease striving after perfection and become satisfied with 'second best' they are on the road to mediocrity. Those involved in successful projects will display certain specific attributes to a greater or lesser degree, of which a continual striving to do better than last time is but one. The system of project administration which they develop will also allow for those attributes to be displayed and fully utilised. For instance, every project has to begin with what is often called a 'feasibility study'. Those contemplating the project have to be assured that it is feasible. But feasibility as such is not enough. Hiding behind the question of feasibility is another question: 'Have we got the best possible answer?' To know that more than one approach to the project will have to be studied and it is here that management often fail. They are too easily satisfied. For instance, Professor Frank Lu of the University of Canterbury (New Zealand), says in the introduction to his book on economic decision making:(5)

> Alternatives are not always obvious, and the search for them can be a difficult task. It is, however, an extremely important task, one demanding skill and creativity. One of the essential attributes of a good engineer and manager is a sensitivity to alternatives and the ability to envisage them. This attribute, natural for some, may be improved upon and added to for others by conscious efforts of learning and vigilance.

This assessment of alternatives should not only be active when the project is initiated, but throughout its life. Every project manager is inevitably confronted from time to time throughout the life of every project – we are sure there are no exceptions – with crises that require resolving. It is the choice of the best alternative for the resolution of such crises that leads on to a successful project.

The elements of success

Much has been written about the road to success, particularly in relation to the running of companies. As we look at the advice on offer, we see that the concept of dominance often comes to the fore. For instance, one book bringing us a number of simple concepts that can lead to success – and we are great believers in simplicity – has the title: *The Business of Winning – How to*

Succeed in Business by Really Trying.(6) But we think that 'winning' is the wrong word in this context, since it implies that there is a need to do better than everybody else in order to be successful, but that is *not* so. That is why we have already emphasised that success is to be seen on every side and that there are any number of successful projects. But success has to be earned. It will not come fortuitously. There are many elements involved in success, but dominance is not one of them. A successful company may well be a market leader – we take up one such case when we look at the French company Schlumberger in Chapter 11 – but a company does not have to be a market leader in order to be successful.

We see Schlumberger as a company striving after perfection, but of course it is only one of many. Here, as always, much depends on the 'man at the top', the chief executive, as he is often called. We shall see as we go through our case studies the critical role played by the 'man at the top' of every successful project: the project manager. Many of the factors involved in successful company management also play a role in project management. We have found Standard Telephones and Cables (STC), a UK-based company, a very good example in this respect and have already used them to illustrate the way in which 'one man can make the difference'.(7) The man was Sir Kenneth Corfield, who took over as chairman and chief executive at STC some ten years ago and transformed its managerial approach. A booklet was developed in cooperation with the employees with the title: *The Best Company Book* and four main principles were identified there as governing company practice:

1 Be efficient and profitable, giving good service to the customers
2 Do business straight and honestly
3 Treat all employees with respect and help them develop and contribute fully
4 Have an open and participative style of management

We shall see, as we go through our case studies, the way in which these principles are worked out in the project management teams set up to run the projects we are analysing and the way in which they contribute to success. STC gather all their management together once a year to hear what the company is doing and to exchange ideas. This is called the MIM (Management Information Meeting) and at the *MIM '85* some 2000 delegates attended, the number being almost doubled as compared with the previous year because STC had recently taken over ICL. Some years earlier (1980) a Management Administration Conference was held with the theme: *Managing for Success*. We mention for the sake of illustration one statement made at the conference by Sir Kenneth Corfield:

> ... the human being is far too good an instrument to be used just for sheer motive power. We have machines to do that. Human beings should be able to approach their work with joy and pleasure.

How rarely does that happen in practice. How wonderful it would be if it were always so. But, as we go through our case studies, watch for the signs that those involved in the projects we are looking at are enjoying their work, for that is another key to success. Perhaps we should bring this reference to STC to an end by pointing out that despite their managerial strategy the company, a major operator in the electronics industry, has been suffering from a lack of orders, the shares collapsing on the stock market. Sir Kenneth Corfield has become a casualty, finally bowing to pressure to resign as chairman and chief executive.(8) It is interesting to note that much criticism was levelled at his having a dual role – chairman *and* chief executive – a managerial approach which we do not think conducive to success in the long term.(7)

The role of communications

The focus of every project is the project team, headed up by the project manager. Since every project has both a beginning *and* an ending, a point we made right at the beginning, every project team is temporary – and everyone on the team knows this. They come together for the duration of the project, whether that be six months or several years, they are necessarily drawn from a wide variety of disciplines, and they usually have very different backgrounds, even when they all come from the same company. This creates a very complex communications problem for the project manager, who not only has to communicate effectively with his team but also with the outside world. His team owe him no loyalty: their prospects for the future lie outside the project, even if that is most successfully performed. The truth of this is demonstrated by an article under the title 'International assignment: career or caper?'(9) The advice given to prospective members of the overseas project team is to stay abroad only so long as it contributes to their career, accepting an overseas assignment only if it fits in with their career plan and not just for the sake of adventure. So here is another problem for the project manager to overcome: divided loyalty. He has not only to be completely loyal to the project himself, putting its prospects above his own personal future, but he also has to communicate the same spirit to his team members.

There is no doubt that good communications are basic to successful management. Peter Drucker, the world-famous expert on management problems, declares in his foreword to a book on communications that poor communications is a direct result of ignorance. We do not know:(10)

1 what to say;
2 when to say it;
3 how to say it; and
4 to whom to say it.

Indeed, he asserts that sixty per cent of management problems are caused in whole or in part by faulty management communications.

Most of the projects we shall be considering will be carried out by a construction contractor with an organisation designed specifically for the implementation of projects; and the organisation established for that purpose must be effective in terms of communication, or it will collapse. Mehta, writing on this subject, considers that the matrix type of organisation is the most effective, although he still makes the point that much will still depend upon the skill and capability of the project manager.(11) We have always recommended the matrix type organisation for project management, since we are sure that it encourages effective communication.(12)

The project team must work well together, and the mere competence of the several individuals who make up the team will not ensure this. The various attributes and talents of the team, to which we have drawn attention earlier, have to be blended together to create a harmonious whole. Another writer on the subject points out that each member of the team should know how to cover for other members of the team and have a feel for what they would do in a given situation.(13) In all this the project manager or team leader sets the pace. His attitudes and in particular his trust in and reliance on the members of his team will become infectious, and they will all follow suit. This is the road to success. So once again, as we work through our case studies let us watch out for the impact of communications, characteristically improved in the case of a team created for a specific objective within a major company by creating a project centre where they all work together, in intimate association with one another.

References

1. Dingle, J., 'Contractors, consultants and the chemical industry'. Speech given at the European Chemical Marketing Research Association Conference, Oslo, 11-13 October 1982.
2. Ireland, E.T., 'Money is an engineering material'. Presidential address at the Institution of Professional Engineers New Zealand, Hastings, 13 February 1984.
3. Kavanagh, T.C., Muller, F., and O'Brien, J.J., *Construction Management*, McGraw-Hill, 1978, 399 pp.
4. Peters, T.J. and Waterman, R.H., *In Search of Excellence – Lessons from America's Best-run Companies*, Harper & Row, New York, 1982, 360 pp.
5. Lu, F.P.S., *Economic Decision-making for Engineers and Managers*, Whitcombe and Tombs, 1969, 172 pp.
6. Heller, R., *The Business of Winning – How to Succeed in Business by Really Trying*, Sidgwick & Jackson, London, 1981, 227 pp.
7. Kharbanda, O.P. and Stallworthy, E.A., *Corporate Failure – Prediction, Panacea and Prevention*, McGraw-Hill, London, 1985, 212 pp.
8. Gribben, R., 'STC chairman bows to "quit" demands', *Daily Telegraph*, London, 3 August 1985, p.17.
9. Limber, T.P., 'International assignment: career or caper?', *Worldwide Projects*, December 1983/January 1984, pp.18+.
10. Parkinson, C.N. and Rowe, N. *Communicate – Parkinson's Formula for Business Survival*, Prentice-Hall, 1977, 205 pp.
11. Mehta, D., 'Communication in project management', *Economic Times* (India), 10 August 1985, p.6.
12. Stallworthy, E.A. and Kharbanda, O.P., *Total Project Management – From Concept to Completion*, Gower, Aldershot, 1983, 329 pp. See the section on 'the organisational matrix' (Chapter 13).
13. Dinsmore, P.C., 'Better communications increases management efficiency', *Asian National Development*, October 1984, pp.42-4.

Part Two
THERE IS STRENGTH IN COOPERATION

5 Motivate and succeed

We have now outlined the management concept in substantial detail and have seen that whilst the project manager has a key role to play he would get nowhere without the project team. We believe that the successful project is, above all, a result of good management, but good management itself is far more than just sound administration. There must be motivation and we would like to coin the phrase: 'motivation the means – success the end'. All the case studies we are now going to review and analyse are of successful projects, so that in all cases sound motivation driving those involved towards a declared objective will be there, but our very first case study brings us a display of motivation *par excellence*.

We are now going to Japan. The recovery of Japan from the ashes of World War II so that it now leads the world in many areas is nothing short of a miracle. It is said, for instance, that the pace of the rise in productivity in Japan is much faster than anywhere else in the world.(1) This is illustrated by the following table:

	Output per hour of work (1983 prices) US$	Annual rate of growth (1977-83) %
Japan:	17.61	3.9
France:	19.80	3.5
United Kingdom:	11.34	3.3
West Germany:	22.22	2.5
United States:	18.21	1.2

This 'miracle', to which we shall refer many times for the lessons it brings us, is said to be largely due to the fact that Japanese managers are essentially team builders. They lead, rather than manage, and do this by a process of 'consensus', rather than by passing down instructions. There is therefore free and honest communication up and down the management structure, which builds up a 'family' type of relationship, with its warm, cooperative atmosphere and strong team spirit. Physical factors such as 'open plan' offices encourage the interchange of ideas and information between colleagues, seniors and juniors. To foster this sense of unity and team spirit, managers and workers alike in many Japanese companies wear identical white overalls. Indeed, so strong is this identification of the individual with the company that if you receive a visit from a Japanese engineer, he does not identify himself via his qualifications, but says: 'I am a Mitsui man', or 'I am a Mitsubishi man'. When you get to know them better, you are able to discern the company from the 'style' of the man you meet. Thus the whole company is a united team, but within that whole the Japanese have for years practised the use of the task force and the project team to resolve a problem or accomplish a specific task. This has been done not only 'in house', but also almost 'in nation' as we shall now see.

There are two outstanding examples from Japan of this nationwide cooperation to achieve a specific end, one in the field of microelectronics, the other in the field of robotics. In both cases, key personnel were taken from various companies to project centres for development research, but were later returned to their respective companies. In both the cases quoted, the basic research had been done elsewhere and was available 'off the shelf' from the technical literature. The Japanese used this published data as their base upon which to build.

Nationwide cooperation

The role of the project team, which would now have as members the best brains on the subject nationwide, rather than companywide, is to develop the specific item for which the team has been brought together (computer or robot) to the point where the main technological problems have been solved. That achieved, they go back to their individual companies with the relevant knowhow and compete fiercely in the marketplace for sales, first at home and then worldwide.

Their efforts, especially outside Japan, are to some extent conserved by regulation through centralised government agencies, such as the Ministry of International Trade and Industry (MITI). These government agencies, together with the banks, play a vital role, their watchword being cooperation rather than competition. Thus resources are conserved, rather than frittered away without result. For instance, major overseas tenders are the subject of considerable consultation among possible tenderers on a platform such as MITI, who assess the situation and then decide on the company best suited at that time to go all out for that particular contract. The project may well involve a large number of different companies, but then the chosen company acts as leader of a consortium, coordinating a cooperative effort. The government agencies and the banks then play a supporting role, extending finance, arranging credit or a subsidy: anything that may be required to meet the international competition.

It is interesting to see that this same idea may now be coming to fruition in the USA. Researchers there are starting a collaborative project to enable companies to make more use of high-power lasers for jobs such as welding and thermal treatment.(2) The project will be led by the Battelle Institute and they are asking companies that want to participate in the project to pay a fee. Then all the participants will share in the patent rights of any inventions and receive the engineering drawings. Thereafter, presumably, they will compete against one another in the further development and use of the techniques that are developed. But to return to Japan.

Now the robot

Who hasn't heard of a robot? Nevertheless it is probably as well to define our terms. The Robot Institute of America defines a robot thus:

> a programmable, multi-function manipulator designed to move material, parts, tools or specialised devices through variable programmed motions for the performance of a variety of tasks.(3)

On the other hand, the Electrical Machinery Law of Japan defines an industrial robot as:

> an all purpose machine equipped with a memory device and a terminal device (for holding things), capable of rotation and of replacing human labour by automatic performance of movements.(4)

The Japanese Industrial Robot Association (JIRA) feels that a robot cannot be defined. The association does however classify industrial robots – largely by the method adopted to input the information being used. Thus:

Manual manipulator: a manipulator that is directly operated by a man.

Sequence robot: a manipulator, the working step of which operates sequentially in compliance with pre-set procedures, conditions and positions.

Fixed sequence: a sequence robot as defined above, for which the pre-set information cannot be easily changed.

Variable sequence: a sequence robot as defined above, for which the pre-set information can be easily changed.

Playback robot: a manipulator that can repeat any operation after being instructed by a man.

Numerically controlled robot: a manipulator that can execute the commanded operation in compliance with the numerically loaded working information on, for example, position, sequence and conditions.

Intelligent robot: a robot that can determine its own actions through its sensing and recognitive functions.

A study of this analysis makes it clear that the American definition of robots excludes manual manipulators and fixed sequence machines. Therefore, when we begin to compare the statistics in relation to robots in the USA and Japan, the data concerning the number of robots installed should be evaluated with care, in order to see whether they include the manual manipulator, defined as a robot in Japan, or exclude that class of machine, as defined in the United States.(5)

In 1961 three industrial robots were sold worldwide – two to General Motors and one to the Ford Motor Company.(6) Despite the fact that this development started in the USA, that country has now been totally outdistanced by Japan. The US market was very resistant: there were fears about lost jobs, loss of the human touch and a lot of misunderstanding. Thus the US company Unimation, failing to develop a receptive home market, licensed its pioneer robot technology to the Japanese company Kawasaki in 1968. This company mobilised substantial effort at home in the cooperative manner we have just outlined, in order to improve the design and adapt it to Japanese conditions. This buying in of knowhow is a common Japanese tactic and provides a quick and cheap start, since the royalty payments would have been a fraction of what it would have cost Kawasaki to start from scratch.(7) Beginning with this bought-in US technology, Japan forged ahead, bringing robots into ever wider use in manufacturing industry. There is no doubt that the chronic labour shortage in Japan has given impetus to this programme of robotisation, but without the appropriate motivation nothing would have happened. Primarily because of the high degree of cooperative effort in the initial stages, Japan has been much quicker than other countries in adapting robots to serve a wide variety of different purposes.(8) Government commitment also helped, there being an allocation of some US$35 million a year for the support of robot research, nearly double that committed in the USA. The end result has been that robots in Japan now make a very substantial contribution to the manufacturing process, not only as labour-saving devices, but in ensuring better and sustained quality production.(9)

Robots were initially the creation of the science fiction writer. The great Isaac Asimov first introduced robots into his writing in 1939, but in his foreword to a book on robotics some forty years later said:(10)

> I did not at that time seriously believe that I would live to see robots in action . . . yet here we are . . . robot replaces man on a job simply because a robot can do it.

He goes on to make the point that the robot replaces 'mindless drudgery'. Robots are also the ideal replacement for man in hazardous situations.(11)

The assessment of the number of robots now operating in Japan and elsewhere in the world varies from source to source, but all who write on this subject agree that Japan is far ahead of any other nation in its application of robots. The number of robots in operation in the USA in 1983 was assessed at some fifteen thousand, whereas in Japan it is said to be nearly four times as many, some sixty thousand. In addition, many of the robots operating in the USA were made in Japan. Babani, reviewing the present status and seeking to look into the future, presents us with the following data:(12, 13)

Robot population

	1981	1985	1990
Japan:	9 500	27 000	67 000
USA:	4 500	15 000	56 000
West Germany:	2 300	8 800	27 000
USSR & Eastern Europe:	6 000	21 000	–

It appears that there are substantial cost savings. The operating cost of the average robot is said to be of the order of US$6 per hour, including maintenance, whereas a workman doing the same job would cost US$23 per hour. This is in the USA and according to the chairman of General Motors, Roger Smith, 'everytime the cost of labour goes up a dollar an hour, another thousand robots become economical'.(14)

The factory of the future

There seems to be no doubt that Japan will continue to lead the world in robotics since there the science fiction fantasy of robots making robots is already a reality. The world's most advanced computer-controlled factory, operated by Fanuc (only established in 1980) has 60 employees and 100 robots producing some 40 different kinds of servo motor at a total rate of 10 000 per month. Servo motors are at the heart of almost every robot. The significance of these figures is seen when comparison is made between a factory using robotics – the technical term is 'flexible manufacturing systems' (FMS) – and one using conventional methods, as set out below:(15)

Yamazaki Machinery Works

	Conventional	*FMS*
Investment in plant (US$ million):	14.1	18.2
In process inventory (US$ million):	5.0	0.2
Manufacturing cost: (US$ 000):	21.6	22.9
Profit before tax (US$ 000):	–891.0	4,347.0
Labour cost (US$ million):	3.9	2.3
No. of workers:	215	13

So far so good. But Japan is already heading towards the unmanned factory. MITI have set up a US$50 million fund to be used over eight years for this purpose and it has become clear that Japan favours automation of *all* their manufacturing operations. It seems that in that country at least the emergence of what is called the 'Luddite' mentality is not feared. The Luddites were bands of English artisans in the early nineteenth century who raised riots for the destruction of machinery, fearing the loss of their jobs. It now seems to be believed that in any society there is always a way to utilise surplus human resources displaced by increased productivity, whilst it is asserted that the level of employment in a society has *nothing* to do with that society's level of productivity.(16) It is of course recognised that those who are displaced by the onward march of the robot will need retraining, but the Japanese already have retraining courses in regular use for their employees, since it is considered good practice to move people from one job to another in any event. The aspect that is continually emphasised is that the robot takes the drudgery out of routine work.(17)

All this seems very different to the motivation for the use of robots in the USA. There the growing use of robots is seen as inevitable if that country is to meet the continuing and growing competition from Japan, but robots are adopted with reluctance. It is said that they take people's jobs away. Nevertheless, the robot is the only hope if the USA is to head off economic decline, since the manufacturing machinery in current use is rapidly becoming obsolete.(12) To quote James A. Baker, a vice-president of General Electric:

> Our machines are old, our processes primitive, our quality and our productivity a disgrace. American industry faces three choices: automate, emigrate or evaporate. The alternative to automation is the loss of all jobs as companies die or move offshore.

To change the product a factory is making called for retooling – a massive investment before the advent of the robot. Robots only need to be reprogrammed. Robots are said to increase productivity by up to 35 per cent on installation, since they require no breaks, no days off, no paid vacations and they neither go slow or go on strike. They also guarantee a consistent, high-quality product. Thus American industry has no choice but to robotise, since otherwise it will just fade away.

Let's get back to basics

The Japanese success with robotics is undoubtedly due to what we might call their 'management style'. The success of Japanese products worldwide can be attributed in part to their successful adaption to robotisation, but that in turn is but a consequence of successful management. To what, then, can we attribute the outstanding success of Japanese management?

In part it is a consequence of their national characteristics, something that cannot necessarily be imitated by others. They love their work, have a strong sense of motivation, sensitivity to the feelings of others and an assured identity.(18) The Japanese *like* to work: more for pleasure than for the reward it brings. They also like to learn. They also have complete loyalty towards their employer, probably because of his 'from cradle to the grave' care of his employees. Another significant factor is their knowledge that they have no natural resources in their country of any significance and must therefore live by their wits and hard work. Even though the average Japanese is now relatively rich, he is well aware of the poverty of earlier generations and the ever-present danger of relapsing to that sad situation.

But whilst all this cannot necessarily be applied in other countries, with very different histories and cultures, its consequences in terms of management techniques are quite clear. There is no mystery about it. The elements of management in Japanese society that have contributed to success have been carefully analysed and a multitude of papers and books written on the subject. In one typical study, five Japanese electric companies were compared with Western Electric, a US company, to establish the realities and dismiss the myths surrounding productivity in Japan, since high productivity is a major factor in their success.(19) The myths were found to be:

> Lower absenteeism
> Greater corporate loyalty
> Harder working employees.

On the other hand, the realities were established as:

> More engineers per worker
> Selective hiring
> Substantial pay differences
> Unique capital structure

The lessons that were then drawn for American managers were:

> Establish an elite labour force
> Screen labour to select the best
> Have close contact with feeder schools

Make heavier investment in plant and equipment
Frequent contact between engineers and workers
Have pay policies that reduce the quitting rate
Motivate – by pay and promotion

The above concepts are perhaps well summarised by Yoshiki Mitsui, the president of Mitsui High-tec, when receiving the nations' prestigious Blue Ribbon Medal from the Japanese government for the phenomenal success of his company. He declared a three point creed for success:(20)

1 To manufacture products useful to people throughout the world
2 Uphold the principle of reciprocal gains and seek to achieve mutual benefits
3 Create a paradise for workers on the basis of a spirit of equality.

Summary

How can we apply the above to project implementation? The first point made above is not strictly relevant, in that our objective is the project itself: no more. But the other two are a reflection of the several recommendations made to American management by Weiss and quoted above. We would further venture to sum them all up in turn with one word: *motivate*. That, above all, is the secret of the Japanese success. The necessary motivation cannot always be introduced in precisely the Japanese fashion, because their culture and concepts are very different to those prevailing in the West, but Weiss has drawn attention to those aspects of management that deserve attention and will stimulate motivation.(19) As we continue with our case studies we shall see yet other ways in which motivation can be established in the project team and so contribute to a successful project.

References

1 Article: 'A time to dismantle the world', *Economist*, 9 November 1985, p.21-3.
2 Article: 'Laboratory seeks research partners', *Financial Times* (London), 14 November 1985, p.14.
3 Potter, R., 'Robotic basics', proceedings of the 13th Inter-

national Symposium on Industrial Robots, 1983.
4. Dorf, R.C., *Robotics and Automated Manufacturing*, Reston Publishing Company, 1983.
5. Vitner, G. and Shenkar, O., 'Motivational implications of different robot types', *International Jnl of Operations & Production Management*, Vol. 5, No. 2, 1985, pp.50-57.
6. Humphreys, Betsy, 'Working robots: have they arrived?', *Cost Engineering* (USA), Vol.27, No.1, January 1985, p.15-7.
7. Byrne, J.A., 'Whose robots are winning?', *Forbes*, 131, 14 March 1983, p.154.
8. Freehlich, L., 'Mighty oaks take time', *Datamation*, January 1983, p.113.
9. Reeve, Ron, 'Where are the robots?', *Computerworld*, 10 June 1985, pp.ID25-32.
10. Engelberger, J.F., *Robotics in Practice – Management and Application of Industrial Robots*, Kogan Page, London, 1980, 291 pp.
11. Lambrines, J. and Johnson, W.G., 'Robots to reduce the high cost of illness and injury', *Harvard Business Review*, 62, May-June 1984, p.24.
12. Reed, D., 'Robots march on US industry', *Readers Digest*, May 1985, pp.188-192.
13. Babani, A., 'Robots – Malthusian explosion', *Herald Review*, 14 July 1985, pp.42-3.
14. Foulkes, F.K. and Hirsch, J.L., 'People make robots work', *Harvard Business Review*, 62, January-February 1984, pp.94-102.
15. Koren, Y., *Robotics for Engineers*, McGraw-Hill, New York, 1985, 347 pp.
16. Yoshioka, H., 'Computer applications for design and manufacture in Japan'. Paper presented at the International Symposium on Electronics for Productivity, New Delhi, April 1983.
17. Cook, J., 'Shakeout', *Forbes*. 134, 16 July 1984, p.87+
18. Sono, Ayako, 'Four keys to success', *Journal of Japanese Trade & Industry*, No.2, 1985, p.49.
19. Weiss, A., 'Simple truths of Japanese manufacturing', *Harvard Business Review*, 62, July-August 1984, pp.119-125.
20. Ohne, M., 'Idealism and persistence send Mitsui High-tec to the top', *Journal of Japanese Trade & Industry*, No.2, 1985, p.39.

6 Success – through international cooperation

Later, when we come to consider some successful projects in developing countries, we shall have something to say about what is termed 'technology transfer'. Whilst the major international construction contractors have made much of their efforts in this field, advertising training programmes and cooperating in the construction of highly sophisticated plants in backward areas, technology transfer is not the 'magic wand' that it was first thought to be – transforming the 'have-nots' into the 'haves'.(1) Technology, unfortunately, is *not* a physical asset, although it is sometimes assumed that it is. Process manuals and operation manuals are not enough: in the ultimate analysis technology transfer is really education and training. To be effective this has to be given 'on the job'. Then individuals build up practical working experience. This also means that the real technology transfer takes place at the basic working level, not in the board room where the papers are handed over, and ultimate success is the result of long-term educational programmes.

But international cooperation does not always involve technology transfer in the sense in which we have just used it. There can also be cooperation between equals, and then it becomes an *exchange* of technology, with both parties well able to assimilate what is being brought to them. South Africa offers us some very interesting examples of this type of cooperation, that has resulted in the completion of some very successful projects. Outstanding in this respect has been the Sasol Two and Sasol Three projects, which are remarkable in many ways, including their size.

The Sasol projects

The name 'Sasol' stands for *South African Coal, Oil and Gas Company* when written in Afrikaans, the Dutch-related language of the South Africans. It is more than twenty-five years ago now that Sasol One was first built to produce liquid fuels from coal, which South Africa has in abundance. Sasol One came on stream in 1954, and since then this operating company has built upon this particular technology, even offering consulting and advisory services to interested companies overseas.

With this background, the design and construction of Sasol Two was begun in 1975. The Fluor Corporation, of Irvine, California, was appointed as managing contractor and the plant was to be located at Secunda, some 94 miles east of Johannesburg in the Eastern Transvaal. The plant was completed and came on stream in 1980: we present an aerial view of this massive project in Figure 6.1. Whilst Fluor operated as managing contractor, a number of other international contractors were also employed to provide specialised equipment and processes, as listed in Figure 6.2. The heart of the process is the transformation of the solid coal to gas, achieved in a gasifier where, coal having been charged, steam and oxygen are then introduced, raising the temperature to some 2 200°F. In this intense heat, the molecular structure of the coal is broken down, releasing carbon monoxide, carbon dioxide, sulphur, nitrogen and other substances to form a raw gas, which is then further processed. Lurgi of West Germany were the specialist contractors for the design and supply of the gasification section, to be seen in Figure 6.3, the operating experience of Sasol also making a significant contribution in this area.

But that is by no means the end of the story. The contracts for Sasol Three were being awarded even before Sasol Two had been completed and commissioned. This indicates a high degree of confidence both in the process and the contractors who had been building Sasol Two. Sasol Three was to be largely a 'chinese copy' of Sasol Two, using the existing design drawings and the temporary facilities already available. So now two projects were being handled in effect as one, bringing economies in both cost and time. As a result Sasol Three came on stream very quickly after Sasol Two, early in 1982. The total investment in the combined project was of the order of US$6.5 billion, taking the US dollar as equivalent to 1.15 Rand, as it was then. We do not propose to enter into the detail of the management of the project, although there are a number of interesting lessons to be learnt, because that has already been done by us elsewhere.(2) What we

SUCCESS – THROUGH INTERNATIONAL COOPERATION

Figure 6.1 Sasol Two in operation
This aerial photograph gives a vivid impression of the size of the complex.
(Photograph by courtesy of Fluor Corporation, Irvine, California, USA.)

wish to emphasise at this point is the way in which the local South African companies were able to contribute to the project development and successfully assimilate the technology coming in from abroad *because* they had the appropriate capabilities at all levels.

Sasol Two and Sasol Three
Secunda — Republic of South Africa

International engineering contractors employed
for specialist plants and services

Badger, Cambridge, Massachusetts, USA.
Deutsche Babcock, Oberhausen, West Germany.
Fluor Mining & Metals, Redwood City, Ca.
L'Air Liquide, Champigny, France.
Linde, Munich, West Germany.
Lurgi, Frankfurt-a-Main, West Germany.
Mobil, New York, New York, USA.
Universal Oil Products (UOP), Des Plaines, Illinois.

Figure 6.2 Engineering contractors on Sasol Two
A listing of the international engineering contractors who provided engineering, plant and equipment for Sasol Two and Sasol Three.

Figure 6.3 Gasification section – synfuels production
Here we see the gasification for the Sasol Two Synfuels Plant, completed in 1980. The scale of the installation can be judged from the cooling tower in the background. (Photograph by courtesy of the Fluor Corporation, Irvine, California, USA.)

Engineering in South Africa

The Union Corporation Limited says of itself, in a brochure titled *A Decade of Engineering with the Union Corporation Group* that it is one of the most progressive organisations in South Africa. It continues:(3)

> Its [the Union Corporation Group] mining and industrial developments have provided the basis for challenging and satisfying careers for engineers. In the 1970s the Union Corporation group spent over R1 billion on capital development . . .

The brochure is designed for the recruitment of young mechanical and electrical engineers. The company offers extensive training facilities and declares that there are plenty of job opportunities. Much stress is laid on the comfortable facilities for such employees: bachelor trainee engineers are housed in fully furnished rooms, with communal lounges and reading rooms, all at a nominal rental. Senior employees live in houses on stands varying in size from a quarter to one acre and offering spacious gardens. All this in established communities, with primary and secondary schools to matriculation level as well as facilities for advanced technical study. A pleasant picture. Recruitment takes place both locally and in the United Kingdom. All this demonstrates in a practical way the point that we made earlier: that growth in technology and its successful application *must* be rooted in long-term educational programmes. That is essential to the successful use of technology, and especially the high technology now so much to the fore.

The same brochure outlines ten projects successfully completed during the decade, including one headed 'Richards Bay Minerals'. We are told in that context:

> Mining of the beach sands by Richards Bay Minerals started in 1977 using a standard method of dredging, concentrating and separating as practised in Australia and the USA. Rutile, zircon and ilmenite are separated in the initial stages. The ilmenite is later smelted to produce titania slag. Major shareholders in this R250 million project are the Quebec Iron and Titanium Corporation, which has also contributed its unique ilmenite smelting technology, the Industrial Development Corporation and Union Corporation.

Here we have technology transfer – from Australia and the USA, but more particularly Canada, for application and use in South Africa. We thought it would be interesting to take this project as a case study, to see how the cooperation worked out in practice.

Titanium, a most expensive metal, is indispensable these days, being used in substantial quantities in the production of military and civil aircraft engines, apart from its use in chemical plants where severe corrosion would otherwise be in prospect. Not only is titanium metal highly resistant to corrosion, but it is strong and light. It is most commonly used as an alloy: a typical alloy would be IMI 318, containing 6 per cent aluminium and 4 per cent vanadium.(4) This particular alloy has a density of 4.42 g/cm^3. That can be compared with aluminium (2.75) or stainless steel (7.75). Its use now extends far beyond the aircraft industry for which it was first developed. One most interesting application, because of its biocompatibility and good fatigue strength in body fluids, is in the replacement of hip and knee joints, bone screws and other surgical devices. But to come to the mine and the smelter where it all starts we have to go to Richards Bay, Natal.

Initiating the project

The extensive sand dunes along the coastline of South Africa north of Richards Bay are rich in heavy minerals. This has been known for a long time, but their exploitation had to await the development of Richards Bay as a harbour. Then the Industrial Development Corporation (IDC), as a result of extensive investigations, established the feasibility of separating rutile, zircon and ilmenite, the minerals present in these sands, but since the ilmenite was not readily marketable, the project was not considered to be commercially viable. At that time (1973) the Quebec Iron and Titanium Corporation of Canada (QIT) were the only successful ilmenite smelter in the world. That company had been looking for a higher-grade ore for processing and the ilmenite fraction available from the sand dunes of Richards Bay seemed to fit the bill. So QIT joined hands with IDC, the government agency and Union Corporation (UC), whom we have just been looking at, to implement this particular project. The consortium formed two companies: Tisand, to undertake the mining of the ore, and Richards Bay Iron and Titanium, to carry out the smelting operation, both wholly owned by a holding company, Richards Bay Minerals. In addition to the three companies primarily involved, two insurance companies took a minor share, so that the shareholding in Richards Bay Minerals was finalised as follows:

	%
Quebec Iron & Titanium Corporation:	31.8
Union Corporation:	30.0
Industrial Development Corporation:	20.7
South African Mutual:	10.0
Southern Life:	7.5
	100.0

You will notice that the company taking the technical lead in the project has the major shareholding. The Union Corporation were to provide the local mining and construction knowhow, whilst the interest of the rest of the shareholders was purely financial.

After some two years spent in feasibility studies, the project was finally approved in December 1975 and design and construction commenced immediately, with the first products coming from the mine in October 1977, followed by the smelter, which came into operation early the following year. Following several years of successful operation, expansion of the ilmenite smelting unit is now being planned.(5) But to return to the initial scheme, let us first look at the process in some detail.

The process complexities

The operation starts with the excavation of an artificial fresh water pond in the sand dunes, on which dredgers and a separation plant are floated. The heavy minerals are separated out as a concentrate and the tailings, clean sand, are left behind as the plant works its way slowly along the dunes, excavating ahead and filling up behind, so that the pond also moves forward. The concentrates, in the form of a slurry, are then pumped some 5 kilometres inland, where they are processed in the smelter. The main products are:

Rutile: a feed material for the pigment industries.
Zircon: used in refractories and for ceramics.

These two products, both directly marketable, are separated out. Then the ilmenite is smelted in an electric arc furnace, yielding:

Iron: this is low-manganese iron, used for the manufacture of ductile castings
Slag: this is titanium oxide slag, from which the metal can be recovered by further processing

The techniques for the two major process operations, mining and smelting, came from across the world. The mining process came from Australia and the smelting process from Canada. Mining Deposits Ltd of Brisbane had considerable engineering and operating experience in the particular process to be used for separating the minerals from the sand, whilst Quebec Iron and Titanium Corporation were bringing in their smelting techniques. The actual plant design and engineering of the smelter was carried out by Hatch Associates Ltd of Toronto. Apart from these two specialist operations, all the other engineering was entrusted to local companies, together with the construction on site. Almost everything was purchased in South Africa, the only significant exceptions being certain specialised items such as the furnace transformers, process computers, HT switchgear and special refractories.

Project execution

Project management expertise was introduced by the appointment of Davy Ashmore of the UK (now Davy McKee) as construction management contractor. Their responsibility was to oversee the project as a whole – design engineering, procurement and construction. Whilst the bulk of the design engineering was carried out in South Africa, process design was carried out in both Canada and Australia. Davy Ashmore acted on behalf of the owner, Richard Bay Minerals, as illustrated in Figure 6.4.

Davy Ashmore acted as the owner's 'agent' for the entire project. To ensure effective project management and in particular project cost control the appropriate procedures were all laid down beforehand, the conventional S-curves relating time and cost being used to monitor the project. All procurement was on the basis of competitive tendering, vendors' capabilities being investigated beforehand and a list of qualified bidders prepared. Civil works

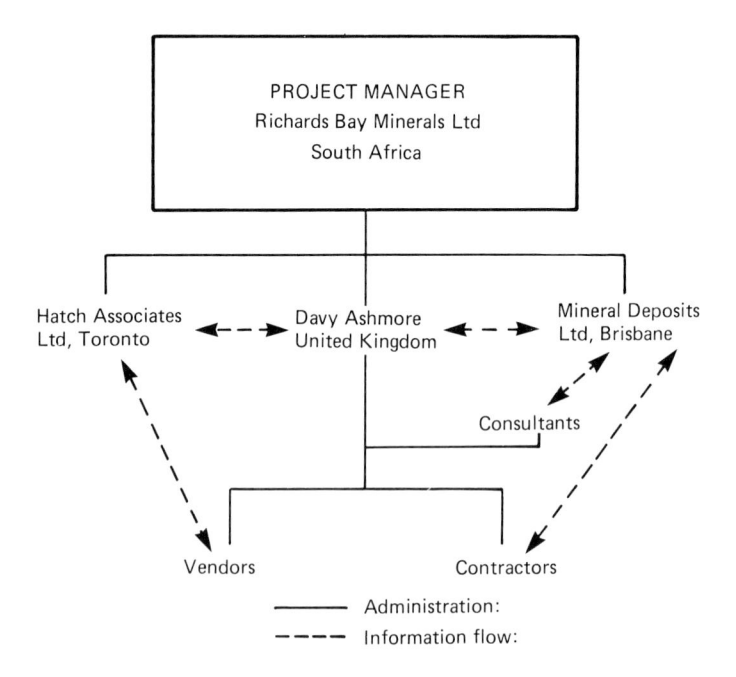

Figure 6.4 Organigram – Richards Bay Minerals Project
This outline organigram illustrates the basic relationships between the several companies employed on the project.

were let on the basis of a schedule of rates related to an estimated bill of quantities. Mechanical, electrical, instrumentation and piping work in the process areas was let on a fixed price (lump sum) basis, the design being well developed and the scope of work thus precisely defined before the work package was put out to tender. This approach was to some extent dictated by the nature of the local resources: if a range of construction disciplines had been offered, competition would have been severely limited.

Everything that happened on the project was carefully documented. This is not to say that the procedures were elaborate, but what happened at every stage was on record. For instance, in order to follow the procurement process through the stages of requisition, quotation and then purchase orders, a specific form was developed, the PIA (Purchase Instruction Authority). This was just another title, from its description, to what we have referred to as the bid analysis form. We present one such typical form as Figure 6.5, just to illustrate the degree of detail. What we wish to emphasise is that the procedures adopted were routine: the procedures that are familiar enough to those with the appropriate experience. Further, the application of the procedures was flexible. We are told, for instance, that whilst such a document was normally reviewed by the project managers group before a firm order was placed, nevertheless in exceptional circumstances and to save time, the project manager had the authority to make a commitment by telex. But in due course, the PIA formalities would have to be gone through, so that the back-up documentation was complete.

Project cost control

The basic tool for project cost control was the S-curve. This is hardly the place to elaborate on this particular technique in any detail, but those who are not familiar with this simple approach to project cost control can readily read about it elsewhere.(6) The costs incurred on the project at any point in time can be compared with the budget cost and related to physical progress. In view of the volume of data this particular monitoring system was computerised, in order that the results might be available soon after the event. A special cost monitoring section was set up with the following tasks:

> Prepare and maintain a project code of accounts

BID ANALYSIS

Item _____ Tag number _____
Amount allowed in control estimate _____ Clients code of accounts _____
Delivery required by schedule _____ Prepared by _____
                                                  Date _____

Suppliers

Name				
Conformity with specification				
Quotation details				
Price				
Duty payable (if any)				
Carriage				
Terms				
Delivery				
Other relevant information				
Estimated total price				

Purchasing recommendation

Reasons

Engineering recommendation

Reasons

Project Engineer _____ Date _____

For Clients' use

Client

Approved for purchasing from

Reason if different from engineering

Project Manager _____ Date _____

Figure 6.5 Bid analysis form
This form is designed to make sure that all the relevant aspects of vendor selection are reviewed and compares the bid, or tender price, with that in the budget, or control estimate.

Prepare budget estimates and PCA's (Project Change Authorisation)
Measure progress and use it for the approval of the monthly payments to contractors
Review extras, including costing and price negotiation
Issue a monthly contract status report
Issue a quarterly forecast of work to completion
Measure progress on all purchase orders and contracts
Forecast the cash flow quarterly
Develop the asset register

The reports issued by this cost monitoring section were fundamental to the assessment of project status. They included:

Monthly budget system reports
Quarterly forecasts, by areas, for orders and contracts
Monthly commitment system report, by areas, for orders and contracts
Invoice report (in same detail as foregoing)
Monthly management report
Quarterly cash flow report, including assessment of escalation and currency variation costs
Credits receivable through tax benefits (this was for the Asset Register)

We have entered into some detail here in an attempt to portray the meticulous detail which is required for proper project cost control, in order to ensure that management is well informed and thus able to act in an informed manner. What we have just said about this particular project will apply in substance to all the other successful construction projects we shall be looking at. The control techniques used will vary in detail, the titles given to the forms used will be different, the computer programs used are also likely to be different, but the fundamental management and cost control concepts remain precisely the same. However large and complex the project, they should remain simple. This is achieved in the main by dividing the project up into what are usually called areas, which are physically recognisable and can then be separately costed and controlled, as if they were projects on their own. This was done with the Sasol projects to which we referred earlier, and this was the device adopted with the Richards Bay Minerals project. Sasol Two, for instance, was divided up into nearly seventy separate areas for project management purposes, and Sasol three would have largely mirrored that.

The lessons

Richards Bay saw a project completed on time and within budget, the two basic criteria of success. The project management structure was unusual, in that there were three separate management groups all reporting to the owner's project manager, as illustrated in Figure 6.4. These three groups were very different in terms of national origin and hence outlook. This meant that a special effort had to be made to ensure the development of a team spirit, with recognition of a common goal. The organisational structure was complex, in that there were both Canadian and Australian consulting engineers, and a significant number of overseas purchases – from countries as diverse and as widely scattered as Austria, Australia, Belgium, Britain, Canada, France, Japan, the USA and West Germany. All these orders called for expediting, scheduling, inspection, currency transfers, import permits and long transit times.

Further, the site itself was remote. The nearest city was Durban, some 200 kilometres away. Whilst the project area had excellent facilities for access and construction – roads, the railway, electric power and water – the entire region was in the very early stages of development, so that there was no infrastructure. This meant that there was no regular transportation facilities. The position at site was further complicated by exceptional rainfall (25 cm in two days) at a critical time during construction on site. This not only cut off the main road to Durban but disrupted the telephone, telegraph and telex facilities. Despite such problems costs were contained within budget. How?

We are sure that sound management played a powerful role, but project management was assisted by the fact that construction went on whilst there was a business recession in South Africa. This meant that there was very intense competition for the work and prices were cut to the bone. Many tenders were believed to be 'below cost', whilst some were termed by those who lost the order 'absolutely ridiculous'. But the project received the benefit of the market situation and the policy of seeking fixed price contracts ensured that the initial price advantage was retained. This particular project went ahead just before Sasol Two got under way. Had it been a year later the purchasing climate might have been very different and prices much higher. Factors of this sort, external to the project, are entirely outside the control of the project manager and his team, but they are there to be taken advantage of. Good management will seize upon and utilise to the full all the available resources. With this project, senior management served as a powerful driving force, propelling the project towards its successful end, whilst tight cost monitoring ensured that total project cost stayed within budget.

Summary

One essential element in a successful project is seen to be effective cooperation between all the various parties involved. When they are drawn from three different continents, as they were with the South African projects we have now looked at in a little detail, care has to be taken to ensure that they are all working together towards a common goal. In terms of technology and managerial ability, the several partners in the project were effectively equals and this can lead to strains unless the management structure is clearly established right at the beginning. In both the cases we have reviewed this was accomplished by appointing a managing contractor, wholly responsible for the construction site. This ensured that what happened on site was properly coordinated, that there was no conflict of interest, and that there was no possibility of separate parties blaming one another when things went wrong.

When we come to consider projects where the parties are not equal, and technology transfer is involved, we shall see that the stresses and strains are of an entirely different type. But they can still be met and overcome, with a successful project the end result. All these problems are concerned with what we might call 'human relations': the principles of project management, planning and cost control, remain the same. They need no elaboration because there are a number of separate and perhaps very diverse parties involved. On the contrary, they should remain simple and straightforward.

References

1 Simplicimus, John, 'Sometimes technology works: sometimes it stumbles', *Worldwide Projects*, April/May 1981, pp78+, 5 p. (John Simplicimus is the pseudonym of an international consulting engineer.)
2 Stallworthy, E.A. and Kharbanda, O.P., *Total Project Management*, Gower, Aldershot, 1983, 329 pp. See Chapter 16, 'A case study'.
3 Brochure: 'A decade of engineering with the Union Corporation Group', issued by Union Corporation Limited, Marshalltown, South Africa.

4. Brochure: 'Titanium Alloy IMI 318', issued by IMI Titanium Limited, Witton, Birmingham, UK.
5. Rogers, J., 'RBM plans expansion for South Africa-based ilmenite smelting unit', *American Metal Market*, 19 July 1985, p.5.
6. Kharbanda, O.P., Stallworthy, E.A., and Williams, L.F. *Project Cost Control in Action*, Gower, Aldershot, 1980, 273pp.

7 Cancel and succeed!

The theme of this part of our book has been the fact that there is 'strength in cooperation', but what happens when there is no cooperation and perhaps even violent opposition? Looking around the world for successful projects, we also encounter projects that were cancelled or curtailed, perhaps even built and then closed down shortly afterwards. Was that failure? Not necessarily, because it takes courage and resolution to terminate a project *at the right time*. More often than not the decision is delayed: delayed far too long, with the result that substantial unnecessary losses are thereby incurred. We think, therefore, that the termination of a project at the right point in time can also be considered a success. The project manager makes the right decision at the right time in those particular circumstances – and we need to be able to recognise when that is. More than that: we need courage and determination to make the decision and see it through. All too often a plant that is an inevitable loss maker is still completed. David Davis, for instance, warning us to beware of false economies, quotes a case typical of many in recent years:(1)

> The new plant has had a 100 per cent cost overrun and an 8-month completion delay and now, six months after startup, it runs at less than half the capacity planned in the original design. The workforce is disgruntled. After a series of production crises, the customers are increasingly impatient, the original project manager has been fired and the plant manager is feeling shaky.

There is no doubt that when one is faced with a serious overrun in either cost or time, the whole project should be reviewed – not only the cost estimate and the plan. It should be completely reappraised for viability and then either abandoned or re-budgeted, as thought appropriate. Minor cost cutting, in an attempt to come close to the original targets is almost always counter-productive. This often seems the easiest course, but it is a panic reaction. The decision to review, re-engineer, re-cast or cancel is a hard decision, but the *right* one. If the calculations are not acceptable on review, then a company should always abandon the project. However, the number of unprofitable, lossmaking profits that make it to the operating stage serve as continuing proof that their sponsors often balk at this particular decision.

The 'point of no return'

But there comes a time when it is too late to cancel. This was demonstrated earlier, in Chapter 3 (see Figure 3.2). There we discussed the use of early warning signals to enable action to be taken before the 'point of no return' is reached. As time passes the cost commitment grows steadily, until a time comes when it costs more to cancel than complete. From then on the wisest thing to do is to complete, so as to ensure that a 'working asset' becomes available, but up to that point in time cancellation should always be considered as a possibility. The regular routine of authorisation for expenditure in many major companies involves a rigid financial routine, whereby the estimated cost of the project is authorised in stages, with project appraisal at each stage to check whether the estimated targets are going to be met. If not, then cancellation *must* be one possibility that is examined and costed. This is not defeatism, just plain common sense. One of us, looking back to the time when he first entered the project construction arena – and that is many years ago now – still remembers the simple practical example one seasoned engineer gave him at that time. His wife, he said, often offered him another cup of tea, urging him to accept, even when he did not want it, because 'there was still another cup in the pot'. But he pointed out that it did not stop there: there was additional sugar and milk called for. That was unnecessary waste if that additional cup of tea was not really needed. That is the concept we should apply to project cancellation. If there is no profit in it, cancel. Never throw good money after bad. We used this same principle when considering failing companies that had reached the 'point of no return'.(2) In such cases *we* then advocated 'euthanasia', or mercy killing. That is, the company should be allowed to die. Let us see how that works out in practice by taking a few projects by way of example.

The feasibility study

The first step with any project should be a feasibility study. This is designed to answer a number of very relevant questions about the proposed project, such as:

> Where shall we build?
> What shall we build?
> What will it cost?
> Will it show a profit?
> How will we do it all?

Answers to all these questions and many more should be provided before any decision is taken to proceed. And if any of the answers are unsatisfactory, then the project should be abandoned. This is where the consultant has a very important role to play, because so often those immediately involved in a prospective project are biased. They *want* the project, irrespective of considerations that should cause them to pause: that is natural enough. So often specific individuals have put much personal effort in what becomes for them their 'pet project' – we have often seen this as the route to failure – that impartial assessment becomes crucial to success.

The purpose of the feasibility study is an impartial assessment of the probabilities. The length of time devoted to a feasibility study will vary. Sometimes it may take only three months, on another possible project it could take a year or two and cost a great deal of money. Indeed, in one case, which we shall consider below, the study went on for years. But that is *always* money well spent, even if the project never goes ahead. The reason for that we think very obvious: without careful preliminary assessment, many millions of dollars can very easily be just thrown away.

Examples are many, scattered worldwide. One that has received much public attention over the years is the Channel Tunnel, proposed to be built between England and France, across the Straits of Dover. That particular project is almost a study in futurology. Six different schemes were formally put to the British and French governments at the beginning of November 1985, ranging in estimated cost from £2.1 billion to £5.2 billion. The construction time would be from three to five years, dependent upon the particular scheme finally chosen. The economics of the various proposals are being challenged, the environmentalists fear the worst and the existing ferry services claim either that some forty thousand jobs are at risk or that the introduction of new larger ferries will cut costs so much that the 'fixed link', as it is called, could not compete.(3) All in all we have a glorious mixture of political and economic considerations but we need to remember that the government decision, approving one of the six schemes submitted, is but the *beginning*: the project has still to be brought to a conclusion. Until it is finished we will not know whether it will be completed on time and within the budgeted cost. Even if that target is achieved, the project is not necessarily a success: it has still to make a profit.

On budget, on schedule

Let us examine that theme – that the real success is a project making a profit and that to complete a project 'on budget, on schedule' is not always the end of the story. That phrase appears as a headline on the front of a glossy brochure describing the 'US$2.1 billion Great Plains Project'.(4) The background to this project is interesting. We have just giving consideration to the Sasol projects in South Africa. Following upon the oil crisis of 1973, a lot of interest was displayed, particularly in the USA, in the production of synthetic fuels, and one method is from coal. This led to the introduction of a new word into the language, 'synfuel', and the setting up in the USA of the Synthetic Fuels Corporation by an Act of Congress in 1980. The objective was to encourage the development and manufacture of synthetic fuels in the USA by giving financial support to suitable projects, thus reducing the risk for the private investor.(5)

Against this background a number of major synfuel projects were put forward, but only a very few have gone ahead in the face of falling oil prices and the slackening in the demand for energy. Of all the countries in the world, the USA was undoubtedly a most appropriate country for the production of synfuels, having tremendous resources of cheaply won coal. After the second oil crisis in 1979 the coal industry was characterised as 'a somewhat frumpy middle-aged ballerina rushed out of retirement to fill an anticipated gap in a show that must go on. Suddenly the old girl is back in demand'.(6)

The only proven commercial process was the coal liquefaction process – the synthol process – in a major plant in South Africa. Whilst the effectiveness of the process was not in doubt, its relative efficiency and hence the economics of the process were suspect. The motivation in South Africa was strategic; in the USA however such a project had to be economically viable. It is here that the Synthetic Fuels Corporation had been expected to play a vital role by offering the appropriate support. Much criticism has been levelled at its operations, reflected in a report issued by a US Senate Committee late in 1983.(7) Nevertheless, the Great Plains Coal Gasification Project came on stream in July 1984.

This project, successful in itself, merits attention as yet another major project completed on budget and on schedule. America's first commercial-scale synthetic fuels facility and large by any standard, it is a pioneering achievement. Built by Lummus Crest, who acted as overall project manager and were also responsible for design, engineering, procurement and quality control, the completed project is a testimonial to effective pre-planning and cost estimating, followed by efficient schedule maintenance and cost control. Severe weather, a remote site and financing difficulties contributed to its problems. Studies had to be prepared that were critical to the obtaining of loan guarantees from the federal government, and successful completion is an outstanding example of effective cooperation between private industry and government.

Project financing

But that is not really why we thought it appropriate to look at this particular project. We feel it should be seen in the context of the energy scene in the USA. This was the first project of its kind in the USA, and intensive efforts were made to obtain federal loan guarantees. Despite strong Congressional support these efforts failed in 1975 and 1976. However, in November 1979, the Federal Energy Regulatory Commission issued an order authorising construction, and final approval with a loan guarantee of US$2.02 billion was given in 1981, construction starting in August of that year. The project was completed in the summer of 1984 and is now delivering syngas to a network of pipeline systems serving customers throughout the eastern half of the USA. But not a word is said about the profitability of the operation. The process is said by critics to have a low thermal efficiency, which may make the process obsolete very quickly. The operating costs are substantial, there being a high usage of water, gaseous effluents need intensive treatment and there are substantial volumes of solid waste, such as ash, to be disposed of. In the case of this plant, dewatered ash is returned to the mine, where it is buried in order to comply with governmental regulations. We gather that the continuing operation of the plant is under threat and it may be abandoned.(8)

So the question remains, despite the fact that the project was built 'on budget, on schedule': can it be operated successfully. The problem is financial, not technical. The cost of production far exceeds the maximum selling price: the difference between the two has therefore to be subsidised by the government. This makes it clear that in speaking of 'successful projects' we may well need to define our terms. We see success as the meeting of defined targets. Here the defined targets were indeed met. The continuing operation of the plant is another subject, governed by political decisions.

Now we go cross country

By way of contrast, let us now look at a project that was first abandoned, but later restarted and finally successfully completed. This is a 60 cm gas pipeline built across 200 km of difficult terrain in Nigeria – ranging from dense rain forest in Bendel State to rocky outcrops and savanna in Kwara State – in some fifteen months and on time. The successful completion of this project was no fluke, but can be directly attributed to sustained and effective project management. Project management is a science as well as an art: something that can be taught and learnt, for this project was locally planned and managed. The technology transfer, a theme we develop in detail in Chapter 13, had been most effective.

This gas pipeline was built by the Nigerian National Petroleum Corporation (NNPC) to serve the Ajaokuta steel mill, one of several such units planned by the Nigerian Government as part of its industrial development programme. The pipeline starts from a gas treatment plant located at Oben, in Bendel State, and runs northeast to Ajaokuta, in Kwara State, as shown in Figure 7.1, terminating in a metering station. The pipe run, buried about one metre below ground, includes five major river crossings.

The project was first conceived in 1977, and a contractor appointed who mobilised the site work far ahead of the arrival of the pipe. When the pipe failed to arrive, the contractor had to demobilise, the contract was terminated and compensation paid to the contractor. An example of the theme of this chapter: they knew when to cancel.

However, the project was revived some three years later, with the steel plant it was designed to serve due to start production in March 1983. This time is was laid down right at the outset that construction experience in a developing African country would be an essential pre-qualification for any contractor employed on the project. This was to learn from experience, something we advo-

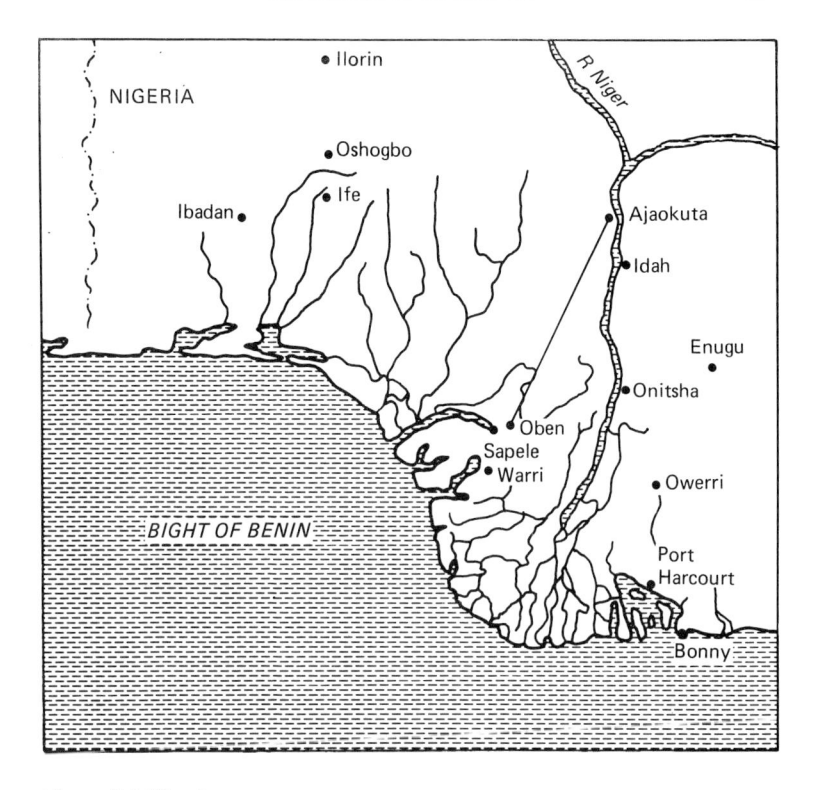

Figure 7.1 Nigeria
This map of Nigeria shows the geographic location of the Oben to Ajaokuta gas pipeline.

cate incessantly. So in mid-1980 invitations to tender were issued to five prequalified contractors, of whom Entrepose of France emerged as the lowest bidder and were awarded the contract.

Choice of consultants lay between Imeg of London, who had prepared the tender documents in 1977 and Earl & Wright of the USA, who were design consultants on the earlier contract. Both were invited to submit proposals, but it was found that most of the personnel of the American consultant associated with the earlier assignment had since left the organisation. This had not happened with Imeg, who were therefore at a distinct advantage and so won the contract. The project management organisation is illustrated schematically in Figure 7.2, showing on-site teams supported by home office services. Both these contracts were let on what is called a reimbursable basis, with certain cost ceilings. The project leader was Mr D.F. Obianyor, to whom we are indebted for much of the information on the management of this project.(9)

```
┌─────────────────────────────────────────────┐
│  ┌─ ─ ─ ─ ─ ─ ─ ─ ─ ─ ─ ─ ─ ─ ─ ─ ─ ─ ┐    │
│  │      NNPW Project Division         │    │
│  │         management                 │    │
│  └─ ─ ─ ─ ─ ─ ─ ─ ─ ─ ─ ─ ─ ─ ─ ─ ─ ─ ┘    │
│                    │                        │
│                    ▼                        │
│        ┌─────────────────────┐              │
│        │ Project leader Obia Nyor │          │
│        │  and project team   │              │
│        └─────────────────────┘              │
│                    │                        │
│                    ▼                        │
│        ┌─────────────────────┐   ┌─ ─ ─ ─ ┐ │
│        │       Imeg          │   │ Home  │ │
│        │ Construction supervision│◄──│office │ │
│        │    consultants      │   └─ ─ ─ ─ ┘ │
│        └─────────────────────┘              │
│                    │                        │
│                    ▼                        │
│        ┌─────────────────────┐   ┌─ ─ ─ ─ ┐ │
│        │     Entrepose       │   │ Home  │ │
│        │Construction contractor│◄──│office │ │
│        └─────────────────────┘   └─ ─ ─ ─ ┘ │
└─────────────────────────────────────────────┘
```

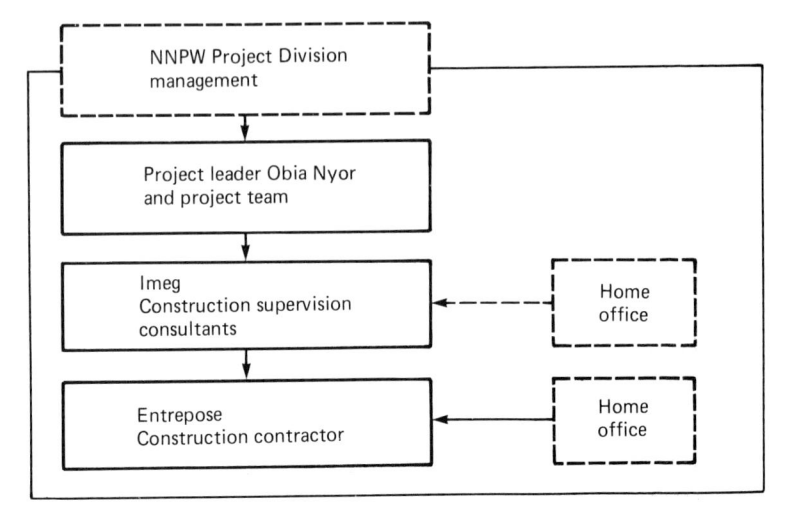

Figure 7.2 Project management on the gas pipeline
A schematic diagram illustrating the project management hierarchy for the Oben-Ajaokuta gas pipeline project.

Problems met and overcome

The interesting aspect of this particular project is the way that the very efforts to avoid the problem encountered when the project was first started and then aborted, led to a completely new set of problems, that then had to be overcome. This time the pipe, some 30 000 tonnes in all and costing about US$9 million, was ordered well ahead, prior to the award of the construction contract. But the pipes had been ordered uncoated and on arrival in Nigeria were stored in a very harsh environment on the Warri waterfront and corrosion set in. The contractor would require the pipes in mint condition, badly corroded pipes would have to be replaced, with related delays in procurement because of the need to secure import licenses in accordance with the government requirements.

The problem was tackled with quick decision and prompt action. Detailed inspection and counting of the corroded pipes, stacked seven high, would have been an impossibly costly and time-consuming task, so a statistical approach was adopted. Random batches only were inspected, disclosing that one out of every seven pipes was so badly corroded that it would have to be replaced. So replacement pipe was placed on order. Meanwhile, all the 17 000 pipes in stock were sandblasted – a six month's job and about 13 per cent rejected – a complete justification of the simple and quick sampling method adopted to assess the potential loss.

Project management *is* cost control

The project team working on behalf of NNPC closely monitored project progress. A payment schedule was established relating to progress, subdivided into activities, with field staff verifying actual progress and signing work measurement sheets which then became the basis for payment. The contract with the consultant demanded a different approach, where a ceiling had been set. The project team had to ensure optimum utilisation of the engineers on the project. This was achieved by close monitoring, specific approval being required for any increase in staff. The efficiency of the approach is demonstrated by the fact that when the project had been completed only 90 per cent of the contractual ceiling manhour target had been expended. This was an outstanding achievement seeing that the actual construction period, due to the problems encountered, had taken some 50 per cent longer than had first been estimated. The wisdom of the reimbursable type of contract in such a context was amply displayed, since it provided the necessary flexibility, coping with change, yet optimising cost. The pipeline was commissioned in March 1983, some 21 months following contract signature and is now supplying 85 million cubic metres a day of natural gas to the steel complex at Ajaokuta.

Summary

This time we have looked at some very diverse projects, with the objective of demonstrating that there can come a time when a project should be cancelled, even though it is not complete. It is an essential part of good management to be able to recognise a failure and act accordingly. We shall finally come to the conclusion that prevention is better than cure (Chapter 20), but if a project is on the road to disaster, good management should discern that road. If the external pressures are so powerful that they cannot be resisted, then the wise course is to cut your losses. Too many, in such a situation, hang on to the bitter end, thus increasing the misery and spreading the disaster. It is human nature, of course. Pride is a very powerful emotion, and people rarely admit that they were wrong. This attitude of mind is the short road to disaster.

References

1. Davis, D., 'New projects – beware of false economies', *Harvard Business Review*, 64, March-April 1985, pp.95-101.
2. Kharbanda, O.P. and Stallworthy, E.A., *Corporate Failure – Prediction, Panacea and Prevention*, McGraw-Hill, London, 1985, 226 pp.
3. Lawson, J, 'Who's who in the Channel link race', and Clifford, C., 'Tunnellers to woo ferries', *The Sunday Times* (London), 3 November 1985.
4. Brochure: 'The $2.1 billion Great Plains Project', published by Lummus Crest Inc., a subsidiary of Combustion Engineering, Inc., of Bloomfield, New Jersey.
5. Kharbanda, O.P. and Stallworthy, E.A. *Management Disasters and How to Prevent Them*, Gower, Aldershot, 1986, 212 pp. (See Chapter 8, 'Synthetic fuels – still a dream'.)
6. Sheets, K.R., 'Synfuels – Washington's $15b orphan', *US News*, 94, 17 January 1983, pp.58-9.
7. Report: 'US Synthetic Fuel Corporation – a report', issued by the subcommittee on oversight of government management, Washington DC. September 1983, 63 pp.
8. Crawford, M., 'Industry abandons Synfuel Project', *Science*, 229, 16 August 1985, p.633.
9. Obianyor, D.F., 'Gasline project management', *Asian National Development*, September 1984, pp.70+. (The author is acting chief engineer for the Nigerian Petroleum Corporation, Lagos, Nigeria.)

Part Three
THE DEVELOPED COUNTRIES LEAD THE WAY

8 A team can work wonders!

The company name IBM is synonymous with computers. This corporate giant has played and is still playing a major role in the life of every one of us, via its sophisticated machinery and related software. It is true to say that what might be called the 'electronics revolution' owes much to this one company. The history of the origins and growth of IBM makes a fascinating story, as told in the book *IBM – Colossus in Transition*: the result of three years' painstaking research.(1) Although IBM has probably less to hide than most major corporations, it has generally been very secretive and suspicious of those seeking to learn of its activities. Nevertheless, the book gives us a good insight into the way in which the company operates, gained to some extent by interviews with key personnel. Looking back over the past history of the company, there are no significant scandals, no inefficient or corrupt senior executives and no major blunders. On the contrary, the IBM story brings us a long list of competent and even outstanding chief executives, admired even by their ex-employees: a company that above all stayed efficient despite its giant size.

The historical background

IBM came into existence in 1924 as the successor of CTR (Computer-Tabulator-Recording), a company founded by Charles Flint in 1910 through the merger of three companies, his own International Time Recording Co., the Computing Scale Company of America and the Hollerith Tabulating Machine Co. Flint himself was essentially a man of action, always on the go and continually involved in a dozen or so ventures in various parts of the world. The man who set the tone of the company, however, was a certain Thomas Watson. His basic philosophy, which seems to have been preserved as part of the 'company culture' right down to this present day, was expressed thus:

> A company is known by the men it keeps. We have different ideas, and different work, but when you come right down to it there is just one thing we have to deal with throughout the whole organisation – that is the MAN.

This, and his admonition to *think*, served to encourage his salesmen to innovate and be creative. His advice in 1917 to a New York audience is equally valid today:

> When practising the art of selling use all your talents ... put everything you have into your efforts; above all, put your personality into them. Never copy anybody. *Be yourself*.

But, whilst thus elevating the importance of the individual, he also stressed the importance of teamwork:

> A team that won't be beat can't be beat . . . Everybody in this company is the supervisor of someone else . . . no man is big enough to instruct everybody how to do his work . . .

Whilst we are going back some seventy years, we have nevertheless quoted Watson at length since his view is valid even today – the emphasis being on teamwork and the importance of giving both the individual and the team full opportunity to use their skills in order to achieve success.

The activities of the company in those far-off days was business machines, but from then on there was no looking back. Beginning as the smallest of the five major companies operating in this area, by 1939 it was the top earner, although its sales were but average, as is illustrated in Figure 8.1. Indeed, at that point in time its earnings exceeded that of its other four competitors combined. This outstanding progress established IBM as one of the few 'blue chip' companies on Wall Street after the depression of the early thirties, and as a result the press hailed Thomas Watson as an 'industrial giant' (*New York Times*) and as the 'most astute businessman in the world' (*Time*). By the end of the Second World War the company still led in terms of sales, but dominated in terms of earnings. It had in fact retained its leadership to the extent that it still earned twice as much as its nearest competitor. We thought it would be of interest to make the same comparison for 1984. The position of IBM over those forty years has so improved, as

	Sales				Earnings			
	1929	*1939*	*1945*	*1984*	*1929*	*1939*	*1945*	*1984*
Burroughs:	32.1	32.5	37.6	4875	8.3	3.0	2.3	363
IBM:	19.7	39.5	141.7	29753	5.3	9.1	10.9	6582
National Cash Register:	49.0	37.1	68.4	4074	7.8	1.8	2.2	561
Remington Rand:	59.6	43.3	132.6	–	6.0	2.1	5.3	–
Underwood:	19.0	24.2	29.0	–	4.9	1.9	2.2	–

All figures in US$ million

Figure 8.1 IBM and the competition
This table illustrates the progress made by IBM in the calculating machine market up to 1945. After that it was no longer mechanical calculating machines, but computers. The postwar growth has been remarkable.

compared with its competitors that it is no longer possible to make a sensible comparison. The two companies who still operate in the same market are no longer in the same league, as the figures demonstrate.

But to continue what we might call the 'Watson story' a little further, Thomas Watson Jr joined the company after the Second World War, presumably having been groomed to take his father's place. His father finally retired in his eighty-second year, in May 1956. The fifties saw severe competition for the computer market worldwide, with many companies battling with IBM for a market share. IBM emerged as clear victors, holding some 65 per cent of the market by 1965. The rest was held by seven other companies, whose market share ranged from three to twelve per cent only. By this time, IBM's business outside the USA was almost equal to its domestic market and its growth over that twenty years (1945-1965) was indeed phenomenal. Earnings grew from US$11 million in 1945 to US$777 million in 1965. Then the 'Incomparable 360' arrived – but that is the story from which we have to learn some lessons.

Efficient communication works wonders

System 360 was developed by IBM using the project team approach. The principal architect was Frederick Brooks, but he had a very large support team. Those in the team with managerial functions met once a week for a half-day conference to review progress, and contact between the team members was continuous and intense. Minutes of such meetings were circulated within a few hours and every member of the team had instant access to all the information that he required. This circulation of information went right through to the programmers, who received copies of material from every group within the project team. In addition, there were annual two-week sessions, where all outstanding problems were resolved. Everyone attending the weekly meetings had the authority to make binding decisions.(2)

The System 360 project team was built up from IBM's top talent and once assigned to the project there were no distractions. System 360 was their full-time occupation: they lived it and quite literally 'slept on it'. Yet, despite this single-minded dedication and devotion to one single goal the project did not go forward without problems. This came about largely because of its size and complexity. During the development of System 360 IBM departed from their usual secretive attitude, allowing an editor of the *Fortune* magazine to interview several members of the project team. The magazine then carried a series of articles with titles that displayed the difficulties: 'IBM's $5 billion gamble' and 'The rocky road to the marketplace'. The articles highlighted personality clashes, errors in judgment and an apparently reckless approach to problem solving. IBM were furious. The articles were lacking in perspective, though accurate in terms of their matter and vivid in description. However, whilst it was felt at the time that the articles were very damaging, it appeared later that the IBM image may well have been strengthened thereby, rather than weakened. The decision to develop System 360 was farsighted and it proved extremely profitable, even compared to their earlier second generation 1400 series of computers. It was also a feather in the cap for Tom Watson Jr. who was thus proved to be as bold and as resourceful as his father.(1)

The measure of success

The development of System 360 cost more and took longer than had been expected. In the past we have seen this as a token of disaster, since failure to complete to plan often results in project failure.(3) But here the context has to be taken into account. IBM were working on a development project in a high technology area, thus involving many unknowns. In their anxiety to pre-empt their competitors, they proclaimed as early as 1962 that the system would be available by April 1964. But at that point in time the system was still being developed. In addition, development costs were escalating, and IBM had to raise some US$370 million of new capital: all of it for the System 360 project.

The first IBM 360/40 computers were installed in April 1965, a year later than had originally been planned, but they were an instant success. Before the end of that year other models in the series – the 360/30s, 50s and 65s – had also appeared and there was a record backlog of orders for this new series of machines. The production problems had been surmounted and the transition from what was called 'second generation' to 'third generation' computers went very smoothly indeed. Within two years the 360 series accounted for nearly half of the total sales of IBM at home and the series was also making great strides abroad, with sales far ahead of those of any of its competitors.

Whilst the competition were well aware of what was happening and was developing its response, no-one was ready to enter the field when the 360 appeared. The development of a new generation in computers is extremely expensive and it was thought that such a major technological advance would take at least ten years. IBM got there in less than half that time!

The project team concept

The establishment of a project team within the company organisation was new to IBM when they adopted the concept for the development of System 360. It was a real achievement for a company of the size of IBM to make a success of their first project handled in this way. They are not the only giant company to approach a project in this way: General Motors, a US$60 billion group, not only adopted the approached but have continued with it ever since, as we shall see when we come to Chapter 10. In sharp contrast, other major companies, such as Boeing, Bechtel and Fluor, use massive project teams as a matter of routine. Indeed, for the last two, both international construction contractors, the project team concept is fundamental to their work, since their entire workload consists of projects. But each project is inevitably a 'one off' and each project team has to be tailored to the specific requirements of that project. Whilst experience from previous projects (accumulated knowhow) must and does help, the degree of novelty has to be assessed and coped with. Location is often one such novel factor: so much so that we have felt it appropriate to demonstrate its significance by reviewing a number of projects in really remote areas. The company structure where projects are the day to day work of the company is inevitably in matrix form, as discussed in Chapter 1 and illustrated in very simplified form by Figure 1.6. Where the project team is taken from a series of functional departments in a manufacturing organisation, as was the case with IBM, the matrix is still there, but the relationship between the team member and the department from which he has come and to which he turns for information and technical support, is probably much weaker than it usually is with a construction company. In such cases the personnel must learn to be able to switch rapidly between the two types of management structure with which he is involved, the project team structure being worked within temporarily, for the duration of the project only: a period that can vary from a few months to several years.

Organisations that do not use the project team concept usually refer a major strategic problem or proposal to a line manager, adding it to his departmental load, or assign its study to planning staff. But this type of approach usually fails to bring decisive action. There is a lack of commitment to the project, for these people have their own work to do, and they see that, naturally enough, as of prime importance. The project team concept brings together a group of people who have nothing else to think about for the time being but *their* project. They eventually go back once again to their own department, division or company, but they go back with an achievement 'under their belt' and they impart a new spirit to their fellow-employees there when they return.

Little by little

The System 360 is of special interest because of its size and duration. It was a major undertaking and the only practical way of handling such a volume of work is to continue the 'project principle' within the project itself, breaking the work to be done into a series of separate, related projects, each with its own team leader, plan and target. Each of these subprojects, if we may call them such, needs to have a clear objective which is within the comprehension of the team leader. Then each specific objective is cleared one by one, and relatively quickly. In major construction projects this is achieved by dividing a project into separate areas and then setting up what are called 'milestones' within the project.

The project team concept seems to work best when a group of some eight to ten persons work together. This is the standard approach in Japan, the *Kacho* (team leader or section head) organising the work of his section.(4) American companies are now taking the lessons offered by the success of Japan and many examples can be seen of its operation in American manufacturing industry. The 3M Company has several hundred such 'venture teams', brought together for a specific task, and later returning to their own departments.

Summary

Whilst the 360 series has been the dominant factor in the growth of IBM over the last decade, the company has not stopped there. It is suggested that it may well become the world's biggest corporation. It already employs some 400 000 people worldwide, has a current turnover (1984) of some US$46 billion, forecast to grow to US$100 billion by 1990.(5) The company is now busy automating most of its product lines, typical of which is a new fully automated electronic typewriter factory capable of turning out 4 000 units a day. This is said to be their answer to the Japanese challenge.(6) However, despite its size the company still only takes some 20 per cent of an electronic equipment market of some US$240 billion worldwide.(7) The rest of the market is shared between some hundreds of companies, so there is no question of monopoly.

What we wish this particular example to illustrate and to emphasise is that the project team concept is *always* the answer, whatever the size of the company. Problems, whether they are direct manufacturing problems, such as improving productivity, or the introduction of a new product, should always be formulated as a project, with a stated objective, to be achieved within a budgeted cost and within a stipulated time. Then a group of people should be nominated, with a project manager, to produce the answer – and they will!

References

1 Sobel, R., *IBM – Colossus in Transition*, Sidgwick and Johnson, 1984, 370 pp. (paperback).
2 Peters, T.J. and Waterman, R.H., *In Search of Excellence – Lessons from America's Best-Run Companies*, Harper & Row, 1982, 360 pp.
3 Kharbanda, O.P. and Stallworthy, E.A. *How to Learn from Project Disasters*, Gower, Aldershot, 1983, 273 pp.
4 Vogel, E., *Japan as Number One – Lessons for America*, Harvard University Press, 1979.

5   Harris, M., 'IBM – more worlds to conquer', *Business Week*, 18 February 1985, pp.84-7.
6   Harris, M., 'IBM graphs fanatical drive to beat Japan in manufacturing', *Business Week*, 11 March 1985, p.62.
7   Harris, C.L., 'Does big blue spur – or stifle – the competition', *Business Week*, 16 July 1984, p.111.

9 Success – even with nuclear plants!

Nuclear power arrived on the scene some thirty years ago now: an awe-inspiring development full of promise for the future. It was anticipated that its use would immeasurably enhance our daily life by providing abundant energy at low cost. The basic source of electricity in most countries has been the coal-fired power station, but it was thought that even in countries rich in coal resources, such as the USA and Britain, nuclear power would take over as the prime energy source, but this has not happened.

As one scans the literature, it becomes very apparent that there is a great deal of prejudice against nuclear power plants. For instance, as early as 1973 Ralph Nader, a powerful advocate of the rights of the consumer, admitted that he could *never* support nuclear power, however safe it proved to be. A few years later another critic of nuclear power, Amory Lovins, admitted that even if he were convinced that nuclear power had *no* safety, proliferation or economic drawbacks, he would still oppose it for political reasons. This innate, almost unreasoning resistance to nuclear power is worldwide, but manifests itself much more powerfully in some countries than in others. France, for instance, has a successful programme for the construction of nuclear power stations, and that success demonstrates the degree to which success in project construction these days is dependent upon public relations.(1)

The United States, on the other hand, presents a very different picture. Whilst the atomic energy industry in the US may well be the most advanced in the world – France has bought in their technology – yet it is now in serious trouble at home. The basic problems are spiralling construction costs and ever more severe safety requirements. The two are, of course, interrelated and the ever more stringent safety regulations are to a large extent a result of public pressure.

A sorry story

Very large plans were made in the sixties for the construction of nuclear power plants in the USA, and by 1980 there were nearly two hundred stations in various stages of construction, concentrated largely in the Eastern States. The history of these plants was none too happy. There were technical problems, but above all the first estimates of cost and time were often doubled. This was said to be largely due to the continuously growing number of regulations that had to be complied with, as illustrated in Figure 9.1.(2) By way of example, the Tennessee Valley Authority (TVA), setting out to build seven nuclear power plants in 1966, found to their misfortune that many of their early assumptions were but myths. Building a nuclear power plant was very different to building the conventional coal or oil-fired unit with which they

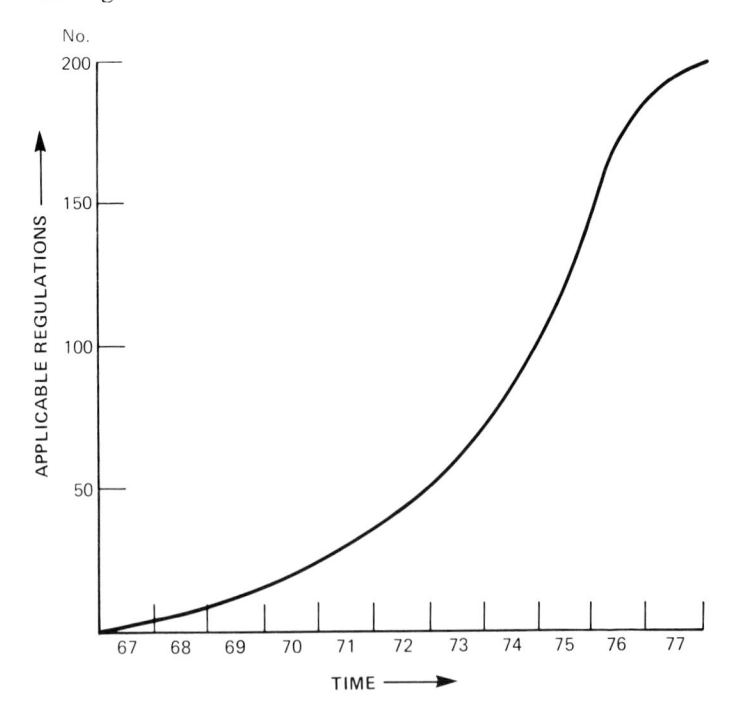

Figure 9.1 Regulations
This graph illustrates the growth in the cumulative total of regulations in relation to nuclear power plants since the late sixties. (With acknowledgements to the Tennessee Valley Authority, see Reference 2.) Following the Three Mile Island and Bhopal tragedies (6) this curve may accelerate upwards once more.

were familiar. A completely new range of concepts had to be developed in relation to safety and environmental protection, whilst the codes and regulations to which they had to conform multiplied.

Since 1980, however, the position in the USA has worsened considerably, with many stations either planned or under construction not even being brought to completion. Further, no new orders were being placed. One of the most momentous cancellations came at the beginning of 1984. A half-finished nuclear power station at Marble Hill, Indiana, was abandoned after some US$2 500 million had been spent. The Marble Hill plant is thought to be the most expensive nuclear plant project ever to be abandoned in this way. Consisting of two units, one unit was said to be about 60 per cent ready, whilst the other was about a third of the way along. But the electric supply company, the Indiana Public Service Company, said that they just did not have the cash resources to finish the project.(3) They were not the only public utility to find themselves in that position. The Washington Public Power Supply System undertook an ambitious nuclear power plant building programme. Five plants, designed to serve some 80 public utility companies, were originally budgeted at about US$4 billion. By early 1982 that had soared to US$24 billion – six times the original estimates. So two of the proposed plants have been cancelled, whilst work has stopped on two others, leaving only one that might reach completion.(4) Altogether a sorry story, the American scene – or is it?

Man bites dog

It is the unusual that makes news. That is why we have brought to you a picture of the calamitous state of the nuclear power station building programme in the USA. Overruns in cost and time, plants deferred and cancelled is the norm in the industry in the USA, so that a project completed successfully *must* be news. Hence the title of an article on the completion of the Byron Plant: 'Man bites dog'.(5) The writer went on to proclaim: 'You've heard all those nuclear disaster stories. Now harken to this nuclear plant success story'.

The hero of this particular success story is Consolidated Edison, who own and operate a number of electric power stations, both coal-fired and nuclear. The plant in question, installed capacity 2 200 MW (4 times 550 MW) was built for a total of US$3.7 billion, or $1 682 per kilowatt. The Marble Hill plant for the

Indiana Public Service Company, to which we referred above, and which was a carbon copy of the Byron plant, had cost some $3 000 per kilowatt when the project was abandoned, so that gives us some idea as to the degree of cost efficiency that had been achieved in construction. It seems that Consolidated Edison are very different to most other utility companies in the USA. In the thirty years since they first started building nuclear power plants, their installations have always cost much less than others in the USA and still do. Their LaSalle plant was built for an investment cost of $1153 per kilowatt, which is as low as that of the latest plant built in Japan: the Fukushima plant for Tokyo Electric.

It is not only in terms of capital cost that Consolidated Edison has been so successful, but also with their operating costs. As a result, this company is credited with one of the lowest costs for power from a new station in the USA. The cost of power generation is said to be 3.1 cents per kilowatt hour, about as cheap as electricity from their older coal-based plants, where the capital investment has been largely written off. In saying this, let us not forget that Consolidated Edison have been subject to precisely the same regulations, market conditions and environmental pressures as all the other utilities operating in the USA. So what was different?

The road to success

Upon analysis it has been found that the success of Consolidated Edison can be attributed to just two factors:(5) *good management* and *knowhow*. The good management includes good project management, whilst the knowhow must be largely the sound application of experience, in itself a significant element of good management, since the chief executive of Consolidated Edison, James O'Connor, has been quoted as saying:

> We've been in this business for thirty years and in my judgment people feel more comfortable with our operating performance than they do elsewhere in the country.

He is equally optimistic about the future:

> The overall increase [in cost] will not be significantly above the rate of inflation.

In other words, the cost in *real terms* of the production of electricity is not likely to rise in the foreseeable future. Indeed, their nuclear power generating systems have been so efficient that their older fossil fuel plants have been relegated to meeting peak demands only. By 1990 the company expect to be producing some 75 per cent of their power needs from nuclear power plants.

But success brings it problems!

One would have thought that the construction of a nuclear power plant on time and within budget would bring its own reward. It did, but it brought penalties too. We have already mentioned the plethora of regulations related to nuclear plants and behind the regulations stand a number of regulatory bodies. Consolidated Edison went ahead with their project so fast that these organisations could not keep pace. The Nuclear Regulatory Commission took its time approving the plant design and issuing a licence. The Atomic Safety and License Board (ASLB) delayed the issue of the operating licence on a variety of pretexts. These delays are said to have contributed an extra US$100 million to the capital cost of the project, apart from the extra costs that arise from delay. Such administrative delays could easily offset all the savings that Consolidated Edison had been able to achieve through good planning and sound project management during the design and construction of the plant at Byron. It did indeed bring them problems, since the delay in commissioning the plant resulted in lower earnings and a higher cost for the necessary finance.

These financial problems made it difficult for the company to borrow at attractive rates of interest, further compounding the problem. However, Consolidated Edison seem to be getting 'out of the wood', as they say. It is hoped that by 1987 they will not need to borrow funds, generating internally all that they require. The company is clearly on the way to getting over their financing problem and achieving ever greater success.

Management the crux

This brief history makes it very clear that efficient company and project management is the secret of success, since with Consolidated Edison they succeeded where so many others had failed. Their success shows us that it is *not* the nuclear industry as such which is to blame. Certainly, the conditions under which such plants have to be built may be arduous, but good management can meet and overcome that situation. Later, we shall be looking at projects built in the remote corners of the globe, where it is the location, above all, that brings the problems that have to be overcome. But they *are* overcome. Here, it is not the location, but the technical requirements and the regulations that present the problem, but we now see that they too can be overcome.

Nuclear energy, particularly in the USA, seems to have a dark and unpromising future, but it could be that in the example of Consolidated Edison we have a ray of hope. Nuclear power can be cheap and very competitive, but at the moment it has the image of being unsafe. Politics have intervened. That introduces us to another aspect of sound management. In France the national utility, Electricite de France (EDF) have some 60 nuclear power plant units commissioned or under construction: a programme which when complete will provide about 50 per cent of the total energy requirement of that country. Whilst there is still a hard core of resistance to nuclear power in France, the public at large seem to have accepted its development. This is undoubtedly due to the great efforts that EDF have made to inform the public, both nationally, and also locally, where the plants are being built. Over a million leaflets have been distributed in response to specific enquiries and more than 20 000 people visit one or other of the nuclear power stations every year. The project manager must recognise the need to keep the public, and especially the local people, fully aware of what is happening on their doorstep. EDF have made every effort at their various sites to weave the construction and operation of the plant in the local economic fabric by helping local firms to contribute and by training local people so that they can be employed there. Yet another lesson in project management.

References

1 Stallworthy, E.A. and Kharbanda, O.P., *International Construction and the Role of Project Management*, Gower, Aldershot, 1985, 301 pp.
2 Willis, W.F., 'TVA's first 10 years of nuclear plant design and construction experience', *Cost Engineering* (USA), Vol.21, 1, January/February 1979.
3 News item: 'Marble Hill owner rejects industry joint venture bid to complete unit', *Nucleonics Week* (USA), Vol.25, No. 25, 21 June 1984.

4 News item: 'Whoops, we cannot pay £1,433 million', *Daily Telegraph*, London, 17 May 1983. ('Whoops' is the nickname of the Washington Public Power Supply System in the USA.)
5 Cook, J., 'Man bites dog', *Forbes*, 134, 3 Dec. 1984, pp.80+.
6 Kharbanda, O.P. and Stallworthy, E.A., *Management Disasters – and How to Prevent Them*, Gower, 1986, 235 pp.

10 Listen to learn

It was in 1973 that Dr Schumacher first published his book *Small is Beautiful*. Since then it has appeared as a paperback: very evidently this is a subject that has broad appeal and the book has certainly been very widely read.(1) Dr Schumacher brought to economics the concept that *people* really mattered and this was most timely. The author sounded a warning: to build *bigger* is not necessarily to build either cheaper or better, but the underlying and perhaps more important point was that in the process of building bigger, the needs and the aspirations of the *people* involved got lost.

But of course, whilst size has some advantages, it has many disadvantages, some of which Dr Schumacher has highlighted. One major disadvantage with large companies is their conservatism, reflected in their inertia, or inability to react quickly to changing circumstances. General Motors is a vast organisation, and it is very evident as we look at their activities through the seventies that the company was not only huge but cumbersome. At the beginning of the seventies General Motors was notorious in the public eye for building cars with the largest petrol consumption of any on the American market – some 12 miles per gallon. As a result their market share dropped from some 52 per cent to 44 per cent in 1972 and was down to 42 per cent by 1975. However, they listened to the message and learned. They also demonstrated that a large organisation *can* move fast if it only approaches the problem properly. Let us see what happened, looking for the lessons as we go.

The background

The emphasis in the motor car industry in the sixties was on market share and effective marketing was thought to be *the* answer to maintaining the market share. The nature of the product and its relevance to market demand was not considered significant. In the words of the then chairman, exhorting his sales force: 'we should not be satisfied until we sell every car that's sold'. An ambitious objective. But nevertheless the market share of General Motors kept falling. Even before the oil crisis there was a trend toward the smaller car and as a result, an ever-increasing volume of imported cars were being sold on the American market, as illustrated in the following table:(2)

	1964	1966	1968	1970	1972	1974
Small cars, as a percentage of US sales:	25	23	25	30	37	43
Imports, as a percentage of total sales:	7	8	11	16	16	18

General Motors finally reacted to this very evident and growing customer preference in 1972, before the oil crisis and the sharp increase in fuel costs that gave it substantial impetus, but their first reaction, in 1970, was apparently expressed in the thought: 'there is something wrong with people who like small cars'. However, what began as something of a fad soon became a question of running cost and the sales figures shouted a message aloud that was then listened to. What happened?

In 1972 the General Motors management set up an *ad hoc* group under the name 'Energy Task Force'. It was in the charge of David C. Collier, then Treasurer and later to become head of their Buick Division.(3) This was a multi-disciplinary group with members drawn from the manufacturing, research, design, finance and economics departments of the company. This is parallel in concept to the setting up of a project team to handle a specific project, which is at the heart of effective project management. But at this point they did not have a project – only a mission and a task.

Six months of intensive work resulted in this group reaching three broad conclusions:

1 The energy problem is here and now
2 This problem will have a profound effect on our business
3 The government have no plans to deal with it.

These three conclusions were discussed in detail at various forums within the company, with the result that practically everyone in management started thinking about it. The group team leader,

Collier, reported back to the Board in October 1973, prior to the oil crisis, although warning clouds were then on the horizon. This resulted in the chairman of the company making public reference to the urgency of 'getting some *downsizing* in our cars'. The emphasis is ours. As a consequence of this all-pervading discussion of the problem, management at all levels was in the right frame of mind, prepared for change. Then came the oil crisis and within two months the decision was taken to aim at the production of a new 'smaller' car by 1976. This was to be done with urgency, using existing designs and components, mainly from Brazil. This new car was to be called the *Chevette*.

At the same time plans were laid for a long-term programme of redesign of all GM cars, to make them more fuel-efficient. The company objective was clearly stated by Pete Eates, the executive vice-president of the Operations Division, who said: 'Our business was family cars and we had to start there. If we had started at the bottom, there would have been a gap for a year or so where the competition would have moved in'.

The project centre concept

In December 1973 a plan was drawn up for a substantial reduction in both the size and weight of the cars to be brought into production by 1977. This was associated with a review of the specific management problems within GM and as a result there was a major reorganisation of the company. One result of this reorganisation was the formation of the *Chevette Project Centre*, incorporating a coordinated but decentralised approach to management, a concept that had proved highly successful in the space programme being run by NASA at that time. Close coordination of management activities is difficult enough in normal times, but is even more difficult in a rapidly changing situation. Yet that was considered to be absolutely essential if the proposed 'crash programme' for downsizing was to be successful.

The main features of the project centre concept are:

> It is *not* a permanent group
> It operates only during the lifetime of the project (in this case the downsizing project)
> It augments but does *not* replace the lead division concept
> It works on parts and engineering problems common to *all* divisions.

The 'lead division' concept means that one particular company division handles a specific technical innovation from initiation through to ultimate production. The project centre, by contrast, handles all aspects of the project, in this case downsizing, until that has been achieved and the project put into production. Then the group can be disbanded and its members returned to the various operating divisions of the company as appropriate. The parallels between the project centre at GM and the project management team for any construction project are clear enough. This means that the lessons that were learnt at General Motors in this context have a much wider application than the automotive industry as such.

In retrospect, the project centre concept turned out to be the most important single tool in the implementation of the bold decision to downsize. It not only eliminated a great deal of duplication and hence redundant effort, but helped to speed the translation of new concepts and developing technology into production items. It proved itself to be much superior, in terms of ultimate achievement, to the persuasion/coercion management technique then prevailing in the various divisions of the company, since it provided an opportunity for individual initiative. People previously working within a division had freedom to work on their divisions' problems without restraint.

Sloan, in writing of his years with General Motors (4) said that 'something was lacking'. He thought that perhaps it was 'ideas, and above all passion and compassion and a commitment to something more . . . than just the business'. The project centre concept allowed these emotions, held in restraint by the very massiveness of the organisation, to find expression. As Schumacher pointed out, people *do* matter, and they will give of their best if they are given the feeling that they matter.

The downsizing project, as executed through the project centre, was General Motor's first comprehensive, new attack on the marketplace for many years and it proved to be a major turning point in the company's history. It also helped to make the management more confident, relaxed, good at both speaking and listening to one another.

The strength of the team

Whilst much of the success of team effort must lie with the team leader – the director, the project manager, call him what you will – the composition of his team is also crucial. Good managers are not 'doers' but rather the developers and encouragers of 'doers'. This management function is all-important and makes the greatest contribution of all to good management and its end result, a successful project and a successful company.

How does this come about? A team should bring together a number of separate but essential qualities. Belbin has identified eight key roles essential to effectiveness, each of these being associated with a particular personality.(5) We have dealt with this subject in detail in Chapter 19 – the project team must team up.

With the optimum mix of individuals having the appropriate qualities, the team can achieve far more than those individuals, operating singly, could ever accomplish: this is called *synergy* meaning that the combined effort of the team exceeds the sum of their individual efforts. This comes as a result of their good interpersonal relations, all uniting to achieve a common, declared goal. We do not know to what extent the appropriate mix was achieved in the project centre created to handle the downsizing project, but the method whereby that centre was put together would certainly allow a sound team to be created. Some 1200 people were assembled, drawn from the various GM divisions, who had been operating almost as separate, autonomous companies. This included some of the chief engineers from the various divisions, and the objective was clearly stated: prepare a complete set of specifications for downsizing, then pass that back to the several divisions for final implementation and production. Once the task had been accomplished (in 1978) the team was disbanded and the team members were returned to their various divisions. However, by then the 'project centre' approach had become a way of life at General Motors and part of its company culture. So the approach was adopted for other manufacturing projects and at the last reckoning there were some eight project centres working in a special project centre building. Two of these were engaged on the development of an electric car, whilst another was applying itself to labour issues.

We wonder whether industry in the West will ever go as far as Japan in this respect, with competing companies forming project teams to achieve specific objectives. Japan has done this in the case of microcomputers and robotics: we have examined the latter for its lessons in Chapter 5. Can you imagine General Motors, Ford and Chrysler, for instance, joining hands in a cooperative effort to develop an electric car and then, the development work complete, allowing the key people on the project, drawn from the three companies, to return to their respective companies to compete fiercely for the success of their own electric car models in the marketplace? And then go on to launch an aggressive export campaign, fighting one another for a share of the overseas market? Yet that is exactly what the Japanese did in the field of robotics, as we have seen.

The real point of the project centre and the project team is that the appropriate momentum is developed in relation to a specific goal, to be achieved within a stipulated period and at a stipulated cost. The target is there. The cost may well present problems, since in the specific case now before us, each project is very much a development project, where what lies ahead is, to some extent at least, an unknown quantity. But everyone involved on the project live it and sleep it, giving it wholehearted devotion until it is completed. People are very ready – indeed eager – to work in this way if the context is right. Unfortunately in massive organisations, especially those involved in mass production, it is very difficult to create specific, realistic objectives and the team spirit required in relation to those objectives. But it *can* be done, as the Japanese have shown very plainly.

To close our study of the downsizing project, it is also of interest to note that whilst the project as such was entirely successful, the benefits to the company were hardly commensurate with that success. A market need had been recognised and filled – and that ahead of the local competition, but there are many other factors as well that affect company management and prospects, as compared with project management. The project comes to an end, but the company does not. It has to go on – from success to success, if it is to remain successful. There can be no letup.

The *Fiero* project

That thought brings us to the *Fiero* project at GM, another outstanding example of what can be achieved by a project team. The downsizing project was generic, guiding a number of divisions within General Motors each producing their own specific new model or models. We now take a look at a project to develop a new car unique in concept and design.

The story begins with Hulki Aldikacti, a turkish-born engineer who was chief of advanced vehicle design with Pontiac (a GM division). He dreamed of designing an inexpensive two-seater sports car, a sort of Porsche at less than half the cost. The idea came to him when thinking of what his own children and their young friends would really like to have. He saw a potential market and began by assessing what the customer really wanted. He studied the habits and aspirations of the younger generation. Such a car would have to be smart looking, one that youngsters would be proud to drive to a party. It had to have a plastic body, so that there was no rusting, and minor damage could be fixed using a simple repair kit. Body panels should be screwed on and thus easily replaceable. If Hulki was to sell the concept to the GM management he would have to link it to their corporate goals and his boss, Peter Estes, president of the division helped him to achieve this.

But to start such a project from scratch demanded much time, effort and expense. So it was decided to skip the planning stage and start to build a prototype, using a small elite project team working to a shoestring budget. This was a great challenge, but once again the project team approach brought success. A small independent company was in effect set up *within* the GM organisation for this specific purpose. A new word has been coined to describe this type of activity – *intra*preneurship – so new that it has yet to find a place in the dictionary despite the fact that much has been written about it, including a full length book.(6)

Intrapreneurship

Before we continue with the story of project *Fiero*, perhaps we should define our terms. Let us first give you our definition of the word 'intrapreneurship' since, as we said, you cannot yet find it in the dictionary.

> **Intrapreneur**: Any of the 'dreamers who do'. Those who take on 'hands-on' responsibility for creating innovation of any kind *within* an organisation.

The intrapreneur may be the creator or the inventor of the idea, but is always the 'dreamer': the one who figures out how to turn an idea into a profitable reality. By contrast, we can define an *entrepreneur* as 'someone who fills the role of an intrapreneur *outside* the organisation'. This second definition picks up the contrast between *intra*preneur and *entre*preneur, the standard dictionary definition of the latter being:

> **Entrepreneur**: Person in effective control of a commercial undertaking; one who undertakes a business or an enterprise, with chance of profit or loss; contractor acting as an intermediary. (*Concise Oxford Dictionary*, 6th ed., 1976)

In all this we see some resemblance between the intrapreneur and the project manager and the resemblance grows when he is given a project team to bring his innovation to fruition.

Back to the *Fiero*

The fundamental concept of the intrapreneur with his own project team is well demonstrated by the answer Hulki gave to Pontiac's chief engineer, Bob Dorn, when he asked: 'How will you build the prototype?' Hulki answered: 'I'll go outside, open up shop, and run it like a small business'. That is what happened, and all without formal approval from the GM board, since it was felt that the concept was so unconventional that it would be rejected forthwith. The chief engineer was convinced of the soundness of the idea and so he and Hulki's boss both supported Hulki and protected him from criticism. There was criticism, since although the project was not formally approved it attracted a lot of talk and attention among both managers and workforce in GM.

Hulki took his team along with him on all major decisions, but decided to form no committees, considering them time-consuming whilst achieving little. Thanks to the single-minded devotion of Hulki and his project team the prototype *Fiero* was completed within six months and driven to corporate headquarters to be demonstrated to the top GM executives. It was an immediate hit, and within a month plans for production had been approved. However, it was not all plain sailing from then on. The project was 'killed' at least three times during the next three years (1980-83), since these were difficult, turbulent times in the auto industry worldwide. But Hulki continued to goad on his 500-strong team with words such as:

> You may have heard rumours that the *Fiero* project has been killed. Ignore the rumours and keep going.

Work on the project was continued and the team were able to cut some two years from the normal timetable for new car development, thus saving many millions of dollars. The end result fully justifies Hulki's action and his setting up of a separate project centre. To quote:

> The *Fiero* experience was a prototype of a better way to product development at GM. In times of rapid change and with the challenge of direct competition, we have to find ways to get cars to market faster.

Hulki showed them the way. His prescription for success? In a nutshell:

* Cut out the paperwork – just one secretary for 26 people
* No meetings (or just 5 minutes, to share a decision)
* Direct communication with those concerned
* Pre-resourcing (partnership with key vendors)

That last item was very imaginative, drawing in potential vendors and their knowhow to contribute to the final design, and is in no way restricted to the automotive industry. It is a good idea in any appropriate context and indeed led to the development of the IBM personal computer (PC).

The end result is to be seen in Figure 10.1. This new model came on the market in September 1984, advertised as the first American-produced mid-engine sports car – the all-new two-seat *Fiero*. There are some seven pages of description in the press release from Pontiac that came to us, ending with the sentence:

> With this extensive list of *Fiero* features and innovations – mid-engine, driveable chassis, 'Enduraflex' skins on mill-and-drill pads, new compounding technologies, separation of fit and function (as with retracting headlamps), fully independent suspension, four-wheel disc brakes, new painting technologies and more – *Fiero* offers quality, value and excitement.

Curiously enough, as compared with UK advertising, no mention is made of the top speed, but much is made of fuel economy. But let us turn from the success itself to the reasons for that success.

Independence is the answer

Having introduced the concept of the 'intrapreneur' what are we really saying? Is not the secret of success here that the intrapreneur, be he manager, project manager, team leader . . . call him what you will, has been freed from the company shackles and is being allowed to act independently, following out his own ideas. Whilst Hulki with his *Fiero*, may be an outstanding example of the concept of intrapreneurship, his success is outstanding more for its context than because of its content. General Motors was remarkable for its inertia. It was not that change was thought to be a bad

LISTEN TO LEARN

Figure 10.1 The Fiero at speed
Here we see the 1984 Pontiac Fiero on the road. The end result of three years team effort: a high quality, fuel efficient, reliable two-seat Pontiac that is fun and exciting to drive.

thing: rather, it seemed impossible to implement change. Indeed, when it began, via the project centre, the concept did not seem to 'take'. One success, with downsizing, did not immediately bring a realisation that this was the way to go. Hulki, it seems, had to battle against conservatism rather than opposition and would not have got very far had he been unable to secure the support of his immediate superiors. But now the concept really has taken hold and the number of companies who are following this policy is growing fast, worldwide.

To take but one other instance, IBM now tolerate competing designs within their organisation, having discovered through actual experience that several small competing design teams, handling specific projects, can easily outperform a comprehensive design *division*, in terms of both cost and time. Each small team is given a specific task and their solution is presented in open forum, where the members of other design teams are present as well as those members of management who will have to make the decisions. This results in the best design, rather than the designer with the best connections to the top, going forward. So we see that whilst the word 'intrapreneur' is new, the concept has been around for a number of years. Indeed, Peters and Waterman, whose study and analysis of America's best-run companies was published some three years before Pinchot's work, discuss the same phenomenon under a different name. They used the word 'champion' to describe the intrapreneur in the large but innovative company, saying of him:(7)

> [he is] so intent on innovation that its [the company's] essential atmosphere seems not like that of a large corporation but rather a loose network of laboratories and cubbyholes populated by feverish inventors and dauntless entrepreneurs who let their imagination fly in all directions.

The term 'dauntless entrepreneur' hardly fits a company employee, whatever his attributes and whatever he does: hence the need for a new word to describe his activities – intrapreneur. The intrapreneur is for us the project manager or team leader of *one* project in a company.

Yet again, to quote Lew Lehr, another notable intrapreneur:(6)

> For many years the corporate structure [at 3M] has been designed specifically to encourage young entrepreneurs to take an idea and run with it. If they succeed, they can and do find themselves running their own business under the 3M umbrella. The entrepreneurial approach is not a sideline at 3M. It is the heart of our design for growth.

So the idea as such is hardly new, but it is now gaining ever wider acceptance in the corporate conglomerates. At General Motors the concept now flourishes, for yet another project, with the codename 'Saturn', is now in hand. The entrepreneurial spirit – or should we not rather say the *intra*preneurial spirit – is well demonstrated by the words of the team leader on that project: 'On a clear day, you can't quite see Saturn'.(8) He and his team have an *objective* and they have both the independence and the freedom to plot their own course to that objective. This is a 'small car' project that will incorporate new manufacturing techniques and is expected to have a 'high technology' marketing plan. Onlookers believe that it stands a good chance of narrowing Japan's present cost advantage in that market.(9) General Motors have a significant cost handicap in that some 70 per cent of their car parts are manufactured in-house, whereas with other car manufacturers this is much lower, allowing them to 'shop around' for the best buy.

We are looking at just a few successful projects, but they are not few and far between – year by year, there are many thousands of them, brought to success by a competent project manager, leading a soundly constituted team. It is not a matter of there being only a few who can display such qualities. Rather, there are very many there only waiting for the opportunity. Bennett puts it thus:(10)

> The task is not to change people. People are perfectly alright the way they are. The task is not to motivate people. People are inherently self-starting. The task is to remove those things that demotivate them, to get them out of their way. Or, more precisely, to create those kind of organisational structures that allow workers to get at problems and act in some independent ways so they can develop their skills solving problems related to their own jobs.

The intrapreneur succeeds when he has freedom to act as an entrepreneur. The project manager and his team will be far more likely to run a successful project if they have freedom to act on their own initiative, freedom to be innovative.

Summary

It is very evident that the subdivision of work into projects and the project team concept is now spreading far and wide through industry and demonstrating its effectiveness in the process. We have now seen that the concept of the project and the project team can be applied with success within large organisations and will contribute much to the success of the company as a whole. But the top management in such organisations have to listen – and then learn from what they hear. They have to listen not only to the voices without, but to the voices within. Do not think that General Motors were extremely fortunate to have a Hulki Aldikacti, or 3M a Lew Lehr. There are many such, but they must be allowed to exercise their gifts.

Our primary interest in this book is the construction project and its successful management, but we now see that there are lessons to be learned from a management technique operated within the major manufacturing companies – that of bringing together a project team to handle a specific project. The project team have clear and limited objectives and they can therefore have a 'success'. Their project has an objective that has to be reached within a limited time: it has a beginning and an end. When we come to apply these same principles to construction projects we see guidance and even a warning to both owner and construction contractor. The project manager and his team *must* have a high degree of autonomy if they are to be successful. But that requires the appropriate organisational structure, a subject we must leave to Chapter 19.

References

1. Schumacher, E.F., *Small is Beautiful*, Blond & Briggs Ltd, London, 1973. Also available as a paperback.
2. Article: 'The small car blues at GM', *Business Week*, 16 March 1974, pp.76-81.
3. Burck, C.G., 'How GM turned itself around', *Fortune*, 97, 16 January 1978, pp.87-91+.
4. Sloan, A.P. Jr., *My years with General Motors*, Doubleday, 1972, 560 pp.
5. Belbin, R.M., *Management Teams – Why They Succeed or Fail*, Heinemann, 1981, 179 pp.
6. Pinchot, Gifford III, *Intrapreneuring – Why You Don't Have to Leave a Corporation to Become an Entrepreneur*, Harper & Row, New York, 1985, 329 pp.
7. Peters, T.J. and Waterman, R.H. *In Search of Excellence – Lessons from America's Best-Run Companies*, Harper & Row, New York, 1982, 360 pp.
8. Edid, M., 'On a clear day, you still can't quite see Saturn', *Business Week*, 12 August 1985, pp.20-21.
9. Fisher, A.R., 'Behind the hype at GM's Saturn', *Fortune*, 112, 11 November 1985, pp.34+ (7 pp.).
10. Bennett, D., *Successful Team Building Through TA*, Amacom, New York, 1975.

11 Striving for perfection

Is there such a thing as perfection? The journal *Cost Engineering* carries a paper with the title 'The perfect plan' and goes so far as to feature the title of the paper on its front cover, but when we read the paper we find it a completely straightforward outline of planning and scheduling concepts: nothing more.(1) Why the title carries the word 'perfect' remains a mystery. The point is made, with which we agree, that 'a project cannot be considered totally successful unless it maintains the initial milestones'. But planning is only one aspect of project management. We are convinced that every successful project is headed by a project manager who fulfils his role to perfection. The project manager is the key to success. It is true that he cannot carry a project on his own: he needs an efficient team. But an efficient team is not likely to run a successful project if the project manager fails in *his* role. Indeed, so important is the role of the project manager in our view that we devoted a complete section of three chapters to him and his team when writing on the subject of project management.(2)

Each and every project manager is different: often they are very, very different from one another. It could not be otherwise, since we are looking at someone who has to excel, and one quality of excellence is without doubt individuality. However, there are certain attributes and characteristics which all project managers have in common – in particular, the quality of leadership and the ability to communicate effectively. Seeking for a successful project where this particular aspect of our subject could be demonstrated, we found ourselves walking in the footsteps of a writer for the *New Yorker* and looking at a company, rather than a project. Earlier, we have been emphasising the differences that exist and have to be recognised between company management and project management, but when we look at the chief executive of a company and compare him and the way he runs his company with the project manager and the qualities he needs to run a project, we find that they have much in common. In a way, running a company is very like running a series of complex projects.

Ken Auletta, seeking to profile a spectacular company, started with a long list of successful companies and then set out to eliminate those without innovation. Those that remained were interesting enough but were mostly led, in his opinion, by uninteresting executives. Further elimination along these lines led him to the firm of Schlumberger and its chief executive, Jean Riboud.(3) The performance of this company has been spectacular, and its success has lasted now for many years. In 1981 it achieved the distinction of having the highest profit margin of any of the world's leading industrial companies. The company is multinational, operating in some 92 countries in the field of high technology. Surprisingly, despite its outstanding performance, neither the company nor its chief executive seem to attract any attention outside the specific area in which the company operates.

A quiet giant

A literature survey reveals little about Schlumberger and Auletta tells us why. The company rarely advertises and when it does this is in speciality journals in its own field, in which it seems to have a virtual monopoly. The journalists have been kept very much at arm's length. This policy meant that Auletta had great difficulty in arranging a meeting with Riboud. However, that was finally accomplished, largely it seems because Riboud equated the *New Yorker* with Schlumberger, as both being the best in their own spheres. Whilst Riboud agreed to provide information with initial reluctance, once he had agreed he did his utmost to provide all that was required, arranging for Auletta to meet both his colleagues and even his critics. It appears that he was an unusual chief executive, ruling his giant company with what is sometimes called a 'loose rein'. His temperament seems to harmonise with what is often termed the 'company culture' of his company. The company combines a tradition of pride in its achievements with humility and a recognition that it has still a long way to go. Having a substantial monopoly in its specialist field, the company has not had to face competition in the normal sense. However, to instil a spirit of competition, Riboud is known to be ruthless in transferring or dismissing executives, whilst setting them almost impossible standards of achievement. There is a constant striving after perfection, which obviously implies that the standard currently being reached can be improved upon.

In this picture we see an immediate parallel with the project manager. Whilst his company may well have had to compete in order to secure the project, his task has nothing to do with competition as such. His task is to complete the project successfully; his objective, the various targets that have been set. He has to motivate his project team to that end. If we see the way in which Riboud inspires his team to bring success, we should get some insight into the management approach that will result in the project manager having a successful project. To help us get the picture let us first review the background against which Riboud works.

Schlumberger

Schlumberger is a French company, with headquarters in both Paris and New York. The company employs some seventy-five thousand people, of whom less than two hundred are located in the head offices. If we assess the value of a company via the market price of its shares, only three companies in the world are worth more than Schlumberger, whom we assess at US$16 billion. These are AT&T (US$48 billion), IBM (US$34 billion) and Exxon (US$27 billion). None of the giant corporations with household names, such as ITT, Colgate and Citicorp, can match Schlumberger's profits, although they are far better known.

The company seeks no publicity, having no public relations department and no lobbyist at any of the world's capitals. The bulk of its income comes from its provision of oilfield services and its success is ascribed to it being 'one of the world's best-managed multinationals'. Its net income and its earnings per share have grown by 30 per cent each year from 1971 to 1981 and its net income in 1982 was 21 per cent of the revenue. This is higher than any of a thousand leading corporations, the median for the 500 reviewed by *Fortune* being only 13.8 per cent.

The company was founded by two brothers, Conrad and Marcel Schlumberger. They were very close, but very different. Conrad was outgoing, passionate and a scientific genius, whilst Marcel, shy and cautious, was nevertheless a shrewd businessman and a practical engineer. The business was started in 1919, initially drawing pictures of mineral deposits by charting the electrical resistivity, but the breakthrough came in 1927, when the technique was found to be applicable in the search for oil deposits. From then on there was no looking back. The wireline logging technique offered by Schlumberger is now used on practically every oil and gas well in the world. The company holds no patents, yet it has nearly 70 per cent of the world market share in logging measurement applications. The business has now been expanded to include drilling, testing and completing wells: pumping and cementing. Its Forex Neptune subsidiary, formed some twenty-five years ago, is now the world's largest oil drilling company. Schlumberger acquired Fairchild Camera and Instrument Corporation in 1979 and now has over forty major subsidiaries. The jewel in its crown is Wireline, which generates nearly half the revenue and two-thirds of the profits. A detailed in-depth analysis has confirmed that Schlumberger has the most consistent, high growth track record of any company quoted on Wall Street.

The managerial and entrepreneural spirit

The management philosophy of Schlumberger has been expressed by Riboud thus:(3)

> Any business, any society, has a built-in force to be conservative . . . if you want to be innovative, to change an enterprise or a society, it takes people willing to do what's not expected . . .

He believes in sowing doubt, rotating people and measuring not just the profits, as is normal, but the man in charge and particularly his enthusiasm for change. For Riboud, only total victory counts. To remain ahead of its competitors technologically Schlumberger must continue to provide challenge and so inspire its technicians. Despite its current lead, Schlumberger still spends over US$100 million annually on wireline research, this being more than the profits of any of its competitors.

That this innovative spirit is the key to success is suggested by Peters and Waterman, who identify Schlumberger as one of the best-run companies in the world and say of innovation:(4)

> The major reason big companies stop innovating is their dependence on big factories, smooth production flow, integrated operations, big-bet technology planning, and rigid strategic direction setting . . . they forget how to learn and they quit tolerating mistakes. The company forgets what made it successful in the first place, which is usually a culture that encouraged action, experiments, repeated tries.

Schlumberger illustrate the truth of this message, since whilst highly successful they continue to innovate. The lessons for the project manager and his team are obvious. Each project, in terms of management and construction techniques, should be an advance on the last. It will be seen that every project that we have ventured to study in this analysis of successful projects has innovative content, sometimes to a marked degree. Not all the innovation is within the project as such – there are companies developing new techniques for the handling of massive modules, as we illustrate in Chapter 15, but it is the innovative project manager who lays hold of and successfully utilises what is on offer.

Successful motivation

Let us turn from the chief executive to his team. They have to have motivation. We are told that Riboud met his counterpart in Japan, the president of Kyoto Ceramics, a company whose sales were built up to some US$600 million in seventeen years. Here was a robotised automated factory with happy workers, a model of efficiency. The key to success here was said to be sound motivation. 'Industry is the great successor to religion', we are told. In other words, the worker has to be encouraged to centre his thoughts and his hopes on his job. That is brought about in Schlumberger by offering training, scope and incentives.

A major activity with Schlumberger is the servicing of oil rigs and this requires constant recruitment and training. For example, Schlumberger recruited 137 electrical engineering graduates to their Belle Chasse Training Centre in 1981. They were given a three weeks orientation course on an oil rig, then another three weeks at the training centre. If successful they become junior engineers and are sent into the field for a further six months of intensive on-the-job training. Over a 30-month period they return to the training centre for five weeks of advanced instruction, take an oral examination and give a presentation on data logging and the use of their tools. Subjected to hours of rigorous questioning, a pass results in promotion. Speed in the execution of their work is of the utmost importance, since it costs a client some US$200 000 a day to maintain an offshore rig which remains idle whilst a Schlumberger engineer answers a specific question or solves a problem. The engineer working in the field has no one to fall back on and this gives him a lot of confidence. He is in full control of a crew and a lot of expensive equipment and his actions bring either success or failure. This calls for devotion to the job. Whilst the financial rewards are substantial, even more important, it appears, is the quality of the job. To quote one such engineer:

> You are your own boss . . . you get lots of responsibility at an early age . . . its really fun . . . it's not a routine job . . . no two days are the same.

This sort of work attracts and shapes competent people. An area manager says that he has the impression that he's running his own company. It is this spirit in their employees, their dedication and complete loyalty to the company, that results in Schlumberger being the best in its field.

But all this can be equally true in respect of a project, since no two projects are alike, the project team work on site, the project manager is in effect running his own company and there is no reason why the same spirit of devotion and loyalty cannot motivate all involved. Indeed, the construction industry is noted for just that. To quote:(5)

> Construction men – however rough and unemotional they may appear – really have an enduring, all-consuming love affair with their profession. They think it, talk it, dream it. The daily challenge it presents is a never-ending lure to all of them.

The approach to perfection

We noted earlier that Schlumberger has a near monopoly in its field, with some 70 per cent of the world market. Its nearest wireline competitor, the Dresser Industries Atlas Oilfield Services Group has a mere 10 per cent. This near monopoly is maintained despite the fact that Schlumberger charge prices higher than any of their competitors. Price, so far as Schlumberger is concerned, is determined by the return expected on their investment and not by the market conditions, a policy instituted by Marcel Schlumberger and maintained to this day. The rise in profits from year to year has been almost continuous, despite the fluctuations in the oil market. In years when oil drilling declined, the Schlumberger revenues continued to rise. Why? Profits rose even when the market in which the company worked was depressed, as in 1982 when the profits of its competitors for oilfield services and its customers, the oil companies, were in decline.

The shareholders have benefited from the success of Schlumberger. One share in 1965, with a market value of US$35, had become 51 shares each valued at US$50 by 1983, without any further investment by the shareholder. That is to multiply the share value some 70 times in less than twenty years. In 1982, net income was 21 per cent of revenue, eclipsing IBM's 11 per cent. Yet again we ask: why? The single most significant factor is undoubtedly a lead in successful technology: a lead the company is determined to maintain. This comes from the inbuilt company philosophy, reflected in the covenant entered into by the brothers Conrad and Marcel at the insistence of their father, Paul Schlumberger, when the company was first formed, that 'the interest of scientific research take precedence over financial ones'. This philosophy, that puts money in its proper place, is further illustrated by the recollections of Anne Gruner Schlumberger. She tells us that her father Conrad once told her: 'Money is earned with great difficulty and you are not allowed to waste it for yourself. Never'.(6) One of the world's wealthiest women, she nevertheless lives very simply indeed.

Schlumberger also has the distinction of being in good standing in the Third World, where multinationals are normally resented. Their operations have never been nationalised – possibly because you cannot nationalise expertise and knowhow. Further, the company has recruited widely in the countries where they work. Hiring local people is not only less expensive but it also lessens political tensions.

Once again, we have lessons for the project manager in project management. Quality of work and harmonious working relationships should not be subjugated to the desire to increase profit. It is often possible to place contracts at prices so competitive that the contractor has no hope of making a profit, but such a policy is self-defeating. It will not lead to a successful project. Of course, the training and use of local people is a subject in itself, but once again the successful project will have maximised the use of local resources, even if that has been done at the expense of much extra effort and trouble on the part of the project team.

The impact of diversification

Perfection is a difficult target to achieve, but to maintain it once achieved: that is even more difficult. Recent acquisitions by Schlumberger have taken the company outside its primary specialisation to some extent. Fairchild was a major acquisition, but Riboud has complete faith in that extension to their activities, which he believes will be the basis of Schlumberger's measurement technology. He sees it as part of the continuing drive for improvement in technology, and warns:(3)

> If we lost the drive, and fear searching for new technologies, or fear taking incredible gambles on new managers, or fear to heed the voices of other countries and cultures, then we will become an establishment . . . Schlumberger will ultimately decline. It is easy to be the best. That's not enough. The goal is to strive for perfection.

The company is continuing to spread its interests, a sign of continuing optimism in the face of decline in the sector it primarily serves, the oil and gas industry. In April 1984 Dowell, a company encasing drill pipes in cement sleeves, became a wholly-owned subsidiary, whilst later that same year Sedco, a Texan company that rents out drilling rigs, was acquired for some US$1.1 billion.(7) Such acquisitions are seen to contribute to Schlumberger company strategy over the past two decades: to be the best oilfield service company in the world and to have a niche in measurement technology. Its course has been mapped by Riboud in the Schlumberger Annual Report for 1984:

> Each cycle has its opportunities and risks. If and when opportunities arise in America, in Japan, in Europe, in the field of semi-conductors, of computer-aided systems (automatic tests, CAD-CAM), of measurement and control, we will move in as we did in the oilfield services . . . We have survived the change of cycle in the oil industry reasonably well. Stubbornly we move forward with the same basic convictions: advanced technology and new products, better service and more answers to the customers, more laboratories and more R&D, better trained, better motivated and more determined people at all levels, in all countries.

To sum up, more of the mixture as before. But the move towards more and more diversification can bring its own problems, unless the diversification is closely related to the mainstream of effort within the company, as seems to have been the case till now. In the parlance of the company financial advisor, this is called 'sticking to the knitting'. That same principle holds good in project management as in company management. Stick to what you know best – this sounds obvious but it is continually overlooked and disaster results.

The secret of success

We have looked at various aspects of the Schlumberger organisation, seeking clues to its continuing success. The company operates in the field of high technology but it has never sought to be a front runner. Perhaps because solid reliability is preferable to technical wizardry. It is the front runners who have to face all the trials and tribulations associated with any new development. Companies like Schlumberger tend to watch all this and then come into the market with a product which is more complete and of the highest quality. This process has been observed in other excellent and highly successful companies, such as IBM, Digital and Caterpillar.(4) Another attribute that brings strength is the complete decentralisation of the company organisation, with a small, lean staff at the two head offices in Paris and New York: staff not tied to a telephone but able to concentrate on long range planning and company strategy. Its extremely independent field force, with over 2000 highly trained and highly paid engineers, who are able to and empowered to make decisions on the spot in the best interests of the client, must also be a powerful factor in the equation.(8)

Yet, despite all these factors, we come back once again to the chief executive and his role. None of this would be effective without the right man at the top, just as the most highly trained, highly paid workforce will never redeem a project if they are led by a poor project manager. Top management and especially the chief executive holds the key to success. The Schlumberger family still own 25 per cent of the shares and although the company employs some 75 000 people it is not a conglomerate – nor ever will be, if Riboud continues to have his way. Despite its size, one Schlumberger executive describes the company as a 'constitutional monarchy with Riboud as the monarch'. In our view this is good, in that it ensures that the successful innovative policies are maintained and pursued. There is nothing wrong with an autocracy so long as the autocrat is fair, just, reasonable and knows what he is doing.

Whilst control remains vested in France, the three top executives being French and the heir apparent one Michel Vaillaud following his appointment as president and chief operating officer in December 1982, the management of the company is widely spread. Other senior executives are American, Scottish and Lebanese in origin. Company recruitment is worldwide, with some 40 per cent of the engineers taken on in 1980 and 1981 for work outside North America coming from the developing countries.

Once again there are lessons for project management. Many of today's projects are very large, some even deserving the title of 'megaproject', which seems to imply that they are going to cost billions of dollars. Such projects need to be scaled down to proportions that are recognisable and manageable. This is achieved by decentralisation, where for instance a project is divided up into a large number of separate physical areas, each of which is processed and handled as a separate project. If this type of project subdivision is not effected, the inertia of the organisation will be such that movement forward becomes almost impossible. It becomes a conglomerate – anathema to Riboud. General Motors was once one such, although things have now changed, as we have shown in Chapter 10. Alfred P. Sloan, Jr, the former head of that company, once said:(2)

> In practically all our activities we seem to suffer from the inertia resulting from great size . . . Sometimes I must be forced to the conclusion that General Motors is so large, its inertia so great, that it is impossible for us to be real leaders.

Schlumberger have avoided falling into this trap and project managers must see that their project administration is such that they retain flexibility and allow for individual initiative by sound subdivision of major projects.

Summary

We have compared the project manager to the chief executive of a company and this comparison is instructive. The project manager has a very special role to play. He is indeed, every time he takes up a new project, the head of a new company with a specific life span, extending from conception to completion of that particular project. Whether he is working for an owner or a managing contractor his position in that respect is much the same. However, the comparison fails in that the chief executive can be an autocrat, whereas the project manager always has to look over his shoulder, as it were, at his management. This means that his management must ensure that the project manager, having been given certain responsibilities, is also given the appropriate authority to carry out those responsibilities. Anything less will result in the project management being much less effective than it otherwise could be. To do this properly requires the preparation of a mandate for the project manager: a written description, brief but explicit and positive, describing the basic objectives of his function, together with some detail of the activities considered implicit in the mandate. Only thus will the project manager have any real opportunity to imitate the chief executive in his authoritarian role.

Since this book went to press, we have heard of the tragic death of Jean Ribould, whose management skills we have highlighted in this chapter. A letter from the Chairman, Michel Vaillaud, in the Schlumberger Annual Report for 1985 opens: 'Grief and shock – this is how we shall remember 1985. Jean Ribould, after 34 years with the company and 20 years at the helm, has left us too soon.'. That same letter highlights the key attitudes of this company towards its employees: priority on continuous training, giving full responsibility through decentralisation, and appraising people on results and on human qualities: an abiding lesson to all project managers.

References

1. Kibler, B.E., 'The perfect plan', *Cost Engineering*, Vol.27, No.7, July 1985, pp.8-13. *Cost Engineering* is the technical journal of the American Association of Cost Engineers.
2. Auletta, K., *The Art of Corporate Success – the Story of Schlumberger*, G.P. Putnam, 1984, 184 pp.
3. Stallworthy, E.A. and Kharbanda, O.P., *Total Project Management – from Concept to Completion*, Gower, Aldershot, 1983, 329 pp.
4. Peters, T.H. and Waterman, Jr, H., *In Search of Excellence – Lessons from America's Best-Run Companies*, Harper & Row, New York, 1982, 360 pp.
5. Halmos, E.E., *Construction: a Way of Life – a Romance*, first published by Westminster Communications and Publications, but now available from the author at PO Box 259, Poolsville, MD 20837, USA.
6. Schlumberger, A.G., *Schlumberger Adventure*, Arco, 1984, 188 pp.
7. Article: 'Schlumberger/Sedco: buy now, profits later', *Economist*, 292, 22 Sept. 1984, pp.77-8.
8. Article: 'Schlumberger's fortunes are measured in oil rigs', *Economist*, 287, 16 April 1983, pp.80-1.

Part Four
THE DEVELOPING COUNTRIES FOLLOW

12 A successful project, but . . .

The Kudremukh iron ore project is one of the largest mining and beneficiation projects in the world. It has been developed in difficult hilly terrain under severe climatic conditions. The heavy monsoon rains last for some four months, and for most of the year there are strong winds and much fog. Indeed, it is said that the Bhadra river valley, where the Kudremukh community is situated, has the distinction of being on record as the third wettest place known on earth. In the monsoon season the average rainfall is some 6000 mm. In 1980, the year the plant was started up, the rainfall exceeded 9500 mm, with 417 mm (17 in) in one 24-hour period in July 1980 – a record. Yet, thanks to proper project planning this US$650 million venture, with a capacity of 7.5 million tonnes per year was completed to a very tight schedule indeed: 40 months to mechanical completion. In addition, the project was completed within budget. The basic reasons for this are said to be:

1 Carrying out detailed design and construction simultaneously
2 Undertaking a number of independent activities in parallel
3 Delivering equipment to site whenever possible fully or partially assembled
4 Standardisation and the use of modular design

The pragmatic and flexible policy adopted by the Indian government also helped substantially towards the successful completion of this project. Let us see how it all came about.(1)

A project in prospect

We set the scene by going back to the early seventies, when a

Japanese consortium expressed an interest in the supply of iron ore slurry to Japan for steel making. That fell through, but in 1974 Iran indicated their interest in a 'captive' source for quality pellet feed for their proposed pelletisation plants, that were going to produce steel by the direct reduction process. Agreement was reached between the governments of Iran and India in May 1974, whereby Iran was to provide a low-interest loan of up to US$630 million over four and a half years against a phased supply of iron ore pellets totalling in all 150 million tonnes. A price formula for the supply of the pellets was agreed, which included built-in variation for construction costs and operating costs. Adequate safeguards were also provided to cover non-delivery by the supplier (India) or non-requirement by the buyer (Iran). Quite a complex contract. All this was first incorporated in a memorandum of understanding, the detailed agreements being signed more than a year later, in November 1975.

The detailed agreement stipulated that the raw material be supplied in the form of filter cake rather than pellets and shipment was to start in August 1980. Delivery was to build up from 3 million tonnes in the first year to 7.5 million tonnes per year from the third year onwards and the initial term of the supply contract was four and a half years. Iran made an advance payment of US$100 million in February 1976 and thus everything was set, including the target date (August 1980) for production of the iron ore.

Advance planning

In anticipation of the finalisation of the agreements between the two governments, the Kudremukh Project Office was set up in November 1975 with Mr M.B. Silgarde, joint managing director of MECON (Metallurgical & Engineering Consultants (India) Ltd) as the project director. A small project team was brought together, with personnel from MECON, HSCL (Hindustan Steelworks Construction Ltd) and SAIL (Steel Authority of India Ltd). These are all public sector organisations with functions as indicated by their respective titles. The work in prospect was eventually allocated as follows:

Work to be done	*Responsible party*
Access road (110 miles) linking Kudremukh and Mangalore	Public Works Department

Power for site construction work	Karanatka Power Corporation
Port development at Mangalore	New Mangalore Port Trust
Design of Kudremukh project	Aureville, Pondicherry
Mobilisation for construction	Hindustan Steelworks Construction Ltd (HSCL)
Operating company	Kudremukh Iron Ore Co. Ltd (KIOCL)
Mining associate and engineering constructor	Canadian Met-Chem Consultants (MET-CHEM)

Within the above list, the two key parties are the operating company, KIOCL and the mining associate, MET-CHEM, who fulfil the roles of owner and managing contractor respectively, as earlier indicated in Figure 1.4 (See Chapter 1). MET-CHEM, a subsidiary of US Steel, were issued with a 'letter of intent' in February 1976, the plant to be complete and ready for commissioning by April 1980. The scope of the services to be provided by MET-CHEM included review of existing data, basic engineering, provision of a definitive cost estimate, procurement, project management including supervision of detailed engineering and construction: assessment of manpower requirements, supervision of commissioning and operator training. For this they were to receive a fixed fee of US$13 million during construction, with a further US$5.2 million during the first two years of operation. There were bonus/penalty clauses relating to both date of completion and the definitive estimate, with a maximum liability of 20 per cent of the fixed fee. They were required to maximise the indigenous content of the project in relation to equipment, detailed design and construction. We mention these details to give a broad impression of the responsibilities normally undertaken by a managing contractor in such cases, for these contractual arrangements were completely typical. Whilst not directly responsible for the total cost of the project, remuneration is affected by the validity of the definitive estimate earlier prepared and agreed with the owner.

The owner, KIOCL, was set up in April 1976 with Mr K.C. Khanna as chairman and managing director and entrusted with the task of ensuring the timely execution of the project in accordance with the agreements entered into with the government of Iran. The period of 40 months to mechanical completion (September 1976 to December 1979) was divided into four major phases, with the first shipment of iron ore concentrate to Iran planned for 23

August 1980. All this concerns the plant itself at Kudremukh. Parallel with the design, construction and commissioning of the iron ore plant were the other construction activities outlined above, equally essential to successful completion and operation of the project.

The initial schedule agreed between MET-CHEM and KIOCL was developed into a detailed set of time-based networks which were computerised and then served as the monitoring tool in relation to project progress. KIOCL had responsibility not only for the activities of MET-CHEM but also the work of the various agencies entrusted with the related development of the infrastructure – roads, port and power supply.

Work starts in earnest

The initial basic design of the plant was carried out by MET-CHEM in Montreal, an engineering team from KIOCL being based there. Gradually the centre of activity shifted to Mangalore where three companies, MECON, Engineers India and Howe (India), undertook the detailed design under the guidance of MET-CHEM. As it turned out, MET-CHEM had to carry out the detailed piping and instrumentation design themselves, since the necessary skilled engineers could not be found locally.

Simultaneously a joint MET-CHEM/KIOCL team of engineers investigated factors such as the availability of skilled manpower and local manufacturing capacity. Equipment procurement called for very close cooperation between these two parties throughout. The specifications were drawn up to match the capabilities of Indian manufacturers and a list of qualified bidders, both in India and abroad, was drawn up using the World Bank system of technical appraisal. Technical discussions with the bidders helped clarify points in doubt and the priced tenders were opened in the presence of those tendering in order to eliminate speculation and any misgivings there might have been.

A total of 80 contracts were let for the civil and structural work at Kudremukh and Mangalore, with HSCL as the prime contractor. At peak, in October 1979, MET-CHEM had a total of 40 expatriates supervising the construction, supported by some 400 Indian personnel, together with a variety of separate agencies used for surveying and quality control. Considering the difficult terrain, harsh climate and the inaccessibility of the site, completion within the time available was a real achievement. Figures in this context do not mean too much, but there was some four million cubic metres of excavation, 200 000 cubic metres of concrete, 29 000 tons of mechanical equipment, 88 000 metres of piping and last, but not least, 2000 houses to be built. Advance mobilisation by HSCL allowed work to commence as drawings became available, whilst a bonus clause in the contract with HSCL for working during the monsoon season also expedited progress. In addition, the necessary construction materials were stockpiled in advance at strategic locations and a number of novel construction techniques were employed to save both time and cost. All this calls for substantial, detailed advance planning.

Problems galore

Do not think that because the project was completed on time and within budget that nothing went wrong. Something *always* goes wrong: good planning should be able to cope with incipient disaster. It is interesting to review a few of the unforeseen incidents, in order to see how the problems they brought were met and overcome.

The Lakhya Dam crisis
The 1978 monsoon brought excessive rainfall, exceeding 850 cm over the period. As a result of very heavy rain one night there was a massive landslide at the partially completed Lakhya Dam, blocking the temporary spillway. The continuing rain filled the lake, threatening the stability of the dam and endangering life and property at Kudremukh itself. An immediate decision was taken to breach the spillway on the downstream side of the dam, the dam survived and was still completed on time.

The Calcutta floods
Flooding in the Calcutta area during the 1978 monsoon caused distress to a number of equipment suppliers. A task force was set up and alternative arrangements were made for the transport of the equipment.

Access road
It became apparent that the road from Mangalore to Kudremukh was not going to be ready on time with the resources immediately available. Help was therefore sought and obtained from the Border Roads Organisation and the Railways Construction Agency, with the result that work was speeded up and the road was available for the transport of the heavy mining equipment when required.

Failure of manufacturer
One of the fabrication companies had a labour problem and was on the point of failure. Immediate action was taken by way of an application to the Madras High Court and the materials in course of construction shipped to other fabricators overnight.

Earth slides
During the 1979 monsoon big boulders rolled down the slopes in the mining area, breaking off some of the spans in the conveyor system. Persistent and sustained work over a period of several days resulted in the repairs being effected, together with the provision of safeguards to prevent future incidents of this nature.

Dock strike
There was a dock strike in North America that threatened to delay shipment of certain critical equipment. The project team in Montreal took immediate action to divert these materials by road to other ports not subject to the strike, thus ensuring delivery on time.

All these incidents were so handled that the basic plan for construction was maintained, but each time it is demonstrated that decisive, resolute and immediate action had to be taken. Each time extra costs were involved and these *had* to be committed. It is a tribute to the cost control of the project that nevertheless total cost remained within budget.

The finale

The initial plan was for mechanical completion by the end of December 1979, followed by commissioning. Review of progress on site indicated that it would be advisable to start commissioning of individual plant units *before* mechanical completion, and this was done. The operating experience gained as each section was started up required modification and improvement, but it was possible to effect such changes without delaying final startup. This constant monitoring of progress against plan and a readiness to modify the initial plan to meet the developing situation resulted in the first iron ore slurry being pumped to Mangalore on 24 August 1980, as scheduled some four years earlier.

The approved capital cost of the project was Rs6473 million (there are approximately 12 rupees to the US dollar). This included Rs1005 million for the development of the related port facilities, so the net estimate for the mining project as such was

Rs5468 million. The actual cost was Rs4838 million, a saving of some 11 per cent on the original definitive estimate. The factors which were seen to make a major contribution to the savings eventually achieved were:

>Economical purchasing, with effective competition
>Timely completion of the various phases of construction activity
>Reduction in interest during construction, since cash drawings were less than anticipated
>A favourable rate of exchange (Rs/US$) during construction of the project

Of these, only the last item is not a result of the sound administration and control of the project by the project team.

If we ask what factors contributed to the successful completion of the project to time and within budget, our answer would be:

>Clearly formulated goals
>Problems speedily identified and resolutely dealt with
>Impact of environmental factors assessed and action taken
>A flexible plan of action
>Constant and rigorous monitoring of cost and progress
>Local (Indian) facilities used to the maximum, *but* with due regard to function, quality, delivery and cost
>No surplus manpower, especially in closing phases of project

This project, the first of its kind in India, offered very special technical and logistic challenges and was to be built to a tight schedule – even by international standards. These challenges were successfully met and overcome. Carrying out detailed design and construction in parallel was a calculated risk, essential for timely completion. It meant that certain changes and modifications had to be made at a very late stage, but the problems thereby presented were overcome.

The very heavy equipment, some of it never seen in India before, posed challenges first in transportation and then in operation. The operating staff had to be trained for the job. That all these challenges were met successfully is a tribute both to the project team and the many contractors employed on this mammoth project. Continuing support and encouragement from the central government and the state government was also of considerable help. One area where central government was of substantial help was through the provision of a blanket foreign exchange release for the project, which left the project team free to make variations within their overall approved estimate and import banned or restricted items provided that could be justified on the ground of quality or cost.

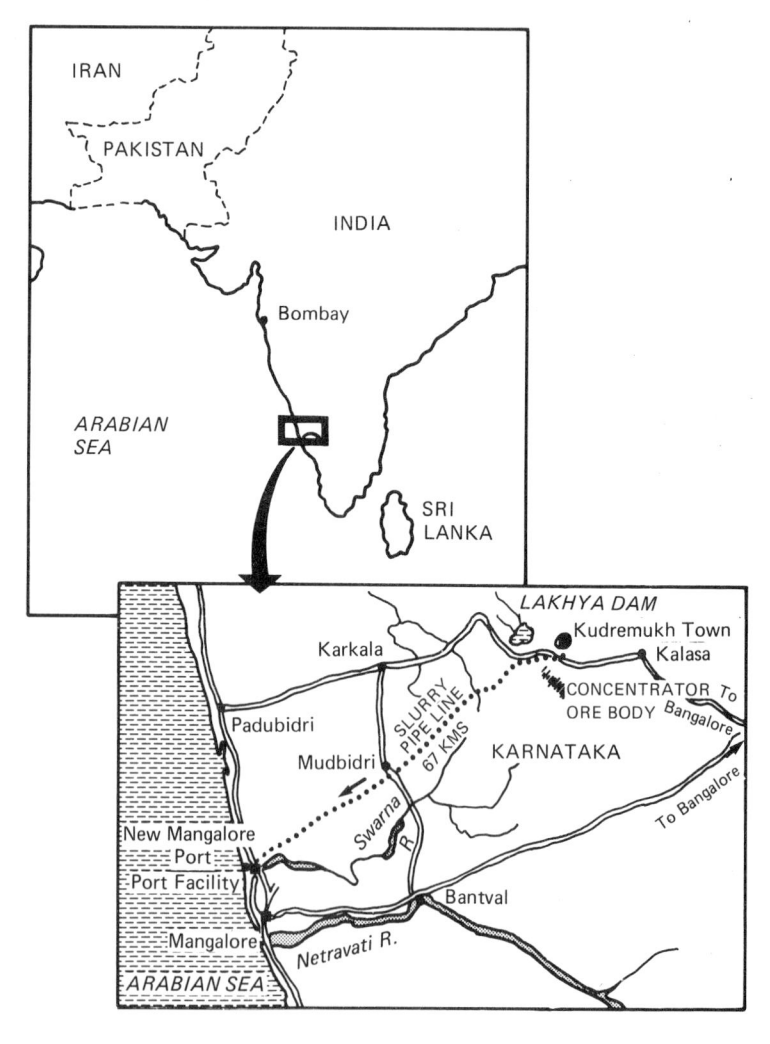

Figure 12.1 The Kudremukh Iron Ore Project
Here we see the location of the Kudremukh townsite, in the Bhadra river valley, and the new port facility at Mangalore. The slurry pipeline route includes a 1.6 kilometre long tunnel through the mountain divide.

The aftermath

A difficult project and well executed – but that is by no means the end of the story. The project was completed ahead of schedule but then languished for lack of a market. The delay in the completion of the pellet plants in Iran and the revolution there brought a great setback. It had become apparent much earlier, following the revolution in Iran, that any dependence upon NISIC as an immediate potential customer for the Kudremukh concentrate was out of the question. The scheduled payments for the construction of the plant ceased in September 1978 with only US$225 million paid out of the agreed total of US$630 million. However, the decision was made that the Indian government would finance the completion of the project and the financial transition was executed so smoothly that many of the executives and contractors involved with the project were only aware of the extent of the problem from reports in the Indian news media.

The situation was to some extent relieved by a trade-type commercial agreement with Romania, whereby the Romanian government export organisation agency undertook to take delivery of 3 500 000 tonnes of iron ore concentrate from Kudremukh over some three and a half years. In consideration for the iron ore supply, Romania agreed to construct a 3 million tonnes per year pelletising plant for KIOCL, using technology supplied by the West German company Lurgi Chemie and Huettentechnik GmbH. Figure 12.1 shows the original concentration plant at Kudremukh, with the slurry pipeline to New Mangalore Port, where the pelletising plant was built. The management of KIOCL showed remarkable foresight in utilising this period of slow market development to embark on a programme of concentrate quality improvement. They realised that concentrate quality must be improved over that initially demanded by Iran, if customers were to be attracted from the Middle East and Southeast Asia. The plant has therefore been redesigned so as to achieve this.(2)

The concentrate sale agreement with Romania was described in the Indian press as a 'distress sale'. However, the sale has allowed KIOCL to tune its facilities, train the workforce and prepare the plant and personnel for the expected production upturn. Meanwhile, during the period 1983-84 Romania exercised its option in increase deliveries by some 200 000 tons and KIOCL is optimistic that the option will be renewed or even increased in the next contract year. Meanwhile, markets are being sought and secured for the pellets from the plant at the coast, which went on stream in September 1985.(3) This plant is said to be the first of its kind in the world and a memorandum of understanding has been signed between KIOCL and Indonesia for the supply of a minimum of one million tonnes per year of Kudremukh pellets, up to 1 750 000 tonnes per year, with India undertaking to buy back sponge iron at a specified level in proportion to the Kudremukh pellets purchased by Indonesia. This is but one of a number of possibilities being pursued. A final note of optimism comes with the news of a decision by the Union Central government to investigate the feasibility of establishing an integrated steelmaking complex in the Mangalore area. A site has already been selected close to the existing pelletising plant by KIOCL for their contribution to this development, the construction and operation of a coal-based Direct Reduction Plant.

Summary

There is no doubt that this project has been an outstanding technical success and much of this has been attributed to project direction by a dynamic chairman and managing director.(4) Mr K.C. Khanna fulfilled the role of project manager and we see once again that a project stands or falls by the qualities and attributes of the project manager. In this case he had a very good support team, and also a managing contractor prepared to exercise initiative. But all this would have been to no avail had there not been detailed planning of the project at the very beginning. The project was planned when the Shah was in power in Iran, to provide raw materials for two steel mills there, but the impact of the revolution that later took place in Iran in no way detracts from the Indian achievement. Indeed, what happened thereafter has been a very adequate demonstration of the way in which determination can surmount the most formidable of obstacles. Kudremukh is still growing, despite all.

References

1 Mirchandani, H.V., 'Kudremukh – inception and implementation', a section in 'Project management – in public enterprises', published by the Standing Conference of Public Enterprises, New Delhi, part of the proceedings of National Workshop organised jointly by SCOPE and the Bureau of Public Enterprises. See pages 4.6.1 to 4.6.22 and 9 annexes, 1983.

2 Shaw, G., 'India's Kudremukh iron ore project – a 1983 update', *Skilling's Mining Review*, 29 October 1983, pp.4-11.
3 Article: 'KIOCL Mangalore plant to go on steam in September', *Economic Times* (India), 14 August 1985.
4 Article: 'Kudremukh – looking ahead', *Business India*, 19 November–2 December 1984, p. 117.

13 Technology transfer is not easy

The population of Indonesia exceeds 150 million. Only four other countries – China, India, the Soviet Union and the United States – have more people. Indonesia is also the world's largest archipelago, with some 13 000 islands, including Java, Sumatra, Bali and most of Borneo (now known as Kalimantan). We shall be looking at a project at Asahan, in Sumatra, and a series of fertiliser projects both on that island and on Java in due course. But first let us look at Indonesia itself, the context in which all these projects have been built.

The government of Indonesia has continually striven to develop its own natural resources and also to ensure that it will ultimately be self-sufficient not only in terms of food and energy, but also in relation to the design and operation of the projects that were being built in that country. To that end it has introduced legislation in 1975 with regard to the use of foreign labour. This fixes the length of time during which expatriate staff may occupy a specific job category. This means that once a plant is built, a large number of jobs must be filled by Indonesians. Whilst there is no fixed deadline with relation to managers, all technicians *must* be Indonesian once the plant is started up. This demands continuous and intensive technology transfer, with the training of large numbers of people, since whilst the country was teeming with prosperous merchants it was sadly lacking in engineering contractors. The continuing invasion of new technology, with the need for the training of large numbers of Indonesians in a wide range of skills, so that they could occupy positions of responsibility in the new industries that were being brought to the country, and the impact of all this on the country, led to one article on the subject being headlined: 'When exchange means change'. And the change has come and is continuing. The commercial stimulation has helped to create a large number of local firms able to synthesise the new demands of industry and the traditional skills of the Indonesian worker. In this way the country is importing technology and then adapting it to its own personality. It seems as though, before embarking on innovation and invention on its own account, it is first going to perfect the technology it has acquired: a most sound and sensible approach.

Technology transfer in action

The work of the M.W. Kellogg Company in Indonesia is an outstanding example of the way in which change has been brought about. Kellogg have been active in Indonesia since 1971, the year in which self-sufficiency in fertiliser production became a national objective. It was then that P.T. Pupuk Sriwidjaja (PUSRI), a state-owned fertiliser manufacturer, decided to expand its facilities near Palembang in South Sumatra. This led to a series of most successful projects, which we have already dealt with in detail elsewhere under the heading: 'Partners in Indonesia'.(1) This partnership in the design and construction of ammonia-urea fertiliser plants led to the formation of a new Indonesian engineering and construction management company, P.T. Kellogg Sriwidjaja (KELSRI). This joint venture company combines the engineering, procurement and construction capabilities of both Kellogg and PUSRI. Formed in the first instance to offer Indonesian clients a local company providing a valuable technology, it is at the same time transferring skills, techniques and systems not only to the KELSRI staff but to many other engineering and construction companies in Indonesia.

To show how these things work together, TOTAL Indonesie was set up in 1968, and oil was struck in 1972 and 1974, first offshore and subsequently in the Mahakam delta. TOTAL is now the operator for the national company Pertamina. It is asserted that, thanks to the experience it can provide, the TOTAL group has, in close collaboration with the national company Pertamina, been able to create a synergy which bears out the Indonesian motto 'Bhinneka tunggal ika' – unity within diversity.(2) Meanwhile, by 1978 Kellogg had completed its fourth large-scale ammonia-urea complex in Indonesia. Built for P.T. Pupuk at Kujang near Dauwan in central West Java, the complex raised fertiliser capacity in Indonesia to more than two million tons a year. The Kujang complex utilises natural gas feedstock provided by Pertamina from various gas fields in Java. The story of the construction of this particular project shows us the way in which the effects spread far beyond the project itself. The site was situated some thirty-five kilometres from the island's northern coast. Shipment of equipment and materials by rail was not feasible and no waterways existed that would allow for barge transport. The only approach to the site was via narrow roads across a plain – and that rice-growing country, criss-crossed by an elaborate network of irrigation canals. But some of the vessels that had to come to site weighed nearly 400 tons! So, during an 18-month period 28 bridges and culverts were reinforced and modified, entire road sections were upgraded and a receiving wharf designed and built on an irrigation canal some three kilometres from the coast. It was thus that the equipment and materials arrived on site in time to meet the construction schedules.

It works!

Technology transfer is undoubtedly working well in Indonesia. The effects, of course, can only be measured after a period of years, but one would expect the ultimate impact on the environment and infrastructure of the country to be both profound and lasting. Much depends upon the sincerity of the various partners involved. With the joint venture company KELSRI, however, it certainly seems to have worked. Their project experience, as detailed in a brochure issued by the company, has already extended beyond Indonesia itself, since it includes a contribution to a fertiliser project in Algeria, where Kellogg France SA was the main contractor. KELSRI provided startup operators in this instance.(3)

Another demonstration of success lies in the actual operation of the plants that are being built, since this is where the local company is in full control. In 1983 Indonesia set a world record in urea fertiliser output. PUSRI, the operating company, produced 900 thousand tonnes of ammonia and practically all of this was successfully converted to urea fertiliser. In achieving this output, PUSRI operated their ammonia plants at 106 per cent of design capacity and their urea plants were also operating in excess of 100 per cent of design capacity: a degree of operational reliability which normally would only be expected in nations with a long history of fertiliser production experience and a workforce with prolonged experience of plant operation and maintenance. Further, the company ran one of their fertiliser plants continuously for 650 days, thus shattering a 1979 operating record of 633 days previously claimed by C.F. Industries of Donaldsonville, Louisiana, in the United States.

Cooperation continues

Let us now take up a specific case and look at it in a little detail. This time the cooperation is between Indonesia and Japan, rather than a Western country. The Asahan project, as it is known, consists of a hydroelectric power plant and an aluminium smelter, completed on schedule and within budget despite all the odds. Costing in all some US$1.8 billion, it was started in 1976 and production began at the smelter early in 1982.

The completion of this major project, accomplished with the full cooperation of the Japanese government, was the realisation of a long-cherished dream for Indonesia. It has special significance in terms of cooperation, for as President Soeharto of Indonesia stated:

> The completion of the Asahan project means that the dream has become a reality through cooperation between Japan and Indonesia. This successful cooperation not only has great economic significance, but is also a sign of a monumental friendship, which will always be remembered from generation to generation.

The project has a long history. The Asahan river region had long been recognised to be a most suitable location for the generation of hydroelectric power. The first water flow survey was made in 1908 and hydroelectric power generation together with aluminium smelting was first planned in 1919. Since then there has been more than one false start. A Dutch company was to begin construction of the power station in 1940, but World War II caused the abandonment of the project. After the War, when Indonesia gained its independence from the Dutch, plans were laid envisaging Soviet aid, but these were abandoned because of political changes. Because of this long gestation period, the project began to be referred to as a 'dream', but it is now a dream fulfilled.

The Asahan project

The project as now built comprises two power stations, a 120 km transmission line and a 3-line aluminium smelter, all located

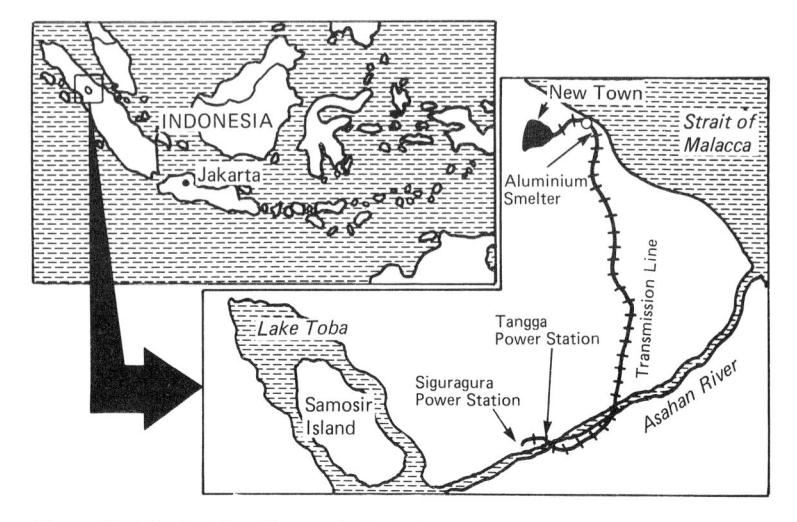

Figure 13.1 Project locations – Indonesia
This map gives the position of the aluminium and fertiliser projects being discussed.

generally as indicated in Figure 13.1. In addition, a very substantial infrastructure had to be developed, including roads, water supply, communication facilities, houses and schools. The end result: Asia's largest aluminium smelter, finally completed late in 1984, and celebrated by a formal ceremony in November of that year in the presence of President Soeharto.

North Sumatra is a very favourable location for such a development, the rainfall being some 200 cm a year, whilst the Asahan river is the only outlet from Lake Toba, some 905 metres above sea level (Figure 13.1). Thus there is a stable and abundant flow of water. There are two great waterfalls, called Siguragura and Tangga, ideal sites for power generation because of the high head of water available over a short distance.

Japan entered into the scheme of things in 1967, when the consulting firm Nippon Koei made a site survey and feasibility study. A loan from the Japanese government gave the project the necessary financial impetus, and three Japanese aluminium companies, led by Sumitomo Aluminium, made a further feasibility study in 1970. Thus the scene was set. Both parties, Japan and Indonesia, were seen to need each other quite badly. The production of aluminium is very energy intensive, requiring as much as 15 000 kWH of electricity per ton of finished aluminium. In Japan electrical power is largely generated from oil-fired power stations, and the cost of the electricity, and hence the cost of manufacturing aluminium, was becoming ever more expensive. In addition, environmental considerations in Japan inhibited further development there. It was considerations such as these that had earlier led Sumitomo Chemical to participate with Colmaco of Australia in an aluminium smelting project in New Zealand.

Indonesia were also well suited with such a project at Asahan. Most of their industrial development had been concentrated on the island of Java, where their capital city Jakarta is located, and the government was anxious to spread industrial development into what were called the 'backward regions'. As a result the government were prepared to rate the Asahan project as a top priority development scheme. Initially, interest was shown not only by Japan, but by Europe and the USA, firms such as Kaiser and Alcoa undertaking feasibility studies. The Japanese sought to cooperate with Kaiser and Alcoa, but the consortium concluded that the total project was too big for 100 per cent private finance and suggested that the Indonesian government undertake and finance the power generation side of the project. This the government refused to do. We consider that to be a most fortunate decision, since had that happened there would have been divided responsibility, with all the problems that brings in its wake. Should the smelters have been completed before power became available, there would have been endless recrimination and contractual disputes. Divided responsibility has often led to disaster, an outstanding example being the Trombay fertiliser plants built in India in the sixties.(4) However, the Indonesian government turned to Japan and sought financial backing from that country to proceed with the project in its entirety – and got it. With the oil crisis on the horizon, and fuel oil prices rising sharply, the project grew ever more attractive, for the hydroelectric scheme offered electricity at a low, stable price.

The financial agreement

The Japanese consortium led by Sumitomo organised a project team consisting of some twenty specialists. The Indonesian team was set up at a high level, experts being drawn from the various ministries. They were led by A.R. Soehoed, who later became Minister of Industry and chairman of the Asahan Development Authority. The Japanese team shuttled between Tokyo and Jakarta, and a series of intensive meetings was held, often lasting to midnight. There were conflicting interests, but these were resolved with seriousness and sincerity. Throughout, there was mutual trust and friendship, which resulted in an agreement being reached which was equitable in every respect. The objective of the meetings was to spell out every aspect in full detail, so that there would be no doubts or disputes at a later stage. The master agreement was finally concluded in December 1974 and it is thanks to the skill and care with which that agreement was drawn up that disputes were largely avoided and the project was successfully completed to schedule. Meanwhile time was passing and the project cost was escalating. The Japanese consortium was therefore expanded to a total of 12 companies, to increase its fund-raising capacity.

Both the Japanese and Indonesian governments, realising the national importance of this project to both their countries, agreed to finance it in its entirety, sharing the cost. For the Japanese, financial support was governed by the following considerations:

1 The project was of national importance, serving to maintain Japan's competitiveness in world markets
2 The project contributed to Japan's policy of promoting the development of aluminium manufacture overseas, in view of the rising cost of electricity at home and related environmental considerations
3 The project would promote both cooperation and friendship with Indonesia

Following these policy decisions at government-to-government level, the appropriate loans were pledged by the Export-Import Bank of Japan, the Overseas Economic Cooperation Fund and the Japanese International Cooperation Agency. Following conclusion of the financial agreements in July 1975 an investment company, Nippon Asahan Aluminium was set up in January 1976 in Japan, which in turn backed this joint venture with the Indonesian government through a further company called Indonesian Asahan Aluminium. For administrative convenience and the smooth implementation of the project the Indonesian government set up a further agency, the Asahan Development Authority.

Now everything was ready. The plans had been laid and the money was available. Construction work started mid-1976. One of the realities with this type of project, with major excavation works, is that it is *never* possible to be sure just what lies under the ground. In this particular case, following two years' work on the project, the cost budget had to be increased by some US$70 million, to US$1.8 billion, to cover specification changes dictated by the geological and other surveys at the site. Costs were also escalating rather more quickly than had been anticipated when the estimates had been made. All this was dealt with by an adjustment in the financial arrangements, the three Japanese financial institutions increasing their contribution, whilst the Indonesian government increased its stake from 10 to 25 per cent. But notice that both parties increased their contribution and it was an amicable arrangement, without recrimination. To conclude this financial picture of the project, we present in Figure 13.2 an outline of the financial arrangements as they were finally concluded.(5) It will be noted that the equity is only some 22 per cent of the total investment in the project. The wisdom of this is open to question. In our judgment it would be better to increase the equity to a maximum, thus minimising the interest burden. Those investing their money get their return by a different and in our judgment a better route: dividend payments coming from the profits made. But of course the return on the investment is not so certain, since if profits fall, return on the investment will also fall, whereas via the other route, both the interest and the repayments *must* be found at an agreed rate. Then, if profits did fall, the two governments involved would have to provide further funding to maintain the

Construction cost			US$ × 1000
Power stations:			530 000
Smelters:			1 040 000
Infrastructure:			220 000
Total construction cost:			1 790 000

This total investment in the project was found as follows:-

Equity

Indonesian Government	(25%):		97 500
Nippon Asahan Aluminium	(75%):		292 500
Total equity	(22.2% of cost):		390 000

Loans

Indonesian government:		150 000
Overseas Economic Cooperation Fund:		270 000
Japanese banks:		980 000
Total loan funding (77.8% of cost):		1 400 000

Figure 13.2 Investment in the Asahan Project
This analysis of the funding for the Asahan Project is typical of the approach to such joint ventures. Care has to be taken to ensure that the burden of interest and loan repayment can be found from the ongoing operational profits.

agreed repayments. It is very evident that banks are not really interested in taking what we might call the 'operational risk', which is a pity.

The benefits

Following successful completion of this project, it is of interest to examine its benefits to both parties, Indonesia and Japan. The President of the Republic of Indonesia hailed it as a 'monument' to the close relationship existing between the two countries, and a symbol of cooperation that should serve as an example to future generations. Whilst Japan lent substantial financial support, that country would benefit from a cheap stable source of aluminium, a vital raw material for its manufacturing industry.

The benefits are, of course, most visible in Indonesia itself. A modern industrial complex has been set up in what had been till then a backward area. The social and economic benefits to Indonesia and the island of Sumatra in particular can be summed up as follows:

> Effective utilisation of local resources, providing great scope for further expansion via the electric power source now available. This will improve living standards greatly in North Sumatra.
> During construction employment was provided for, on average, 5000 Indonesians. The Indonesian labour force peaked at some 15 000. Now, in operation, there is continuing employment for some 2500 Indonesians.
> Substantial technology transfer, local contractors being involved in construction work which for them was a 'first': an underground power station, arch-type dams and aluminium smelters. A training centre was set up in Indonesia and some 100 young Indonesians were sent to Japan for training as key personnel.
> A substantial increase in the export trade, with the shipping of the aluminium ingots to Japan. At the same time, the local downstream aluminium processing industry no longer had to depend upon imported ingots, but had a cheap local source of supply.
> The infrastructure, and especially the ports, roads, electrical distribution network, were all greatly improved, whilst there was the provision of a hospital and schools.

Yes, the benefits have been substantial and it should not stop there. It has been demonstrated that these two countries, Japan and Indonesia, have much to contribute to one another not only economically, but culturally and politically. No wonder that Keijiro Seo, the President Director of the joint venture and deeply involved in the initial planning of the project, was moved to write:(5)

> As the head of the [joint venture] which has propelled the project from the beginning and will manage it in the years ahead, I feel deeply moved by this success story.

Those few words highlight for us once again a vital element in every successful project. Essential qualities in the project manager and his team and hopefully present in all who worked on the project are: personal involvement and enthusiasm, a sincere commitment to the project and its successful completion.

This most successful outcome also illustrates the point made in a paper relating to the implementation of projects in developing countries, that the owner has to take a major responsibility in relation to project decisions.(6) Further, he must invest in experienced people, even though this may not show an immediate direct return.

Summary

We have looked at a nation of some 150 million and have seen a strong commitment to learning. The knowledge brought to the country from abroad has been avidly assimilated and applied. This is the first essential attitude that must be seen in any successful project: a willingness to listen and to learn. A willingness that begins right at the top, with the project director or manager. We are *never* too old to learn. We shall meet that lesson more than once as we go through the successful projects we have chosen to review.

The other essential attitude is that of enthusiasm and commitment, which also has to pervade every member of a project team. We can well imagine that in Indonesia, the benefits to those engaged on the projects we have been looking at would have been so obvious that the enthusiasm and personal involvement would hardly need stimulation, but in the developed countries it can be much more difficult. In such circumstances the project manager, recognising the powerful influence for good and ultimate success that personal involvement brings, may well have to take continuing and positive steps to inform his workforce and so involve them personally in the ultimate aims and benefits of the project they are busy with. One little story springs to mind in this context which illustrates very well both the need for such motivation and the way in which it can be introduced. Two bricklayers are working side by side and each is asked in turn what he is doing. One replies wearily, 'Laying bricks', but the other answers with enthusiasm, 'Building a great building'. If all engaged on a project can look at the 'building' rather than the 'bricks', then success is at the door.

References

1 Stallworthy, E.A. and Kharbanda, O.P. *International Construction and the Role of Project Management*, Gower, Aldershot, 1985, 301 pp. See Chapter 20: 'Partners in Indonesia'.
2 Article: 'When exchange equals change – the effects of technology transfer in Indonesia', *TOTAL Information*, No.98, 1984. Published by Compagnie Francaise des Petroles, Paris.
3 Brochure: *P.T. Kellogg Sriwidjaja – Engineering and Construction Management*, published by Kellogg Sriwidjaja from Jakarta, Indonesia, November 1983.
4 Kharbanda, O.P. and Stallworthy, E.A., *How to Learn from Project Disasters*, Gower, Aldershot, 1983, 273 pp. See Chapter 8: 'The Trombay fertiliser plant complex'.
5 Seo, Keijiro, 'Asahan project – a shining example of economic cooperation', *Journal of Japanese Trade & Industry*, No.2, 1985, pp.20-23.
6 Baldwin, P.L. and Henty, C.J. 'Some suggestions for improving the implementation of fertiliser projects in developing countries', *Fertiliser Society*, London. A 30 page booklet issued in October 1978.

14 Joint ventures in China

During the past decade there has been a complete transformation of certain areas of the world, largely as a result of the discovery and subsequent exploitation of petroleum and natural gas reserves. Regions such as the Middle East and the Sahara have become active and prosperous centres of industry. Towns have sprung up alongside the petrochemical installations. In other parts of the world there is the taming of both the Arctic and Equatorial regions. Port facilities have come into being, roads and airfields have been developed, first to serve the construction projects and then the infrastructure that inevitably comes in their wake.

Indeed, not the least important of the changes that this industrial development has brought about is in the development of a sociocultural environment. The increase in wealth coming into a previously undeveloped region has been accompanied by a development of the local culture and mores. A substantial proportion of the available funds go towards the provision and maintenance of school, sporting, religious and artistic facilities. Cultural exchange between the citizens of the host country and the expatriates is stimulated, even though that is by no means the primary objective and sometimes even deprecated. There are, obviously enough, positive efforts to ensure the transfer of the process technology and operational knowhow, such as we have seen going forward in the case studies we took in the previous chapter ('Technology transfer') but the resulting industrial cooperation between the industrialised and developing countries involved brings with it significant progress in communication and mutual understanding at all levels. Nowhere is this more noticeable than in China.

China is changing

Chongqing, in the province of Sichuan, is said to be the world's largest city, with a population approaching 14 million and an area of some 8600 square miles. It is true that greater metropolitan Mexico City has a population of some 18 million, but Mexico City itself, which is more comparable to Chongqing, has only an estimated 11.5 million people. However, the aspect of interest to us is that this great city was given the economic and administrative powers of a province in 1983, and now has the power to negotiate contracts worth up to US$5 million directly with foreign companies without consulting Peking.(1) Since then the city government has signed deals worth about US$100 million with some seventy foreign companies. Chongqing is of particular interest because it is thought that what is good for Chongqing will be good elsewhere in China. Things are stirring there and there is growing prosperity. The influx of visitors has shown that the city is woefully short on transportation facilities. The municipal planning commission's vice-president is quoted as saying:

> There are not enough trucks, cars, trains or taxis. We have to plan to import more

As we said, what is true of Chongqing is true of China as a whole, so we see US and European motorcar makers being attracted to this vast and now demanding market. In 1983 American Motors Corporation acquired a 31 per cent stake in Beijing Jeep Corporation by investing some US$16 million, and the jeep *Cherokee* is now being assembled there. In 1984 Volkswagen of West Germany followed, signing an agreement with the Shanghai Automobile and Tractor Industry Corporation (SATIC), which produces a wide range of trucks, buses, tractors, motorcycles and cars. It is proposed to introduce the VW *Santana* on to the Chinese market, firstly at an estimated annual rate of 15 000 units. This will be followed by other models. The Volkswagen agreement with SATIC provides for VW to take over complete management responsibility.(2) So we see intimate cooperation which then leads on to joint ventures.

All this is recent, resulting from the drastic changes in attitude that have been taking place in China, but there has been a long history of trade between China and various Western countries.

More recently, following the change in what we might call the political climate in China, there has been an upsurge of interest in that country because of its vast potential and many companies have sought to promote their products and projects there. For instance, GEC Telecommunications claimed a breakthrough at the beginning of 1985, in that they had secured two separate contracts for pushbutton telephones, in all, 25 000 instruments. This was followed by orders for private switching systems. These orders, worth some £1 million, are seen by GEC as an invaluable introduction to the enormous Chinese market. China had by then announced plans to spend £25 billion to update its telecommunications networks and Yang Taifang, the posts and telephones minister has been quoted as saying that the number of telephones in China would increase from just over 5 million to some 10 million by 1990 and to 33 million by the year 2000. We mention these figures just to give some idea as to the potential market. This initial sale of equipment may lead on to the establishment of a joint venture, to which we will return shortly. Going hand in hand with this growing commercial association is an endeavour to cultivate cultural, industrial and educational links between Britain and China. One method that has been adopted to further this has been the 'twinning' of towns. For instance, in 1984 Coventry in the UK was twinned with Jinan in the PRC and this has led to exchange visits involving students and teachers. But to return to the industrial relationships being established between China and the rest of the world, let us now look at the way in which the relations between the USA and China have grown over the past decade.

Growing cooperation

The easing of tension between the USA and the People's Republic of China following President Nixon's trip led to the famous Shanghai Communique of 1972, that enabled re-establishment of American trade with the PRC. The commercial interest of US entrepreneurs in China was rekindled. That vast country had always been viewed as one of enormous economic opportunity and at long last a number of US companies have signed trade agreements with various national agencies in the PRC. These range from straightforward reciprocal trade agreements, such as the approval of a US airline service to China in exchange for China's national airline's ability to serve the USA, to projects, joint ventures and co-production agreements.

These trade agreements have created the opportunity for US companies to become involved in major mining and construction projects ranging from the proposed Three Gorges Dam across the river Yangtze to the development of a massive open-pit coal mine. This latter project is based on the decision of the government of China to use coal as a primary energy source. Under the plan, foreign companies will be invited to act as consultants to the Chinese, providing technical expertise ranging from planning and equipment acquisition to the actual mining and distribution of the coal. So we see increasing cooperation: will it be a success? Well, there have already been a number of successful projects in China and it is interesting to see what they have led to. We see success building upon success.

China takes time and patience

Trade between the USA and China reopened in June 1971 and since then a number of US firms have signed sizeable contracts to deliver various plants to that country. Outstanding amongst these has been Pullman Kellogg (now M.W. Kellogg). Kellogg began by negotiating with the People's Republic to build a single fertiliser ammonia plant. By the end of the decade eight Kellogg-designed ammonia plants were operating, from Heilungkiang in north-east China to Yunnan province in the southwest. Linked to each of them was a urea plant designed by Kellogg's Dutch subsidiary, Kellogg Continental BV. This undoubtedly had something to do with the fact that Kellogg Continental's predecessor company had supplied China's first urea plant in 1963. No doubt a successful project, or the follow-up would not have been there. The spread of these installations across the country is to be seen in Figure 14.1. Four other Kellogg-designed process plants bring to 20 the number of major facilities engineered by that company since trade between the US and China was resumed. One consequence of this cooperation is that Chinese engineers and technicians have travelled largely to the offices of the American company in Houston and Amsterdam, whilst several hundred of its own employees have worked in China over the years. This has had a cultural impact which is of some significance. Let us look at it, first of all, from the point of view of the Americans involved in negotiating and operating these contracts.

With a background of experience as extensive as any company in China, M.W. Kellogg report two main lessons:(3)

   1 Selling in the Chinese market is costly in terms of the consumption of time of key personnel
   2 Negotiation with the Chinese requires a degree of patience

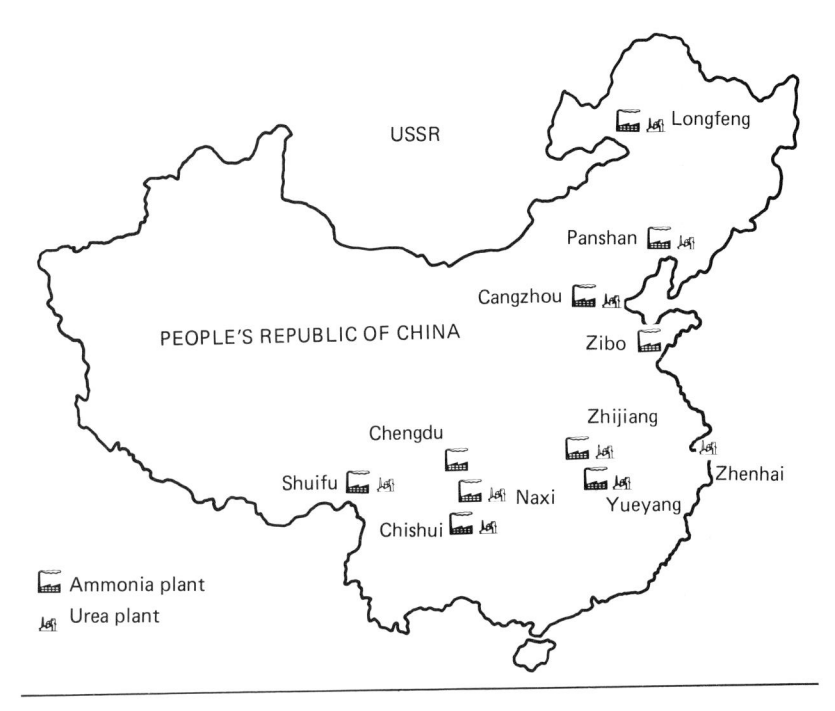

Figure 14.1 Ammonia and urea plants in China
This map shows the wide spread in location of the M.W. Kellogg-designed ammonia and urea plants. (Data by courtesy of the M.W. Kellogg Company, Houston, Texas.)

that few American business executives have ever had to exercise

It also seems that these negotiations were considered by the Chinese to be very private. Anything more than the simple statement of contract award, following upon the signing of the contract, would have been regarded as commercial exploitation of themselves: something to be deprecated. They also considered it unfair and an act of unfriendliness for one company to pass on to another its experience in negotiation. Yet again, it was learnt that a raised voice, an expression of anger, a common negotiating tactic, was not only offensive to the Chinese, but indicated a sad lack of self-control. This would result in their losing confidence in the ability of that particular individual.

We mention these matters primarily to demonstrate that there was a learning process going on – on both sides, no doubt, although we have only heard from one side of the negotiating table. The ability to learn is one of the hallmarks of those involved in successful projects and this is the aspect that is of immediate interest to us. We see also that the problems associated with differing cultures are not limited to the construction site, but can also extend to the negotiating table and have to be remembered in the boardroom.

The move to joint ventures

The growth in bilateral trade is now leading to the establishment of joint ventures in China. For instance, a high-level delegation from Sichuan, one of the richest province's in the People's Republic of China, visited GEC Telecommunications in Coventry in the Autumn of 1985 to discuss a multi-million pound project to manufacture GEC digital telephone exchanges in China. Notice that it is now the *manufacture*, not the *supply* of the equipment that is under discussion. This change in the pattern of cooperation has come about so that the utilisation of local resources might be maximised. Thus, GEC has entered into an agreement with the Sichuan Telecommunications Exchange Equipment Factory to discuss the establishment of a joint venture using Chinese labour with British technology and expertise to manufacture GEC Lyric digital PABX equipment and UXD5 digital public exchange equipment. The proposed factory would have a turnover of around £20 million a year and would be a smaller version of a factory making such equipment in Coventry. China plans to increase the number of telephones in the country from the present level of some 5 million to 33 million by the year 2000, so the potential market is really vast.

Not only new plant has been provided, but also on occasion what we could call second-hand plant. The Shanghai Steel Structure Factory bought the existing steel fabrication plant of the Isaacson Steel Company of Seattle 'lock, stock and barrel'. Everything went, and also included in the purchase price was the provision of a team of eleven technicians from the Isaacson Steel Company, to work in Shanghai for three months supervising plant erection and training the Chinese plant operatives.(4) The Seattle plant, although modern, was proving uneconomic, largely due to intense competition from cheap steel coming from South Korea and so the decision was taken to shut the plant down. Sold for scrap, the plant would have had little value, but when the Chinese came on the scene, they bought a modern fabricating plant which, although no longer competitive on the US market, was capable of great things on the Chinese market. This is not the only purchase of its type, and it illustrates yet another type of cooperation. But let us return to the development of joint ventures in China.

A headline in the English-language newspaper *China Daily*, published from Beijing on 15 November 1984, 'US company keen on joint ventures', followed the signing there of protocols between the M.W. Kellogg Company and the China National Technical Corporation (CNTIC), which will create two joint venture companies within the People's Republic of China.(5) One joint venture has the objective of developing an extensive expatriate residential community within the PRC, a 'total residential city' consisting of housing, educational and recreational facilities and the municipal infrastructure to support it. The other joint venture consists of a consulting organisation to help other foreign companies set up joint ventures in China. This would provide, on a fee basis, 'searches for potential partners, feasibility studies, investment advice and aid in current negotiations' for foreign firms planning to enter into joint ventures in the PRC. It is interesting to note that despite a relationship with officialdom in China extending over more than ten years, these particular negotiations took more than a year to complete, illustrating the need for patience to which we referred above.

The potential is well illustrated by the comment of Chen Jin-Hua, China's minister of the petrochemical industry, who is also president of the China Petro-Chemical International Company (SINOPEC), during an interview with a reporter in Houston whilst there for the signing ceremony:(6)

> We have one billion people. Our president has estimated we have the capacity to internally produce only about one ounce [of synthetic fibre] for each person in our country.

This demonstrates the great difference between the development of the petrochemical industry in the Middle East and its potential development in China. The countries of the Middle East, whilst they have the natural resources, do not have any substantial domestic market for the petrochemical products that they can manufacture and have therefore to rely mainly on exports to maintain profitability. In China, however, there is a huge population that can readily absorb whatever is produced and more: a population four times that of the United States or all the EEC countries taken together. Truly a vast market, that has been exciting the imagination of Western companies for years.

Implicit in a joint venture is the sharing of both the profits or the losses. It appears that this is a substantial step philosophically for the Chinese and it is to be hoped that these joint ventures will indeed be a success, since the Chinese negotiators have said more than once that 'nothing's good unless there is profit'.(7) So this now seems universal!

The agreements discussed above were followed, some two months later (December 1984) by contracts between M.W. Kellogg and the appropriate agencies in China for two major processing facilities, the installed value of which is estimated to be in excess of US$75 million. One was for the modernisation of an existing 80 000 tonnes per year ethylene facility in Ganzu province, whilst the other was for a coal gasification facility for installation in Shanxi Province in northern China. This latter plant, to be installed at the Fularji Heavy Machinery Works, part of the Ministry of Heavy Machinery and believed to be the world's largest steel manufacturing complex, is to produce reducing gas for steel production. It is expected to be the forerunner of a series of such gasification plants in China. So the potential is there. Indeed, one executive officer with Kellogg has predicted that the company's ongoing activities in and with China 'could signal the opening of a single market as big as our total worldwide markets of the mid-1970s, the 'boom years' of the engineering and construction industry'.

The social scene

The ability of expatriates in the project team to adapt to local conditions plays a significant role in the ultimate success of any project, together with their ability to work beside the local people engaged on the project. We have already looked at the way in which such problems have been handled in other developing countries, but one would expect China to be a rather extreme case. There have been difficulties, but they have not been as great as might have been expected. Perhaps this is due in part to the provision of a home environment so far as that was practicable. M.W. Kellogg report that the Chinese made extraordinary efforts to duplicate the American lifestyle in the accommodation that they provided at the various sites for their personnel. The plants that they were building and the daily work in which they were involved would be familiar indeed. Figure 14.2 illustrates one such plant, but whilst its outline is familiar, the detail tells us immediately that we are in the Far East. For ourselves, that is as far as we can go:

Figure 14.2 A typical installation
This ammonia-urea complex at Zhijiang, Hubei province, can accept both natural gas and naphtha feedstocks. Like its seven sister plants in China, the facility is based on licensed Kellogg ammonia process technology and Stami-carbon urea process technology. (Photograph by courtesy of the M.W. Kellogg Company, Houston, Texas.)

we cannot distinguish between one script and another.

That introduces us to the problem of translating the Chinese script into that which we are using here. It appears that a phonetic system has been developed – the Pin Yin phonetic system – which enables the translation to be standardised. The intention is to prevent doubt and confusion, which arises particularly when we come to proper names and place names. For instance, the names of the various provinces we have been quoting, together with the place names given on the map, Figure 14.1, have all been spelt in accordance with this new system.

But to return to the living conditions set up for the expatriates, it has been said that even in the far reaches of China's northernmost Heilungkiang province, it is still possible for a group of Americans to order filet mignon, scrambled eggs, a grilled pork chop, or even a slice of apple pie.(3) That was written by an American, and thereby gives us a little insight into their eating habits. The wife of one expatriate commented on their social life as follows:(8)

We have found our relationships with the Chinese to be most

rewarding on both business and personal levels . . . Their hospitality has been no less than remarkable. They have been anxious for our people to see their country . . . We have been treated to numerous plays, operas and concerts and have had virtually free access throughout Peking. We have been accompanied on visits to the Forbidden City, the Great Hall, the Reclining Buddha, the Summer Palace, the Great Wall, the Marco Polo Bridge, the Ming Tombs and the site of the Peking Man discovery.

Perhaps it is there that we should leave China, with its 'Shiang Su duck', its 'ping pong' tables, its 'yuan' (two yuan = US$1.00) and its world-famous acrobatic troupes.

Summary

We believe that the primary lesson to be learnt from our brief review of developments in China is that success breeds success. It is very clear that had their early experiences with American contractors led to disappointment, then the establishment of joint ventures and the like, a truly remarkable development in view of the insularity of the Chinese, would never have been made. China is a very large country indeed and there are quite substantial differences among the Chinese in the various parts of the country, not only ethnic and physical, but even in their philosophy of life. They are a friendly people, in general honest, truthful, courteous and very willing to cooperate. When one is speaking of a country with almost a quarter of the world's entire population and a total area of nearly 10 million square kilometres it is obviously most dangerous to generalise, but it seems that there should be no significant problems in human relations, despite the wide cultural differences that patently exist. We would expect China to be a fruitful source of successful projects in the years to come.

References

1 Rheingold, E.M., 'China: change sweeps Chongqing', *Time*, 1 April 1985, p.33.
2 Article: 'China's auto industry – enter the US', *Update 4*, 17 October 1985, pp.16-17.
3 Editorial: 'US technicians in China: the Pullman Kellogg story', *US-China Business Review*, September/October 1978.

4 Article: 'A steel plant heads for a new life in Shanghai', *Business Week*, 12 December 1983, pp.28-9.
5 Lattin, Clark P. Jr, 'Time and patience achieve rewards in China', *Financier* (US magazine), May 1979.
6 Article: 'US company keen on joint ventures', *China Daily*, No. 1032, 15 November 1984.
7 Thomas, K., 'Pact to be revealed this week', *Houston Post*, 14 November 1984.
8 Article: 'Pullman's work in China', *Perspective*, Summer/Fall 1979. *Perspective* is an employee magazine of Pullman Incorporated.

Part Five
CONQUERING REMOTE AREAS

15 Transport the key to success

We declare in the title to this chapter that transport is *the* key to success. Perhaps we should have said that it is *a* key to success, but effective transport plays such an important role in every project that we may still be right. Without effective transport no project can proceed. Transport is needed to get both men and materials to the site where the work is taking place. When we start to study projects being built in remote areas, we come to realise some of the problems that have to be met and overcome in relation to both the transport of men and materials if the project is going to be successfully completed. Projects built in the open sea demand a helicopter service to ferry the people working on the project to and fro. A project built on the Falkland Islands resulted in a ferry service from Cape Town to the islands once a fortnight for the same purpose whilst the project was under construction.

When we turn to the bringing of materials to a remote site, we find the situation further complicated by the desire to reduce the number of people working on the site to a minimum. This has resulted in larger and ever larger prefabricated constructions – they are usually called *modules* – that have to be transported to the construction site, sometimes half way across the world. But it is of no use building ever bigger modules unless the means to get them to the site is also there.

Nothing stays the same

All industry is in a continuing state of growth and development. Nothing ever stays the same. We may well be familiar with the fact that the motor car industry produces new models every year, but this applies in manufacturing industry as well. If we consider a company building a process plant to manufacture a certain product, and then finding perhaps two years later that sales are so successful that it needs to build another plant to manufacture 'more of the same', yet that next plant will never be the same as the one completed two years' earlier. Not only will two years manufacturing experience have disclosed areas where improvements can be made, but all the vendors and subcontractors who contributed to that first installation will have improved their products and services as well. New computer facilities may well improve and simplify process control: new construction plant may well speed erection on the site: new process technology may well add another dimension. Wherever one looks there will be change: even where the requirements are identical, no process plant will ever be a 'Chinese copy' of the one that went before. Though why the Chinese should be credited with slavish imitation we have never understood. But colloquial sayings may sometimes contain hidden truths, since our friend the *Concise Oxford Dictionary* tells us that to 'beat the Dutch' is to do something remarkable.

The Dutch, a seafaring nation, were pre-eminent for a great many years on the high seas with their seagoing tugs and even today they still have a leading position in this field. However, the importance of maritime towing has declined insofar as the transport of large objects is concerned. This has come about as a result of the development of a variety of specialised purpose-built vessels to achieve the same end. We now have what are called dock vessels, self-propelled pontoons and heavy-lift module carriers available for such work. Yet in this relatively new branch of transport the Dutch still play a leading role, their market share of the tonnage in current use being estimated at more than 50 per cent.

To illustrate the continuing development in this field, when we looked at the construction industry worldwide we mentioned that the Dutch company Mammoet Transport, a Ned-Lloyd subsidiary, had on hand a new heavy-lift vessel that would be the biggest of its kind, capable of transporting a 2000-tonne module across the world.(1) Built at the Hitachi Zosen shipyard at Innoshima, Japan and delivered in August 1985, that vessel is now in service. We present details of its size and capacity in Figure 15.1. You will see that it has container capacity and this was a novel feature that could contribute much to its operating economy. One of the problems when transporting anything from one place to another is the 'return load' and here we have a neat solution to that difficulty. Indeed, the very first journeys made by the *mv Happy Buccaneer* were with container loads. Then it brought a 720-tonne vessel from Japan to the Total refinery at Flushing in Holland. We see the

TRANSPORT THE KEY TO SUCCESS

MV Happy Buccaneer

Length o.a.	145.86m
Length p.p.	135.80m
Breadth	28.30m
Depth	14.80m
Draught open	7.02m : Deadweight 9 493 tons
Draught closed	8.22m : Deadweight 13 740 tons
Gross tonnage	16 341 tons
Net tonnage	4 902 tons
Service speed	14.6 knots (Trial speed 16.6 knots)
Engines	2×5, 220HP (Hitachi Zosen Sulzer 6ZAL40)
Bow-thruster	1 200HP
Lifting capacity	1 100 tons (2×550 tons)
Aux. hoist	2×25 tons (Trolley type)
Ro/Ro capacity	2 500 tons (Ramp length 7.5m, width 20m)
Lower hold	68.88m(L) × 20.6m(W) × 5.4m(H)
Tweendeck	112.56m(L) × 20.6m(W) × 5.4m(H)
Deck	112.0m(L) × 24.0m(W)
Bale capacity	19 908 cmb
Container capacity	1050 TEUS or 508 FEUS + 34 TEUS

Figure 15.1 Specification – *The Happy Buccaneer*
The above table details the principal particulars of this twin screw heavy lift Ro/Ro vessel. (Data provided by Mammoet Shipping B.V., Amsterdam.)

equipment being unloaded and placed on a modular transporter at the quayside in Figure 15.2. From here it sailed to Rotterdam, where it took on board several heavy loads destined for Kuantan, East Malaysia, for a power station under construction.

The modular transporter, seen so clearly in Figure 15.2, is a well-known construction tool for the transport of very heavy loads on the roads, but even that is growing with the times. Mammoet, in cooperation with Scheuerle of West Germany, a well-known constructor of hydraulic platform trailers, has developed a new generation of platform trailers. Described as a 'self propelled modular transporter', it is incredibly easy to manoeuvre. Fitted with a sophisticated microprocessor controlled steering and hydraulic suspension, all the wheels can turn to any position within 360 degrees, enabling it to drive forwards, backwards, sideways, diagonally, in a circle and even carousel-wise.(2) Just to illustrate the complexity and flexibility of this 64-wheeled transporter, of which two are in use in Figure 15.2, we present in Figure 15.3 an outline diagram. The units can be combined together in many different ways, depending on the weight and size of the load to be carried, being controlled from one central cabin.

Figure 15.2 The *Happy Buccaneer*
Here we see the *Happy Buccaneer* completing its first assignment. (Photograph by courtesy of Mammoet Transport B.V., Amsterdam.)

Live site working

Construction projects fall into two major classes: the first where the project is a distinct and separate facility, often on what is called a 'green site'; the second where a new plant or process unit is being built in the midst of existing facilities. It is this latter which is called 'live site working' and such projects often present substantial problems in terms of access, and much ingenuity may have to be exercised to meet those problems.

We have just been looking at modular transporters in use, and in Figure 15.2 we see a 720-tonne vessel on its side, ready for further transport. But what if there were not the room to manoeuvre that length on site? You solve that problem by transporting the vessel upright. Mammoet were given the job of transporting a 380-tonne vacuum tower, 12 metres diameter by 36.5 metres high to the Pernis Refinery of Shell Nederland Raffinaderij. It was brought by water from the RDM works where

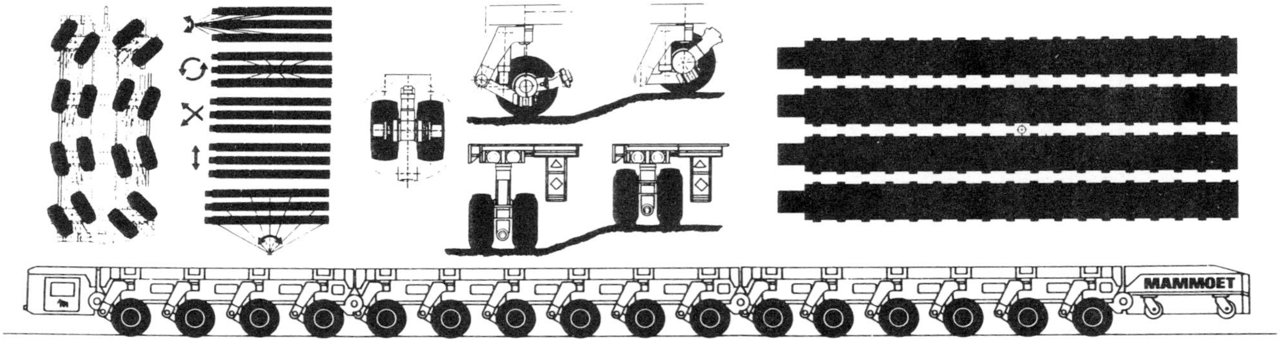

Figure 15.3 The latest modular transporter
This transporter (seen in use in Figure 15.2) is considered to represent a technical breakthrough in heavy land transport. (Drawing made available by courtesy of Mammoet Transport B.V., Amsterdam.)

it was built to the Vondelingweg in Rotterdam, where it was offloaded on to the modular transporters. It is here that the unusual departure from tradition took place. For the first time ever for such a vessel, it was tilted up and placed on the transporter in the vertical position.(3) You see it moving at some 2 km per hour down Vondelingweg in Figure 15.4, where 86 lampposts had to be taken down to allow for its passage. At site the column was placed on climbing jacks and moved opposite the 40 anchor bolts waiting for it. The Shell magazine *Profiel* concluded its own story of this outstanding achievement with the words:

> Above all, the excellent collaboration between Mammoet, the Pernis Transport and Security Service and the Rotterdam police proved that the safe delivery of exceptionally large plant units need no longer be a problem.

This transport of a major item in the vertical position is always possible with the modular transporter, though unusual. Just what *is* possible is well illustrated by the response which Mammoet made to an advertisement by Van Gend & Loos, a major transportation company in The Netherlands, who advertised on TV there that anything they couldn't carry was impossible to transport. The advertisement was illustrated with a huge truck returning empty from the Eiffel Tower, in Paris. Mammoet engineers made detailed calculations, and then asserted in their advertising that even the Eiffel Tower could be transported in one piece. It should however be said that whilst it is theoretically possible to transport the tower, estimated to weigh in total some 9000 tonnes, on a transporter system with 1152 wheels, it is not strictly feasible at present for more than one reason. The prime reason that occurs to us is the difficulty in ensuring that the structure would not topple – that was the problem with the movement of the reactor that we have just been studying. However, loads of up to 4000 tonnes can and have been transported in this way without trouble.

Innovation everywhere

The Dutch, of course, are not alone in this field. McDermott International, a US-based company operating worldwide, has announced the forthcoming delivery of *Derrick Barge 102* to the North Sea by March 1986 in the following terms:(4)

TRANSPORT THE KEY TO SUCCESS 181

Figure 15.4 A vacuum column on the road
This column was carried by two self-propelled 12-axle modular transports (SMTs) with 48 wheels each. The transport took place by day, and only one thing required constant regulation: the column's position on the trailers, since its centre of gravity was very high. (Photograph by courtesy of Mammoet Transport B.V., Amsterdam.)

McDermott International, Inc., a Panamanian registered company, signed a contract on 25 June 1984 with Mitsui Engineering and Shipbuilding Company Ltd., Tamano Works, Tamano City, Japan, for the design, procurement of materials and equipment, and construction of the self-propelled, dynamically positioned, semi-submersible crane vessel *Derrick Barge 102*. Delivery of the *DB 102* to McDermott is scheduled for December 1985 at Tamano, Japan. McDermott will sail the vessel directly to the North Sea by traversing a route from Japan to Singapore, around the tip of South Africa, then up the West Coast of Africa with arrival in the North Sea area during March 1986.

Notice the bold, positive terms in which this announcement is made, with firm delivery/arrival dates a year ahead of the event. It seems that this confidence is based primarily on the successful record of Mitsui in this context, for McDermott go on to list 14 vessels built over the past twenty years for them by Mitsui, all delivered on schedule. Our theme is successful projects – does it not seem from this that behind every successful project there must not only be a successful project team but successful vendors and contractors? *Derrick Barge 102* already has its first commitment, for we see an announcement to the effect that Phillips have awarded McDermott the installation contract for the Ekofisk waterflood platform, on which project that barge will be used.(5) Cost and schedule are major concerns in the marine construction industry – the success of projects depends upon them. McDermott claim that with lifting abilities that far surpass those of previous vessels, the *DB 102* can dramatically reduce both costs and the time required – the two essential elements in achieving success on projects.

We thought it would be of interest to present an outline drawing of this latest development in 'seaborne tools', and an elevation is given as Figure 15.5. The significant difference for potential users comes, of course, in crane capacity. The term 'outreach' is used to describe a crane's actual capability as determined by calculating its usable reach. It is claimed that the outreach of *DB-102's* cranes sets a new standard for the industry. The *DB-102* will be fitted with two cranes, each having a fully revolving capacity of 4720 tonnes at 42.6m maximum radius. The accommodation on the *DB-102* is also substantially greater and has been materially improved. There are four dining rooms and one cafeteria-style galley, whilst ten offices and two conference rooms are also available for the customer. This gives us some insight into what is on offer: truly a 'floating hotel' as well as a massive work vessel. These facilities are to be found on 10 floors, air conditioned in summer and heated in winter. The facilities for off-duty personnel include lounges, movie theatres, card rooms, a swimming pool, sauna and weight lifting/body conditioning room and the vessel can operate for 60 days without resupply.

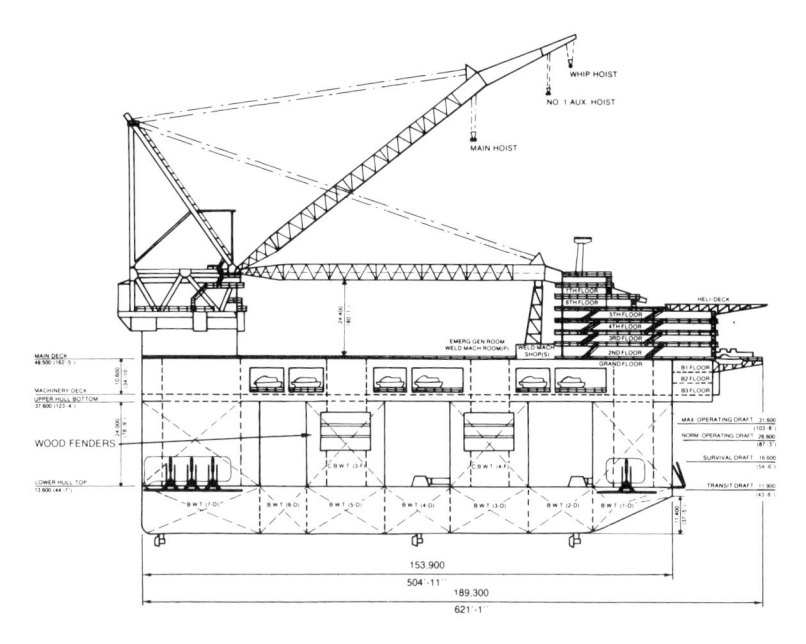

Figure 15.5 Derrick Barge 102
Elevation drawing of the *DB-102*. The plan view tells us that there are two identical cranes. The entire vessel is electrically powered, with six 4,600-kw diesel-driven generators providing up to 27,600 kw. The projection on the extreme right carries the lifeboats. (Drawing reproduced by permission of McDermott International, Inc., London.)

Superlatives all the way

At every turn we take in this industry we meet superlatives: largest, heaviest, biggest, costliest – and sometimes even the word 'cheapest'. A brochure describing the activities of Wimpey worldwide presents us with a picture, to quote, 'of dawn breaking over the mighty BP Magnus jacket, under construction at Nigg Bay, Scotland'. We are further told that 'at 40 000 tons, Magnus is the world's *heaviest* yet fabricated. The Magnus Field Production Platform is situated some 230 km from Sullom Voe in the UK North Sea, and is the *deepest* and *most northerly* located platform. Matthew Hall Engineering were appointed as the topside management contractor for this project and as we read an article describing the project, superlatives continue to appear.(6) We are told that this project was to be BP's single *largest* offshore investment, that the accommodation module is to the *highest* standard of comfort, and that the design of the platform incorporated a large number of 'firsts'. The article concludes by saying that following thorough preparation 'all the modules were placed in six and half days, a record for the North Sea'. This was for a total of 19 modules, weighing up to 2450 tonnes and giving a total platform topsides operating weight of some 35 000 tonnes.

Looking after the workers

So far, we have been looking at the way in which equipment and materials are brought to site, but those working on the project have both to get there and stay there in order to work. The only effective means of transport for these men are the helicopters which shuttle to and fro. Whilst one or two accidents to helicopters in this service have reached the headlines, the safety record is in fact outstanding, considering that there are upwards of 20 000 movements a month in this area of the North Sea. At every location there is in effect a hotel (or hotels) and an airport, the helideck. Men coming off shift can relax with a shower, a high-class meal and a movie.

The 'sky hook'

Cranes of various types play a very important role in every construction project. Figure 15.6 shows us a Demag CC4000 Crawler Liftcrane at work, one of the largest of its class in the world and the only crawler version of this model in the United States at the time of writing. It weighs more than 500 tons, has a maximum lifting capacity of 880 tons and can be fitted with boom lengths of up to 504 feet. It looks at home at the Richmond Refinery of Chevron, in the USA – but what if our site is at some remote location? It is here that the specialists enter the field once again. There are companies who specialise, and are therefore very experienced, in the provision of construction equipment anywhere in the world. One such is Morgan Equipment, with its head office in San Francisco. In Chapter 16 ('Coping with the environment') we take a close look at the Ok Tedi project, built in the jungle of Papua New Guinea. Figure 16.5 shows the company moving a barge carrying construction equipment upriver. Morgan Equipment delivered more than US$65 million worth of parts and services to this remote site, including 325 pieces of earth-moving and other heavy construction equipment. In addition, the company was responsible for the servicing of the equipment on site.

TRANSPORT THE KEY TO SUCCESS

Figure 15.6 Bechtel's heavy-lift crane in action
This crane is crawler mounted and so self-propelled. It placed all the vessels seen, including the three 600-ton reactors in the centre of the photograph. (Photograph by courtesy of the Bechtel Power Corporation, San Francisco, US.)

This company are also working in the People's Republic of China, having concluded a contract with the China National Coal Development Corporation for the designing and overseeing of the construction of the largest heavy mining equipment maintenance and engine rebuilding facility in the world, at Ping Shuo, some three hundred miles west of Beijing.

The history of Morgan Equipment is a success story in itself. Founded in San Francisco by Harold Morgan in 1958, his personal philosophy, expressed in the phrase 'the harder we work, the luckier we get', has carried him in twenty five years from a US$500 partnership to chief executive officer in the US$185 million company that bears his name.

Summary

We have seen that for a successful project there must be the appropriate transport and site facilities and that the two go hand in hand. The successful project team has to have the support of successful vendors and contractors, who are able to provide it with the facilities it needs. There is continuing innovation in this field of endeavour, and the successful project manager will be keeping himself fully informed not only as to what is available, but what is in prospect. He will find full scope for the exercise of initiative and much ingenuity.

References

1 Stallworthy, E.A. and Kharbanda, O.P., *International Construction and the Role of Project Management*, Gower, Aldershot, 1985, 301 pp. See Chapter 21, 'Transport across the world'.
2 Feature article: 'Innovation keeps Mammoet in the lead', *Mammoet Mail*, No.6, December 1983, pp.2-5. *Mammoet Mail* is the house magazine of Mammoet Transport B.V., Amsterdam.
3 Article: 'Vacuum column transported in upright position', *Mammoet Mail*, No.7, August 1984, pp.23-4.
4 Brochure: 'Derrick Barge 102', issued by McDermott International, Inc., North Sea Division, Brussels, Belgium.
5 Feature: 'North sea headlines', *The Cost Engineer*, Vol.23, No.2, March 1985, p.17.
6 Article: 'B.P. Magnus production platform', *The Cost Engineer*, Vol.21, No.7, 1983, p.11.

16 Coping with the environment

There is no doubt that the biggest challenge offered to project management lies in the environment and we find it remarkable that a number of outstandingly successful projects can be found in locations as widely separated as the Arctic Circle in the north, the Falkland Islands in the far south, and the steamy, humid jungle of Papua New Guinea less than four hundred miles from the Equator. That is before we look at some major projects undertaken in the deeps of the North Sea, the subject of our next chapter.

We go first of all to Finland. This country has been an independent republic since 1917 and its foreign policy is one of active neutrality. This is reflected in its foreign trade, Finland's major trading partners being the Soviet Union, Sweden and Great Britain. Finland, in terms of land area, is one of the largest countries in Europe, but her population is one of the smallest, with some 4.8 million inhabitants. The basis of the Finnish economy is wood processing and the metal industries and the country has achieved high technological standards both in these industries and many others. This means that it has technological knowhow to export and this it has been doing very successfully. One of the most successful areas in this respect is in the field of construction projects, where the export activity is now more than 10 per cent of the total construction activity in Finland. An outstanding company in this field is Finn-Stroi Limited of Helsinki. Beginning with construction projects in the Soviet Union, it is now expanding its activities across the world to South-east Asia and Northern Africa.

Finn-Stroi Limited

The story of Finn-Stroi is a success story indeed, both in terms of

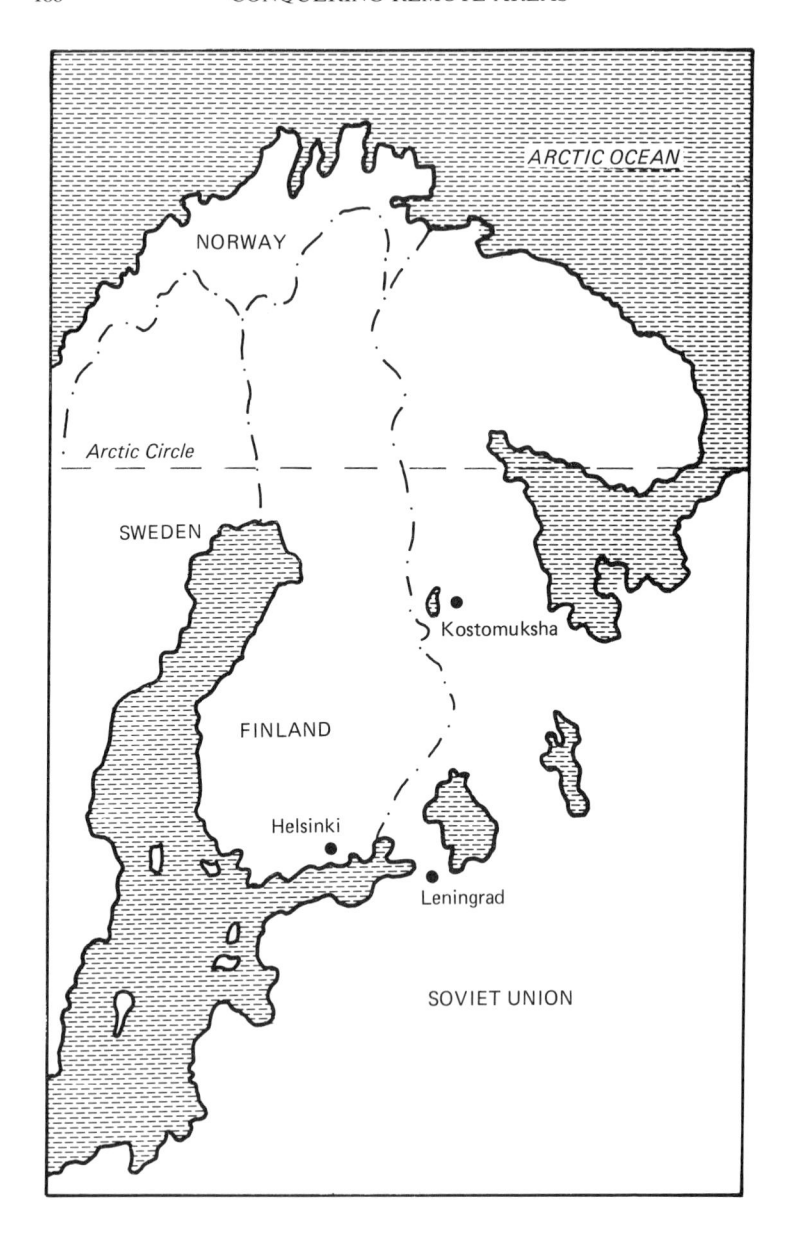

Figure 16.1 Kostomuksha
This outline map shows the location of the town of Kostomuksha, in the Soviet Union about 40 km. from the Finnish border.

the company and the projects it has undertaken. The company was established in 1972 and is privately owned.(1) Its shareholders include 14 Finnish building contractors and the company, which operates as an international general contractor, was founded to implement major construction projects outside Finland. It says of itself that it 'aims at meeting client objectives effectively, economically and on schedule' and the projects completed to date illustrate its competence. The growth of the company since its formation has been quite rapid and it has established a sound reputation for meeting schedule deadlines.

Of the many projects handled by the company, perhaps the most outstanding is the Kostomuksha new town/mining project in the Soviet Union, which is said to be the biggest project ever handled by a Finnish or even a European contractor. The value of the project in total is over US$1 billion.(2) It has been a successful project, judging by the fact that it was completed on schedule, the owner was very satisfied and what is more, the contractor has made a reasonable profit on a fixed lump sum contract. Let us now see what sort of a project it was.

Kostomuksha

In 1945 Soviet geologists discovered an iron ore deposit of some two thousand million tons at Kostomuksha, with an iron content of the order of 35 per cent. The deposit is near the surface, making open-face mining possible after removal of the surface layer. The location of Kostomuksha is indicated in Figure 16.1. To mine this ore a complete new town has been built, together with an industrial complex, the project going forward in three stages. Development was started as a joint Finnish-Soviet venture, the intergovernmental contract being signed on 31 October 1973. Rail and road connections from Finland to Kostomuksha were built between 1974 and 1976. The project then went forward through Finn-Stroi via three separate contracts, the first of which, with the Soviet foreign trade organisation V/O Prommashimport, was signed on 18 May 1977.

There was no industry and only quite a small community at Kostomuksha before the project was launched. The Finn-Stroi contracts included the construction of the industrial installations, the town, the road network and municipal engineering. In all there were some six hundred subprojects. The construction work was carried out by Finnish workers: employment peaked at 3700 during stage 1 and at about 3000 during stages 2 and 3. These workers, drawn mainly from northern and eastern Finland, spend the week at Kostomuksha, returning home each weekend, crossing the border with a pass approved by the authorities of both countries. The complex was inaugurated in June 1985.

There is no doubt that the planning and programming of the project has made a significant contribution to its ultimate success. Design went forward in parallel with construction, and in order to reduce the time span and ensure close coordination, major subprojects have been divided into smaller installation sectors in a logical manner. Each sector then has its own schedule and its own target for completion. Thus in spite of the scale of the project, it has been possible to establish and maintain a very tight construction schedule. Good programming and close cooperation between client and contractor have ensured proper progress and completion on schedule. After mining, the plant produces pellets of iron ore concentrate. Production began after completion of stage 1, at the rate of 3 million tonnes per year. Following the completion of stages 2 and 3, pellet production has risen to some 9 million tonnes per year.

A dairy on the permafrost

What we find remarkable is that although the Kostomuksha Mining Complex is located in the far north of the Soviet Union, just south of the Arctic Circle, no mention is made in the brochures issued by Finn-Stroi dealing with the project of the climatic conditions, its challenges and its problems, nor how they were coped with. One must assume that to Finn-Stroi these were routine and thus a demonstration of the role that experience can and should play in such projects. The same company also carried out the Norilsk Dairy Project and here the local conditions get a mention, but *not* in the context of project construction. Norilsk is located in the USSR in Siberia, north of the Arctic Circle, in a region of permafrost, some 3000 km east of Moscow. The weather conditions are severe, with winter nine months long and temperatures down to $-50°C$. The discovery of large nickel and copper deposits in 1922 led to the founding of the Norilsk mining complex and Norilsk is currently an industrial city with some 260,000 inhabitants. Finn-Stroi had the job of building a dairy to serve the entire city: a project worth some US$35 million. The local conditions receive a mention because of the relatively unusual nature of this particular dairy. Because of Norilsk's location, fresh milk is not available in sufficient quantity, so that the milk products from the dairy are being based on milk powder reconstitution. The reconstitution department produces some 25 000 litres per hour of milk, and the factory produces not only milk but a range of milk products, such as kefir, ryazhenka, sour cream, quark, mayonnaise and ice cream. The project was completed in 34 months, including startup trials and the training of the operators.

Once again, careful planning was at the heart of successful project completion. Because of the location, prefabrication in Finland was used to the greatest extent possible, construction work on site thus being reduced to a minimum. However, the project's high level of prefabrication (some 70 per cent) demanded careful coordination and a shipping strategy. The prefabrications had to be shipped from Helsinki via Murmansk across the Arctic Ocean to the port of Dudinka, and then by train to Norilsk and everything needed had to be contained in three shipments at the appropriate time of year. A sizeable problem in logistics, but the challenge was met and the project has been a success.

Now we go to the Antarctic

Perhaps it is not quite fair to describe the Falkland Islands as in the Antarctic, but they are certainly about as far south as Helsinki is north. The first British settlement on the islands came in 1766, the Islands becoming formal colonies in 1833. They came into worldwide prominence on account of the war between Argentina and Great Britain in 1982. One consequence of that war was the decision by the British Government to build a major airport on the islands: Mount Pleasant Airport. The first stage of that airport has been successfully completed, being opened on 12 May 1985 by his Royal Highness Prince Andrew. The opening of the airport was featured on a special issue of four stamps by the islands, one of which shows the ship which first brought some 13000 tons of plant and equipment and was then converted into a floating jetty for use as a bridgehead at East Cove for the duration of the contract.(3) Figure 16.2 shows the location of East Cove and the airport site, some five miles away. Stanley, the only town on the Islands, was some thirty miles away.

The Property Services Agency (PSA) of the Department of Environment were given the responsibility for the project and put the work out to competitive tender in March 1983. A consortium of three UK companies, John Laing Construction Limited, Mowlem International Limited and Amey Roadstone Construction

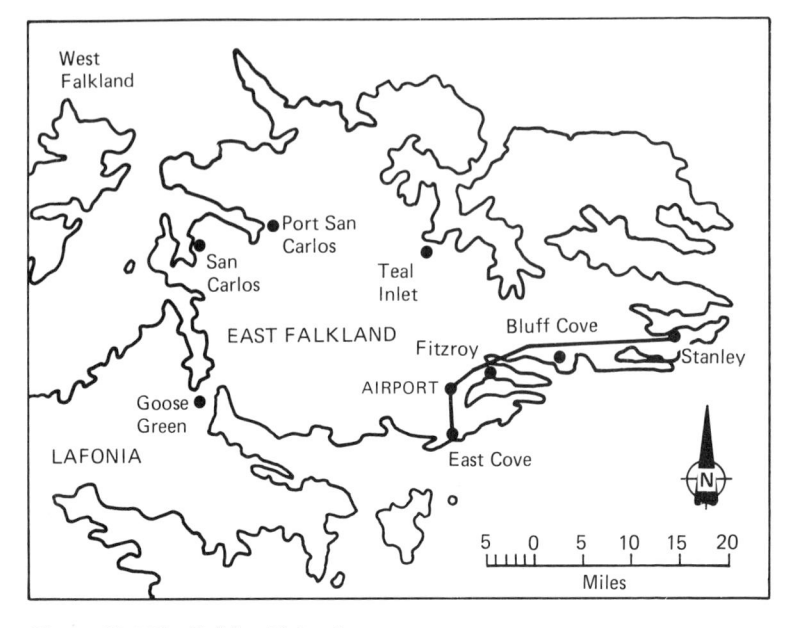

Figure 16.2 The Falkland Islands
An outline map showing East Cove, where the *Merchant Providence* was berthed, the Airport and Port Stanley, the only town on the Islands.

Limited, was established as a Joint Venture (known as Laing-Mowlem-ARC, or LMA) for the prospective project and secured the contract. From then on the history of the project has been as follows:

June 1983 Parliamentary announcement of location of airfield and LMA instructed to proceed

Sept 1983 Ships *Merchant Providence* and *England* with pioneer workforce sailed from UK

Oct 1983 Both ships arrived at East Cove

Nov 1983 Pioneer workers camp established at East Cove and work started on temporary access road to airport site

31 Dec 1983 Turf cutting ceremony on main runway by Commander British Forces

April 1984 Workforce moved to accommodation on site; pioneer camp dismantled for use elsewhere

April 1985 LMA handed over main runway to PSA

May 1985 Official opening and start of regular flying operations.

It was a major achievement to complete this first phase of the project within 22 months of contract award and 16 months from the start of the permanent works – and all this some 8000 miles from home base, with no local facilities whatever. Indeed, it was one of the conditions of contract that the construction force had to be completely self-reliant. The challenges faced, in addition to a short construction schedule, were extensive logistics problems, difficult communications and the absence of harbour facilities adjacent to the site. There was also the requirement to use a British workforce and British plant and materials where practicable and economic. Virtually the only raw materials available on the island itself were water, stone and sand. The contract is estimated to be worth some £200 million and there is no doubt that the novel proposal included in the LMA tender, that of using a ship as a floating jetty head, contributed significantly to the success both of their tender and the project. Figure 16.3 gives an aerial view of the *MV Merchant Providence* anchored firmly offshore. The Bailey Bridge can be clearly seen. A road from the ship leads to a site where, to begin with, there was nothing but a shepherds hut, a few penguins and upland geese. Now there is a thriving town of some 2000 people, more than the entire population of the Islands, but of course in the process of time they have all disappeared once again.

The logistics

The personnel on site peaked at some 2200, who all had mandatory leave every six months. Following the pioneer workforce, who sailed direct to the islands on the *mv England*, that ship was used as a ferry between Cape Town and the islands, the round trip taking about a month. Personnel flew from the UK to Cape Town to take the boat, and roughly three hundred people a month were coming and going, month in, month out. In addition, four chartered cargo vessels sailed in turn from Avonmouth about every three weeks, moving in all over 500 000 tons of materials, plant and equipment, not forgetting 300 tons of food. All this was organised from the project office in Surbiton (a suburb of London), but once work had started on site the project director moved from Surbiton to the islands. Despite all the difficulties the project was completed on time. Now that Mount Pleasant Airfield is in service, there are regular flights between the UK and the islands,

Figure 16.3 The jettyhead at East Cove
The *MS Merchant Providence*, secured to the shore by specially designed struts and anchors and with a Bailey Bridge for access. Cargo ships were discharged using the ship's derricks. (Photograph courtesy of John Laing Construction, London, NW1.)

the trip taking some eighteen hours in all. Perhaps it is also of interest to mention the way in which the problem of communications was overcome. At the outset, the town of Stanley (some thirty miles from the site) was the only link to the outside world, via marine cable. Cable and Wireless set up a satellite link between Stanley and the UK via Intelsat, whilst LMA established a UHV radio link between that facility and the site. LMA had a dedicated line on this system, with the result that the project manager had only to lift the phone in the Surbiton Office and dial one number to be talking to the site 8000 miles away. The system provided not only computer links, telefax and telephones for business purposes, but also enabled the workforce to dial direct to the UK using public call boxes installed in their recreation centre.

The entrepreneurial spirit

We have seen many times in the case studies that we have taken up in this book the contribution that the attitude of the project management team and the workers on the project make to that project. Here we have a conventional setup, with major contractors working for a government department, constructing a conventional airport: a routine project except for its location. The essence of the project was time, and the airport became operational on time because the project management team adopted an unconventional approach. They were innovative, as demonstrated in particular by the setting up of the bridgehead, the ferry service and the charter service for materials. A similar spirit was inspired in the workforce, with the result that a news feature reporting interviews with individual workers on the site quoted them as speaking of the 'fantastic companionship' and saying: 'we're all in this together – we're going to win through together'.(4) The management philosophy called for decision making throughout the organisation, expressed in the injunction: 'don't make decisions too easily – but *make* them!' The fact that the project director was on site, despite its remoteness and despite the eventual ease of communication between site and home office, exemplifies another principle of good project management we consider crucial for a successful project: the ability *and* the freedom to make major decisions *on site*.

Now to the Equator

If the previous project had a set of stamps issued in its honour, the project we are now going to look at has had a whole book written about it. There are indeed very few projects that get to rate a whole book about them. One that occurs to us is the book by Yeomans, *The other Taj Mahal*, which tells the story of the Sydney Opera House. Now we have found another: Dr Pintz's book *Ok Tedi*. The Ok Tedi Gold and Copper Project involves the mining, processing and shipping of more than a billion tons of copper ore that is lodged beneath an isolated mountaintop in north-western Papua New Guinea. The copper deposit lies under more than two million ounces of high-grade gold that will be mined first. It is expected that the mined gold will yield one million ounces of gold bullion. But why does this particular mining project rate a book about it?

This project has one outstanding feature: its location. The ore is located on the top of a mountain in the middle of a rain forest near the Equator. It is one of the wettest places on earth – an average of 8 metres (311 inches) of rain falls annually. The ground is unstable and landslides are a commonplace. The forests are nearly impenetrable. The road which had to be built to the site had to climb steep, unmapped slopes and crossed some of the wettest, muddiest ground known. At the mine site, rain falls an average of 339 days a year out of 365 and the clouds constantly cling to a damp landscape.

Ok Tedi

Begun in 1981, there is no doubt that the Ok Tedi Project ranks as one of the most ambitious projects ever undertaken in the mining industry. The greatest challenge has been getting to the site. Mount Fubilan, in the heart of Papua New Guinea, has steep slopes, but is capped by ores carrying some 100 tonnes of gold. Below that is a core carrying some 350 million tonnes of copper ore. The mining complex has been located on the top of this mountain, at the headwaters of Ok (meaning 'river') Tedi in the Star Mountains, as shown in Figure 16.4. Absolutely everything required on the project had to be shipped to the site from suppliers

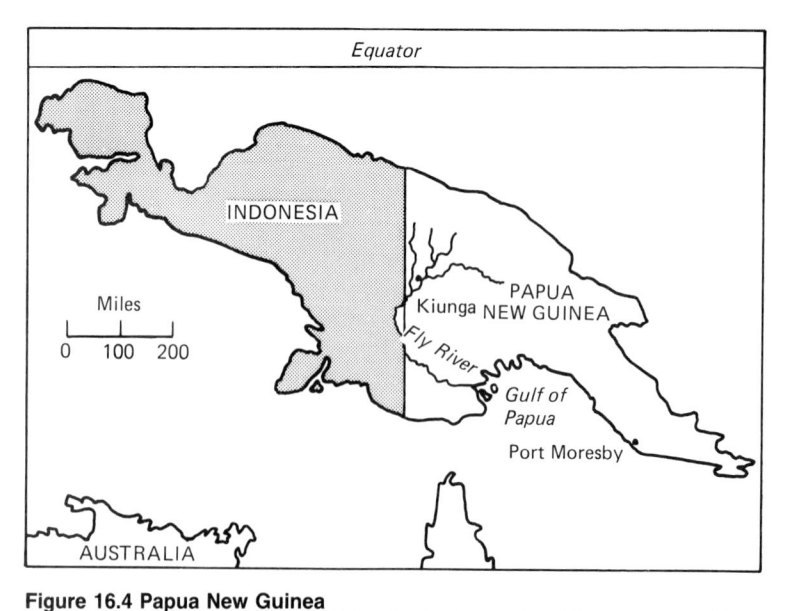

Figure 16.4 Papua New Guinea
The mining site is located some 100 miles to the north of Kiunga, the receiving terminal for shipments travelling 500 miles up the Fly River. The inhabitants there had not seen a white person until 1963, when the first Australian government patrol paid a visit to the region.

spanning the world. The labour, however, *was* recruited locally – but that brought its own problems.

Ok Tedi Mining Ltd is owned by a consortium of mining interests, and a joint venture was formed by Bechtel Civil & Minerals Inc. and Morrison-Knudsen International to provide the design engineering, procurement and construction services required to implement the project. The materials and supplies required for the project entered Papua New Guinea at Port Moresby, the capital, located on the south-east coast (see Figure 16.4). At that port the materials were transferred to barges and shipped some 500 km across the gulf to the mouth of Fly River, a further 800 km up that river to the town of Kiunga, and finally another 160 km up a steep mountain road to the construction site. Figure 16.5 shows us one such barge going upriver. You will notice, as we noticed, that stick-like projection at the front of the barge, on the starboard side. We had hoped that it was a mysterious navigational aid known only to the natives of the Western Province, but upon enquiry it was simpler than that: merely a snag that the barge had picked up as it went upriver.

Earlier we were reviewing a project where prefabrication was maximised: here we have a project where the nature of the local

Figure 16.5 The Fly River
Moving supplies up the Fly River to Kiunga. (Photograph by courtesy of Morgan Equipment Co., San Francisco, USA.)

facilities and the route that had to be taken completely inhibited such an approach, thus demonstrating once again that each project is unique. The first and major stage of the project, the processing of gold-bearing ore, was reached mid-1984. The project has, in all, three stages, stage 2 being planned for completion mid-1986 and stage 3 by mid-1989. With the advent of stage 3, mine production will be increased to more than 400 000 tonnes per year of a concentrate containing both copper and gold. To get there, however, construction camps had to be built to house some 4800 workers, whilst the facilities finally provided include not only the various service facilities at the mine, but also service roads, laboratories, warehouses, offices, a town site for 1250 people, an industrial area, an airstrip, a power station, a cargo wharf, together with an infrastructure of community, educational and government facilities. All in all, the project is said to have cost some US$1.5 billion.(5)

Moving mountains

The objective of the project is, in effect, to move a mountain of mineral ore, but to get that far mountains of materials and supplies had to be moved to the site at the top of a mountain: some 400 000 tonnes in all. Materials came from hundreds of vendors spread across the world: steel from Australia; tunneling equipment from Austria; heavy construction equipment from Japan and high voltage switchgear and transformers from the UK. The grinding mill was probably the single most important item of equipment, the heart of the process, to be used to grind up the ore before the gold and copper are extracted. That came from Canada. Because of its size and weight – over 200 tonnes and some 10 metres in diameter – it had to be shipped in pieces and hauled in special multi-wheel trailers. All this material had to be moved by barge up the Fly River and then onwards by road: just look at both Figures 16.4 and 16.5 once again. Only personal and urgent supplies were flown direct to Kiunga.

The innovative spirit

We have already said that the key to success in project management is to give the contractor's project manager and his team the necessary responsibility and scope to exercise initiative.

The more remote the site, the more crucial it is that there be an innovative spirit in the team, since they are a long way away from help and guidance. The planning of such a project in the first place demands both initiative and innovation, but the pressure becomes much more intense when things go wrong. That is why we continually draw attention to the problems that arise, as we go through our case studies, since it is the manner in which *they* are coped with that brings its lessons in management. But to appreciate the problem, one has first to set the scene, as we have just done for Ok Tedi. So let us now look at a few of the problems that arose on this particular project.

We mentioned earlier the tremendous rainfall (8 metres a year!), yet the project encountered the worst drought in fifty years, that dried up the Fly River supply route for five months. Ironically, rain continued to fall in abundance elsewhere. Fortunately, this was early in the project, but supplies still had to go through, primarily to sustain the road building work. By the time the drought ended in January 1983, more than 5000 tonnes of fuel and supplies had been flown to Kiunga, for onward trucking.

Mention of the road introduces another major setback. A separate contractor was building the 'pioneer road' from Kiunga, some 160 km up through steep, unstable mountainous rain forest. The construction consortium (Bechtel/MKI) was asked to take over the construction of the road, since it was behind schedule. This was due to the failure of the initial road building contractor, thus preventing access to the multiple work sites. Building this missing main access road to the mine was to be a critical path task for over twenty of the project's thirty-three months total duration. To maintain the project schedule, work was then begun on several sections of the road at once, bulldozers being taken apart, airlifted by helicopter, and then reassembled, to start cutting the road in the new place.

A third major setback occurred in January 1984 when some 50 million cubic metres of hillside slipped into the Ok Ma valley, right where a dam had been planned to retain the tailings from the gold recovery process. Once again initiative and the innovative spirit came into play. An interim tailings disposal plan was prepared and implemented. The tailings were to be temporarily deposited in nearby Ok Ningi gorge. This allowed the plant to start up on schedule, whilst the permanent tailings handling system was reviewed and redesigned.

The Bechtel/MKI workforce peaked at more than 4800, of whom 70 per cent were local, from Papua New Guinea. Some of these people had not even seen a wheel until twenty years ago, much less sit in the cab of an enormous bulldozer. Thus there had to be an intensive training effort, first in the classroom and then on the job. Yet, despite the high proportion of 'green' staff, the accident frequency rate was held down to 4.15. This rate is calculated by multiplying lost-time accident cases by a million, and then dividing by the number of hours worked. Thus the smaller the rate, the better the record. To illustrate just how good that accident rate of 4.15 was, the average rate for accident frequency in the US in 1982 was 29.5.

Finally, to let you see the spirit in which this project was carried out, let us quote the contractor's project manager:

> This was a project that you like to tell people you worked on. It was a mega-project, a one-of-its-kind challenge, something that provided much more than just a new mining complex. There's a tremendous amount of satisfaction when you complete something that seems so difficult. It's just a hell-of-a good feeling for all of us to see this job come together knowing what we accomplished to get it there.

A sting in the tail

The successful completion of the first phase of this project, with gold being produced according to plan, undoubtedly speaks volumes for the degree of cooperation that developed between the three major parties involved: the government of Papua New Guinea, the mine owners and the construction contractors. The political problems that were overcome to get the project implemented are reflected in the words of Pintz, the author of the book on the subject to which we referred earlier:(6)

> Ok Tedi was a child born of suspicious parents into a family of siblings [and its completion is] in itself an interesting episode that reflects the growing policy sophistication of developing nations in understanding and dealing successfully with the international business community.

But now this particular developing nation is none too happy, largely because of the impact of falling copper prices on phase 2 of the project: the further development for copper mining. The fall in prices that has occurred during the planning and construction of the project, can be demonstrated by following the fall in the ratio between the base metal and the precious metal price over the years, as follows:(7)

	1970	*1972*	*1974*	*1976*	*1978*	*1980*	*1982*	*1984*
Ratio:	1.0	0.84	0.75	0.68	0.58	0.25	0.35	0.35

(1970 is taken as unity for the copper/gold prices)

For young and growing Papua New Guinea, the project should bring economic independence, generating employment and revenue in what was a very backward, remote area. But the fall in copper prices seems to be making phase 2 financially unattractive to the mine owners and the government is becoming irked by the slow progress towards completion. They have actually gone so far as to ask for an assurance that the copper mining will not be abandoned, but positively pursued once the gold has been extracted. In the words of the Prime Minister, Mr Michael Somare:(7)

> They cannot behave like a boy with a plate of rice and fish – eat the fish and leave the rice.

Let us leave this project there.

Summary

We have reviewed a number of projects, scattered across the world, but all having one feature in common: the environment was extreme. We have had extremes of cold and heat, difficulties with distance and access, yet such projects were successfully completed. We think it becomes very clear that on every occasion the factor that brings success is *experience*. The project manager and the project team have had the appropriate experience. Not the *same* experience, for we have been looking at extreme cases, but *relevant* experience. The construction contractors were employed because they were *already* familiar with the work and could plan to cope with what lay ahead. The strength of the project team resides, every time, in its ability to cope with the unexpected and find a way round, so that the momentum of the project is maintained. We well remember the answer once given to the question: 'However has it come about that we are now six months late?' The answer: 'A day at a time'. The converse is also true. The momentum *must* be maintained: every day must be usefully employed. That is where initiative and innovation should be displayed. A river dries up and essential materials are flown in. Lack of port facilities are overcome by using a ship as a docking berth. Work at sub-zero temperatures is so routine that the day-to-day problems are not worthy of mention. The implications in relation to project management are clear and we will take them up in detail when we come to consider what are the essentials for success, in Part 6.

References

1 Brochure: 'Finn-Stroi Ltd, Finnish industrial projects exporter', published by Finn-Stroi Ltd, Helsinki, Finland.
2 Peterson, A., 'Survey of Finland', *International Construction*, April 1985, pp.29-48.
3 Spafford, R., 'Falklands International Airport', *Stamps*, August 1985, pp.52-54.
4 Feature article in the *Daily Mail*, London, 11 May 1985, pp.6-7.
5 Brochure: 'Ok Tedi – ready for the production of gold', published by the Mining and Metals Division of Bechtel Civil & Minerals, Inc., California, USA.
6 Pintz, W.S., *Ok Tedi – Evolution of a Third World Mining Project*, Mining Journal Books, 1984, 206 pp.
7 Article: 'Ok Tedi – a plate of rice and fish', *Economist*, 294, 23 Feb. 1985, pp.60-1.

17 The offshore challenge

Offshore platform construction began in the open waters of the Gulf of Mexico in 1947 with the installation of the first steel template-type platform in 20 feet of water. A second platform in a water depth of 50 feet soon followed and a new industry was born. That first platform was pioneered by McDermott Inc. of New Orleans. Staying with the Gulf for a moment, in 1981 the largest one-piece jacket, Cerveza, 968 feet tall was fabricated, loaded out and installed by McDermott in 935 feet of water. To facilitate this a launch barge 650 feet long was constructed to convey it to its installation site in the East Breaks field in the Gulf of Mexico. Once again we see the development of 'construction tools' proceeding alongside the ever more demanding construction requirement.

The role of the North Sea

Turning now to the North Sea, Britain's first offshore oilfield, Montrose, was discovered by Amoco in September 1969. Since then North Sea operations have grown to such an extent that Britain now ranks among the top ten oil producers in the world. The investment that has been required to achieve this dramatic development is impressive, running at over £2000 million annually. So far well over £20 000 million (US$30 billion) has been spent in the development of the offshore fields in the North Sea. According to Shell a further £60 000 million (at 1985 prices) will have been invested by the year 2000.(1)

It is said that currently the works being carried out in the North Sea account for between a third and a half of the world's total offshore spending and all this work, involving very high technology, has to be carried out in an extremely hostile environment.

Indeed, the North Sea is generally acknowledged to be one of the toughest areas in which the construction industry has ever had to operate. When exploration began, back in the 1960s, seasoned offshore personnel described it as 'the world's worst marine environment' and it has hung on to that reputation ever since. The North Sea is rarely calm. Storms can blow up with little warning. Gales gust up to 150 knots, whipping waves to heights of more than 30 metres. The depth of the water is a further complicating factor. Most of the discoveries have been made at depths of up to 200 metres.

Because the work that has been done in the North Sea is so demanding, it is full of useful lessons for those involved in project management. Despite the fact that offshore work had been going on for more than twenty years when work began in the North Sea, it soon became evident that a great deal had still to be learnt about offshore construction. Almost every project, it seemed, involved a number of 'firsts'. This meant that every project had a high development content. For instance, a brochure on Total Oil Marine's MCP-01 platform, an intermediate platform for the Frigg Field, in emphasising the outstanding features of the project, makes this very clear. To quote:(2)

> The installation of the transportation system cost some £620 million, and involved Total Oil Marine in several industry records: no pipe of such large diameter had been laid over so long a distance – or, on some days, at such speeds – in comparable water depths before: self-propelled barges were used for the first time to lay double jointed pipes: and the hyperbaric welding technique for joining sections of pipe had never previously been accomplished at such depths. Pioneering technologies were demanded on land, too: the volumes of gas expected through the system required a particularly detailed approach to metering. The resultant system of orifice plates and highly advanced electronics places the company at the forefront of this complex speciality.

The Frigg Field began to deliver gas in 1977. Although only some 200 km from the Norwegian coast, the gas was piped all the way to the British mainland, nearly twice as far, since it was not then feasible to lay a pipe across what is known as the Norwegian Trench, a sort of ditch that runs down Norway's western shoreline, since it was some 300 metres deep. Six years later, what were then termed 'pioneering technologies' had become a commonplace. The Statpipe Project treated pipelaying at a depth of 300 metres as routine.(3) However, other features of that project involved substantial technological innovation.

The continual references to technological innovation in this context establish that these projects are, at least in part, development projects, and this has been true of nearly all such projects in the North Sea. This was in fact the prime purpose of the report published by Shell to which we referred earlier.(1) The cover illustration to the report likened the technological achievement involved in developing the North Sea oil and gas fields to that of putting a man on the moon, and the report said that whilst the North Sea is the world's 'most demanding commercial test bed' it also offers a 'unique shop window for companies to show their skills and capabilities'. Technological innovation, first demanded by the onerous conditions, could have world-wide use and application, to the benefit of all concerned. There are a multitude of examples already, including developments only indirectly related to undersea operations, such as a distress beacon using the SARSAT satellites and a pneumatic line thrower for rescue operations at sea.

Nevertheless, the projects themselves remain development projects and we have drawn attention before to the importance of 'development content' in relation to the targets of time and cost that have to be established for every project.(4) In the early days this was not done, with the result that, taking all projects in the North Sea for a decade or more, the cost and time estimates were continually overrun. Ignoring the effect of cost escalation over the period of construction, there is no doubt that most of those early projects had a cost overrun, sometimes of more that 50 per cent. The reasons for the massive increases in cost that occurred are much the same as for any project with a similar 'development content', namely:

1 Underestimation of the physical requirements
2 Inadequate pre-planning or research
3 Unexpected technical difficulties
4 Design changes during development
5 Shortage of specific resources
6 Management and logistics problems

But things have greatly improved since then and we can now find more than one 'success story' in the North Sea. Indeed, if we assess 'success' in terms of completion on time and within budget there are quite a few projects we could take as examples. For instance, we meet the headline: 'First oil flows from Statfjord 'C' –

ahead of schedule and under cost'.(5) That applies to the platform, which cost £1050 million and was completed £150 million below budget. We are told that this 'success story' can be attributed to using the same management team that built the previous projects, thus bringing forward experience from those earlier projects. Whilst experience certainly has a role to play, we are sure that is only part of the answer. Good project management and in particular effective project cost control *must* also have been in full evidence.

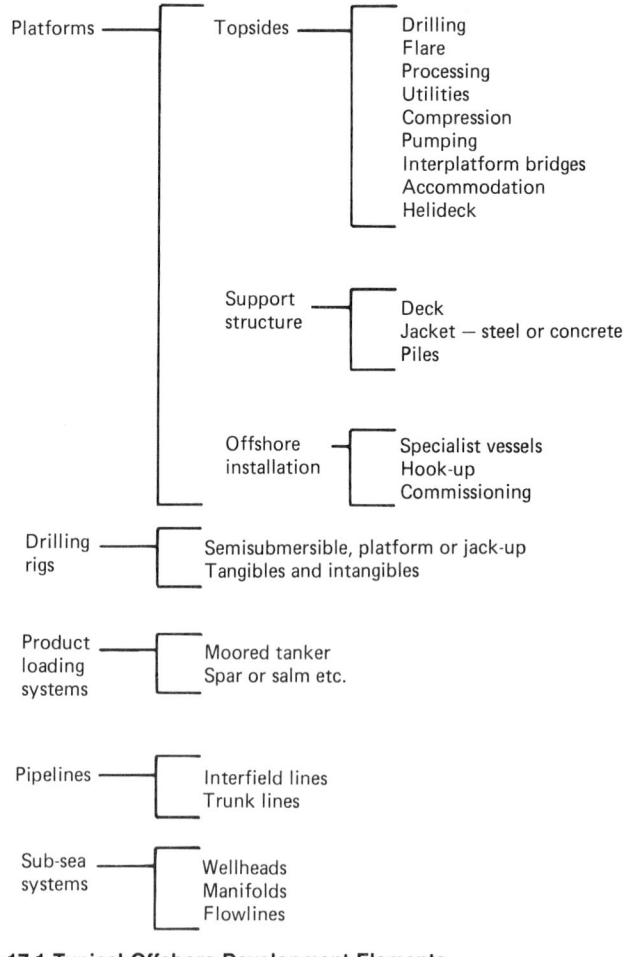

```
Platforms ─────┬── Topsides ──────┬── Drilling
               │                  │   Flare
               │                  │   Processing
               │                  │   Utilities
               │                  │   Compression
               │                  │   Pumping
               │                  │   Interplatform bridges
               │                  │   Accommodation
               │                  └── Helideck
               │
               ├── Support        ┬── Deck
               │   structure      │   Jacket — steel or concrete
               │                  └── Piles
               │
               └── Offshore       ┬── Specialist vessels
                   installation   │   Hook-up
                                  └── Commissioning

Drilling ────── Semisubmersible, platform or jack-up
rigs            Tangibles and intangibles

Product   ───── Moored tanker
loading         Spar or salm etc.
systems

Pipelines ───── Interfield lines
                Trunk lines

Sub-sea   ───── Wellheads
systems         Manifolds
                Flowlines
```

Figure 17.1 Typical Offshore Development Elements
A typical offshore project is likely to contain most, if not all, of the project elements detailed above. (With acknowledgements to Mr. R. Batten (see Ref.6) and the Association of Cost Engineers for permission to publish.)

Continuing development

It is said that between now and the turn of the century some eighty new fields are likely to be developed in UK waters alone. These new fields are expected to be smaller and have complex reservoir geology or be found in deeper waters.(6) Consequently there is likely to be a trend towards using floating and sub-sea facilities as well as what are loosely called conventional facilities. Thus we meet articles with a banner headline such as 'At the frontiers of technology'.(7) In other words, technological development is going to continue apace and North Sea projects will therefore stay 'in character': they will continue to be development projects.

We have said often enough (although we did not invent the saying) that 'project cost control *is* project management' and so felt justified in devoting a whole chapter to this theme earlier (Chapter 2). The growing success in controlling the costs of North Sea projects is undoubtedly due in part to the growing body of experience in the cost control of such projects. Batten, from whose paper we quoted earlier (6) draws our attention to the *Estimating Check List for Offshore Projects*,(8) the first book of its type ever produced. It provides an *aide memoire* for estimators and cost engineers, that they may check that all cost items and cost considerations have been included in an estimate for an offshore development. A typical offshore development project is likely to contain all, or most, of the following elements:

    Platforms
    Drilling rigs
    Product loading systems
    Pipelines
    Sub-sea systems

Each of these elements can be further subdivided as illustrated in Figure 17.1. We mention this to demonstrate the degree of sophistication that has now been reached: a sophistication well illustrated by the material provided for a one day Seminar on 'Cost Engineering Offshore' offered by the Association of Cost Engineers in March 1985. One feature of many of these projects is that the client takes up the role of project manager, rather than handing over to a managing contractor, so we have a paper on 'Client Project Execution'.(9) The presentation of the cost control aspects is delightful in its simplicity, despite the complexity of the projects for which it is designed. When discussing changes in scope – inevitable in any development project – we meet the rule: no change without full evaluation and proper authorisation. We hope that it is *always* obeyed!

Speaking generally, it is becoming unusual for the client to handle major projects, because apart from the benefits that come from employing a managing contractor, it is not economic for him to maintain a project organisation when major projects only come along relatively infrequently. Construction work in the North Sea is somewhat different, in that the clients are major multinationals, often collaborating with one another, so that they have ongoing demands for project management and can build up experience. For instance, the Statpipe Project to which we referred earlier involved not only Statoil of Norway, but a number of oil majors – Elf, Norsk Hydro, Mobil, Esso, Shell, Total and Saga, since they all had a financial interest. Of these, Total, Shell and Esso appointed personnel to the project management team who had specific experience in pipeline operations. For instance, the engineering manager, appointed from Total, had previously been manager of the then world's biggest pipeline project, at Upper Zakum. There is no better teacher than experience.

Now we go to Norway

Compared to most other industrialised nations Norway's energy situation must be considered comfortable. Some 50 per cent comes via the production of hydroelectric power, the rest coming from petroleum products. North Sea development, particularly in the Norwegian continental shelf, has stimulated Norwegian industry in a variety of ways. One problem was what is called the Norwegian Trench, to which we referred earlier. This meant that whilst important oil and gas discoveries have been made, it was not technically feasible at the time the fields were developed to bring the oil and gas to Norway. The Frigg Field, for instance, is only some 200 km from the Norwegian coast, yet the gas is piped all the way to the British mainland, twice as far. But now technology has advanced to such an extent that the trench, some 300 metres deep, can be and has been crossed by pipeline. This is the Statfjord gas gathering project, said to be 'the biggest offshore pipeline operation ever', with a total cost in the region of US$3 billion.(10) We have examined this successful project in detail elsewhere, demonstrating that success was generated from developing experience, with each project somewhat more arduous than the last.(3) Thus experience was built up over the years and then successfully applied.

We would now like to look at this matter of developing experience in another, but related context. All the early support structures built in the sea were steel fabrications, but concrete structures had certain obvious advantages, one in particular being their resistance to corrosion. The real breakthrough for concrete platform technology came in the North Sea in 1973. Given the established role of the North Sea as a forcing house for developing advanced technology, this need occasion no surprise. Mobil initiated the new approach by ordering, in July 1973, the construction of the Beryl 'A' Condeep structure. Shortly afterwards Shell UK followed with an order for the Brent 'B' Condeep. From then on Norwegian Contractors have pursued a path of innovation and design development that has brought continuing success. Once again, as we review the articles on the subject, we meet familiar phrases, such as 'always on time and on budget'.(11) That particular article, The Statfjord Story, deals with the design and construction of three very similar platforms, of which Statfjord 'C', the last, was installed in June 1984. All the three concrete structures were delivered on site, on time and within budget. Looking for the lessons with respect to project management, we see once again the role played by continuing and growing experience. The Statfjord field is one of the largest oil fields to be discovered in the North Sea and is most certainly the largest industrial project ever undertaken by Norway. But to illustrate the value of experience, let us quote:(11)

> When 'C' left Yrkesfjorden for the 430 km tow to location early in June, it was the most complete structure ever towed out to an offshore field, two months ahead of schedule and well under budget. Since then operator Mobil has announced that cost estimates have been reduced further to NKr11.5 billion compared with NKr12.5 billion and the original NKr13.1 billion . . .

Talk to anyone involved in Statfjord C about the reasons for its success and the same phrase keeps recurring: 'the learning curve'. Norwegian Contractors, responsible for all three concrete gravity bases, with a steady flow of orders for Statfjord, have been enabled to improve design, construction techniques and organisation. However the learning curve was most in evidence at Stavanger, where both 'B' and 'C' decks were assembled. Each of the three concrete structures were unique, in that they had to be tailor-made for their specific location. This is due to the different water depths and soil conditions at the location where they were finally installed. However, with respect to the 'deck' which is mounted on the concrete platform, it was decided to make deck

'C' a copy of deck 'B' and improvements in productivity and costs were therefore anticipated and allowed for. But they far exceeded expectations. Whilst a 15 per cent increase in productivity was assumed and hence incorporated in the cost estimates, on inshore work this was exceeded by 30 per cent, giving an overall improvement of 45 per cent.

To illustrate what is involved, let us look at the Statfjord 'B' platform. Built by Norwegian Contractors for Mobil Exploration Norway Inc., the contract was awarded in February 1978, the tow to the field taking place in August 1981. It was said that at towout the topsides were some 85 per cent complete. This compares with Statfjord 'C', where they were said to be more than 95 per cent complete, with only the flare boom and mud processing module left to be installed. The flare boom was left off since it was feared that the extra weight slung out to one side would upset the stability whilst the platform was being towed to the field. The mud processing module was delayed due to changing regulations with regard to the disposal of waste. But to return to Statfjord 'B', Figure 17.2 shows us the structure being towed out to Vats, north of Stavanger, for deckmating, whilst Figure 17.3 shows us the platform after deckmating, during hook-up. It is interesting to note that the cells in the caisson at the base of the structure, used to create buoyancy during transport, are finally used for crude oil storage. They hold up to 2 million barrels of oil. The platform deck weighs some 40 000 tonnes. We also have to remember that the oil from this field is not piped away, but taken away in tankers. The production capacity at Statfjord 'B' is around 150 000 barrels per day, so there is local storage for some thirteen days production.

The emplacement

Having laid much emphasis on the role that specialised transport and specialised 'floating tools' play in the successful completion of projects such as this, it is interesting to note that Statfjord 'C' was towed to site using a team of eight tugs, coordinated by Wijsmuller.(12) They had a combined strength of some 120 000hp. It is estimated that despite deteriorating weather that structure ended up only 9 metres off the theoretical centre, whilst satellite-confirmed figures for the installed structure's verticality and orientation showed it to be near-perfect.(12) The underbase grouting was carried out by Norwegian Contractors using a

Figure 17.2 Towout of the Statfjord 'B' GBS
We see the concrete structure on its way to Vats, north of Stavanger, for deckmating. (Photograph by courtesy of Norwegian Contractors, Stabekk, Norway.)

purpose-equipped barge, the *Concem*. The grout was pumped from barge to platform via flexible hoses. This was another 'first' and it went off successfully. Some 22 000 cubic metres of grout were injected in a more-or-less continuous operation taking in all some 130 hours. Thus Norwegian Contractors completed yet another successful project.

Summary

It is very evident from our review of some major successful projects in the North Sea that the situation is now very different to what it was some ten years ago. Then a successful project was hard to find: most projects overran in terms of both time and money. But now project after project is being successfully completed. Initially, the degree of development, it seems, was too much for the project management teams to cope with successfully, but now there is sufficient experience available. The firms engaged on projects in the North Sea have very clearly learnt from their experience, so that whilst there is still a degree of design development and novelty incorporated in every project as it comes along, the project team copes with that effectively, containing cost and building to plan. Indeed, the knowledge and the experience is still spreading, for now we find courses publicised offering 'Practical Technique for the Management of Small Offshore Projects'. These smaller projects arise during the ongoing maintenance of the

Figure 17.3 Statfjord 'B' after deckmating
This follows on from Figure 17.2. We now see the structure during hook-up. (Photograph by courtesy of Norwegian Contractors, Stabekk, Norway.)

existing fields, and the experience of offshore logistics, so crucial in a major project, is thus being applied as a proven technique.

References

1. Report: *The North Sea: a Springboard for British Industry*, a report commissioned by Shell UK Limited, London. Published September 1982.
2. Brochure: *TOTAL Information*, 1982, No. 189. An information magazine published quarterly by Compagnie Francaise des Petroles, Paris.
3. Stallworthy, E.A. and Kharbanda, O.P., *International Construction – and the Role of Project Management*, Gower, Aldershot, 1985, 301 pp. See Chapter 17: The Statpipe Project'.
4. Kharbanda, O.P. and Stallworthy, E.A., *How to Learn from Project Disasters – True Life Stories with a Moral for Management*, Gower, Aldershot, 1983. See, in particular, the case studies in Part 2 of the book, 'Make failure bring success'.
5. Article: 'First oil flows from Statfjord "C"', *Oil Spot*, Vol. 7, No. 6, June 1985, p.3. *Oil Spot* is the newspaper of Britoil.
6. Batten, R., 'What is Offshore', *Cost Engineer*, Vol. 23, No.3, May 1985, pp.4-9.
7. Article: 'Expert eyes examine floating facilities', *Oil Spot*, Vol. 6, No. 9, October 1984, p.4-5
8. *Estimating Check List for Offshore Projects*, published by The Association of Cost Engineers, 26 Chapel Street, Sandbach, Cheshire CW11 9DS, UK.
9. Plumb, R., 'Client project execution', *Cost Engineer*, Vol. 3, No. 4, July 1985, pp.4-8.
10. Moore, S., 'Up from the deep', *Fluor Magazine*, Vol.XL, No.2, 1983.
11. Gregory, Jenny et al, 'The Statfjord Story', *Offshore Engineer*, July 1984, pp.46-54.
12. Morgan, D., 'C overcomes the elements in near-perfect landing', *Offshore Engineer*, July 1984, p.57-8.

Part Six
WORKING FOR SUCCESS

18 Management remains the crux

The many projects we have examined in detail demonstrate very clearly that successful completion is wholly dependent upon the quality of the project management. A project that is not properly managed can quickly head for disaster. Indeed, so important is the subject of project management that literally hundreds of books have been written about it, from all possible angles. When we ourselves dealt with the subject, rather than deal with the mechanics of project management, we sought to provide the prospective owner with a 'cradle to the grave' view of the important considerations that he has to face at each stage of project development.(1) We did this because, whilst it is the owner who has the greatest financial stake in any project, very little of the literature is directed at him and his needs. The case studies we have had under review in this book concern not only construction projects, but manufacturing projects; it has become apparent, however, that the guiding principles for successful and effective project management remain the same.

It is our considered opinion that the basic principles of sound project management are few and simple. As we have followed our project manager and his project team through one successful project after another, we have seen these principles emerging time and again, so let us now review them one by one.

Coping with crisis

Many of the projects reviewed have had crises along the way. In all probability, they *all* had to overcome unexpected problems of one sort or another, but a problem successfully resolved just passes into oblivion and nothing further is heard of it. When a landslide sends 50 million cubic metres of hillside into a valley where a dam had been planned (Chapter 16: section on 'The innovative spirit') then the incident is very public and the manner in which the problem was resolved open for all to see. But private wrestling with a vendor to make sure that a key piece of equipment is delivered as scheduled is considered to be but part of the daily routine and hardly makes news.

There is no doubt that at such times of crisis swift, crisp decision making is called for and perhaps another little case history might be the best way of illustrating this. This was a very public incident: the story first unfolded in Chicago, and the media headlined what was happening day and night, seeking to prevent further damage, but possibly creating fear in many in the process.

Dreadful news!

One of the first stories about this tragedy ran 'A death blow to Tylenol'.(1) Tylenol is analgesic (pain reliever) manufactured by Johnson & Johnson, known worldwide as manufacturers of baby powder and band aids. It had been promoted as an alternative to aspirin, it being claimed that it was much better, in that it did not cause stomach upsets or other side effects. An aggressive marketing campaign had brought its market share up to some 35 per cent in 1981. But now – dateline 30 September 1982 – the Cook County Medical Examiner reported three deaths resulting from the ingestion of cyanide in a Tylenol capsule manufactured by McNeil Consumer Products Co., a company in the Johnson & Johnson group. The death toll soon rose to seven and the mayor of Chicago, Jane Byrne, urged her audience in a TV broadcast: 'Don't take Tylenol!'

Apparently a deranged killer had tampered with the Tylenol capsules in some chemist's shop, since random samples collected from a wide range of distributors and shops were found to be in order. He was never caught, despite the fact that Johnson & Johnson offered a reward of US$150 000 for information leading to his arrest.

The chairman becomes project manager

The chairman of Johnson & Johnson, James E. Burke, took charge of and full responsibility for the several actions that were taken to meet the crisis. He declared:(2)

It's an act of terrorism . . . we've had crisis before . . . but this is really different – it's historic.

Realising the gravity of the situation he sent David Collins, recently named as chairman of the particular company involved, McNeil Consumer Products, to the company plant at Fort Washington, Pennsylvania, together with a lawyer and a public relations expert to handle the project from there. At the same time, a scientist, another public relations assistant and a security agent went directly to Chicago in the company plane. Collins himself sent another lawyer – a college friend of his – to the Cook County Medical Examiner's Office to act as his 'eyes and ears'.

All this was done very publicly, in itself a very unusual approach, since chemical companies are usually most reticent where the impact of their factories and products on the public are involved. We ourselves are great advocates of openness and here we have an example where openness was practised, not just preached, – and succeeded. A previous incident when the media published the most misleading statement that the company's baby powder was contaminated with asbestos, may have contributed to this open approach. Before the incident with Tylenol, hardly any of the public knew that a 'famous name' – Johnson & Johnson – had anything to do with that particular product, but a survey after the event showed that nearly 50 per cent of the public were now aware of the connection. This meant that the sale of other major products could be seriously threatened and was undoubtedly one of the reasons why the chairman took personal charge. What did he do?

Resolving the crisis

First and foremost, failing to find any clues to the mystery, Burke took the bold decision to recall *all* Tylenol capsules, wherever they were, destroy them and make the appropriate refunds. This involved some 31 million bottles and cost them some US$50 million. It is interesting to note that this 100 per cent recall was opposed by the FBI and the Food & Drug Administration because they felt that the culprit would say: 'Hey, I'm winning. I can bring a major corporation to its knees.' But Burke saw three basic steps that had to be taken:(3)

    1 Analyse the problem
    2 Assess the damage and contain it

3   Get Tylenol back on the market again

The first two phases took the team some two weeks. So open were they with the media that having first declared that there was no cyanide anywhere in the factory, they went back again with a correction when they found that cyanide was used in the quality control department for testing the purity of raw materials. This was embarassing but the company felt that it dare not lose credibility.

Getting the product back on the market was a very different proposition. Just a month after the tragedy Burke impressed upon over 2000 salesmen, working throughout the USA, that they should persuade doctors and pharmacists to continue recommending Tylenol to their customers, but the road to recovery was long and arduous. The product was reintroduced in a triple seal packing at an additional cost of 2.4 cents a bottle and retailers were offered higher than normal discounts. Some 76 million coupons, each worth US$2.50, were placed on the national Sunday newspapers. This programme was variously described as very gutsy and highly imaginative, the company being complimented for 'giving it their best'. The brains behind it all: none other than the chairman himself.

Success the result

Tylenol made a substantial contribution to company profits (some 18 per cent) so profits took a dip – or, to express that somewhat better, the rate of rise was slowed right down, but sales have now substantially recovered.(4) But what concerns us is the project management approach that overcame the crisis. Notice, above all, that the problem, when it came, was immediately recognised as such and faced up to: then dealt with. This has always been a part of what is called the 'company culture' at Johnson & Johnson: admit that a problem exists and learn from it – that is what we have been saying for long enough. And it is most certainly what project management is all about. Burke puts his own personal philosophy in a nutshell thus:(5)

> One of the things we insist on here is that everybody understands that part of their job is to fail. You don't move forward unless you make mistakes.

We would add to that statement the comment that we can learn a great deal from mistakes. We learn best from our own mistakes, if we will but take heed, but we can also learn from the mistakes of others – if we will but listen. That is why this book has had two forerunners, both dealing at length with the mistakes that others have made.(5, 6)

Since writing the above, there has been a repetition of the incident. Once again (February 1986) the product has been tampered with, despite the fact that it has been sold in 'tamper proof' containers. Once again, somone has died. It would appear that whoever is doing this now has the equipment to reseal the containers so that there is no external evidence of tampering. Once again the product has been withdrawn from the market, but this time the reaction of Johnson and Johnson has been different. The product is sold in capsule form and the cyanide is added to the capsule. They have now stated that Tylenol will not be on the market again until it can be offered in tablet form. Once again, the FBI has expressed disapproval of the policy of 100 per cent recall, feeling that it gives the killer the feeling that he can succeed.

Making joint ventures work

Another aspect of management is of course what we might call 'joint management': the situation where a number of separate companies have to work together in harmony if they are to achieve success. Here we are thinking not so much of the consultant-owner-contractor relationship, but where two or more companies join hands to build a specific project. Owners can join hands and we have had several examples of that in our study of projects in the North Sea (Chapter 17). There a large number of oil companies will form a company to exploit a specific field: the term often used is 'coventurers'. This is a most appropriate name, it is indeed a venture. In such cases it is usually the partner with the largest shareholding who undertakes the responsibility for first constructing and then later operating the project. In other cases, such as the Richard Bay minerals project, the shareholding will be fairly evenly distributed and then the company with the local knowledge and construction expertise will build the project – in that case Union Corporation Limited.

What seems to come out very clearly is that success in a joint venture will only come if there is what is called 'communality of interest'.(7) Even then, the relationship will only endure as long as this continues, with continuing benefit to both parties. When one is looking at a success story this aspect is hardly apparent, although we have continually stressed the contribution made to success by all engaged on and involved in the project having a common goal. When one looks at a joint venture that has run a gamut of problems, then this need for communality of interest becomes very clear.

To take one example that caught our eye: Brazil and Paraguay joining together to build a dam. The headline is followed by the comment: 'Binationality has added some strange twists to the creation of the world's largest hydroelectric installation.'(8) One of the 'strange twists' seems to be what is called 'the unequal partnership'. Whilst the contractors on the project have complained that Brazil is dragging Paraguay along, one foreign consultant comments:

> Paraguay is supplying the right bank of the river: that's a pretty important contribution when you consider that Brazil needs the power and Paraguay doesn't.

Clearly there is not really a communality of interest. The problem is apparently compounded by the 'technology transfer' factor, of which we had some outstandingly successful examples in Chapter 13 ('Technology transfer is not easy'). Here it has gone very differently. Instead of cooperation there is conflict, primarily because of the great technical gulf between these two countries, Paraguay and Brazil. The author of the article is a Rio-based journalist and he quotes one Brazilian official as saying:(8)

> If Itaipu [the name of the project] were being built by a Brazilian consortium alone, you could dispense with half the infrastructure and you wouldn't have to train the Paraguayans. When construction began in 1975, we couldn't find a single Paraguayan company capable of building even 30 standardised houses.

Just to give you some idea of the size of this project, built on the Parana River separating Paraguay and Brazil, it is probably somewhere between US$15 and US$20 billion – yes, *billion*! The cost, particularly when expressed in US dollars, is difficult to determine, since the rate of exchange between the dollar and the cruzeiro is constantly changing, with hyper-inflation in Brazil. All in all, it is very evident that the 'cross-cultural' aspect of any project involving more than one nationality, can be of great significance even when the two countries are neighbours.

Bridging the cultural gap

There is no doubt that joint ventures will always be difficult, because even when everyone is looking in the same direction there are not only different management philosophies to be reconciled but also cultural differences. These differences exist even between the nations of Western Europe, but when east meets west the difference can be most marked – and even when 'Middle East' meets West. Many interesting tales can be told and some are even comical. An architect – female – who has worked for British design firms in Oman and Sharjah wrote:(9)

> Late for a meeting with a client in one of the Emirates, I rushed to the street for a taxi. The only one in sight was filled with passengers, but it screeched to a halt. The occupants jumped out, graciously offered me the cab, and away I went. Every designer's illusion? No, as a Western woman working in the Middle East this was a normal occurrence.

The office routines, she says, were much the same. Sitting at her desk she could have been in England, in the United States or, as it happened, in Sharjah. But when she was discussing a projected swimming pool with a young unmarried client he suddenly turned bright red and left the room. Why? He was very much embarrassed by the suggestion that a barrier round the pool was needed to prevent children falling in. This reference to future children he might have was something 'not done'. Conversation about such subjects had to be avoided.

The role of the expatriate

This brings us to yet another aspect of good management: the selection of the appropriate people for the project. We shall look at 'team building' in the next chapter, so let us for the moment consider the implications when people work in a foreign country. There are in our view two distinct areas of interest. First there is the selection of specific individuals, usually specialists, to perform a supervisory role. This is often related to and coordinated with the training of local people to do the work in prospect. Then there is the selection of a substantial workforce working abroad because there is no local labour resource.

To take the latter case first, let us briefly illustrate what is involved by a successful example with which one of us was closely associated. An Indian contractor was employed on the construction of a fertiliser plant at Qatar, on the Arabian Gulf. Whilst the plant was financed by British loans and the project the responsibility of a British contractor, Power Gas (now Davy McKee), an Indian contractor supplied skilled workmen, supervisors and engineers, in all some six hundred men at peak, who worked

Figure 18.1 Fertiliser plant at Qatar
This plant, located at Umm Said, has a capacity of 900 MTPD of ammonia and 1000 MTPD of urea. (Photograph by courtesy of Davy McKee (London) Ltd., who were responsible for the basic and detail engineering, procurement, construction and commissioning.)

alongside their British counterparts. Close monitoring showed comparable productivity, despite the fact that when working at home in India, these same workers had only achieved production rates some 50 per cent of their European counterparts. How was this achieved? Primarily through motivation. All the personnel sent from India to Qatar had a brief induction course before they left. The main thrust of their briefing was:

- Consider yourself as India's ambassador during your term in Qatar. This instilled pride in the team.
- In India you (a skilled welder, for example) have a 'helper' by tradition. You are welcome to have it so in Qatar as well. But your wage level will be lower (some 70 per cent of top rate). You decide.

They *always* opted to work without a helper. The completed plant in operation can be seen at Figure 18.1.

South Korea provides us with another facet of the same problem. This country has been active worldwide in the field of engineering design and construction for a number of years, gaining acceptance through low prices associated with a hard-working and well-disciplined workforce, that has a very high productivity. These work teams have a very clear target when sent abroad: complete the project as quickly as possible, within budget. It seems that *their* major incentive is the desire to be back home once again in the midst of their families, since they always work on construction sites at 'bachelor status', as it is called.

Turning from the mass importation of workers to the choice of specialists, that problem has to be approached rather differently. A mistaken choice can be very expensive, costing perhaps as much as US$100 000 per employee, apart from loss of productivity and the tarnished image that results. One survey of expatriates who had worked in Saudi Arabia led to the conclusion that a careful system of interviews, tests and an orientation programme was necessary, that might reveal potential candidates (and their spouses) and identify those who would be at risk.(10) In other words, such a choice is not easy and requires a specialist approach. There are indeed employment agencies who have developed detailed analytical techniques in this context and their services can well be sought with profit. We are told that persons assigned to work overseas, especially in countries where they have no prior experience, need to be a special breed: culturally sensitive, psychologically adaptive and thoroughly familiar with the host nation's culture and values.(11) Those offering the employment have themselves to be very knowledgeable: hence the wisdom in using a specialist, if there is no prior experience. The problems can be complex, demanding a detailed knowledge of local legislation, taxation, appropriate salary benefits, local facilities and the like.

A word of advice

Experience is, of course, a great help. Yet, despite every painstaking effort to ensure success, there can be surprises from the unexpected and in addition a further cultural shock for the expatriate on return home. The usual tendency is, once an expatriate and having made the first bold move, to continue on that course for many years, moving from project to project – let us say from one successful project to another. But success abroad can lead to problems at home. There may be missed opportunities, bearing in mind the saying 'out of sight, out of mind'.(12) As an aside, and as a reminder of the language problem that is almost inevitably present in all such circumstances, we would tell of the time when an Englishman at a United Nations assembly used that colloquial phrase once in a speech. The phrase came out of the wonderful instantaneous translation system that they have there as 'invisible idiot'!

But to return to our forgotten expatriate. There will always be problems in adjusting once home after several assignments abroad and the return home must be most carefully planned. The advice from a veteran with more than 20 years service overseas is:

* Stay abroad only so long as it contributes to your career plan.
* Keep in constant contact with the home office, retaining possession of a house there.
* Accept an overseas assignment only if it fits in with your career plan: not merely for the sake of adventure.

But the person who now gives that advice did not follow it – after all, he was abroad for more than twenty years. What happened? He fell in love with the job, displaying the motivation and desire for a job well done that we have said continually *must* be seen in every successful project. To quote once again:(13)

> Construction men – however rough and unemotional they may try to appear – really have an enduring, all-consuming love affair with their profession. They think it, talk it, dream

it. The daily challenge that it presents is a never-ending lure to all of them.

The construction industry is the biggest in the world. The opportunities it offers may be demanding and often frustrating, but nevertheless it can be an extremely satisfying way of life. It must be the objective of management to see that this motivation, always there in the beginning, is not stifled but encouraged.

References

1. Article: 'A death blow to Tylenol', *Business Week*, 18 October 1982, p.151.
2. Article: 'The battering of a best selling brand – J&J assesses the Tylenol damage', *Fortune*, 106, 1 November 1982, p.7.
3. Moore, T., 'The fight to save Tylenol', *Fortune*, 106, 29 November 1982, pp.44-9.
4. Article: 'Changing a corporate culture – can Johnson & Johnson go from band-aids to high tech?' *Business Week*, 14 May 1984, p.130+. (6 pp.)
5. Kharbanda, O.P. and Stallworthy, E.A., *How to Learn from Project Disasters – True-life Stories with a Moral for Management*, Gower, Aldershot, 1983, 273pp.
6. Kharbanda, O.P. and Stallworthy, E.A., *Management Disasters – and How to Prevent Them*, Gower, Aldershot, 1986, 225pp.
7. Article: 'Making joint ventures work', *Chemical Week*, 17 August 1983, pp.30-6.
8. Murphy, T.P., 'Three "nations" build a dam: Brazil, Paraguay and Itaipu', *Worldwide Projects*, June/July 1983, pp.28-36.
9. Davey, Lynda, 'How did Arab clients react to a Western female designer', *Worldwide Projects*, June/July 1980, p.1 (with grateful acknowledgements to the publishers, Worldwide Projects, PO Box 5017, Westport, CT 06881, USA, for permission to use)
10. Article: 'Russian roulette, or selecting your overseas people', *Worldwide Projects*, December 1983/January 1984, pp.26-7.
11. Kuhn, D.C., 'Develop people for overseas work', *Hydrocarbon Processing*, January 1978, pp.221+ (8 pp.).
12. Limber, T.P., 'International assignment: career or caper?',*Worldwide Projects*, December 1983/January 1984, pp.18+ (4 pp.).

13 Halmos, E.E., *Construction: a Way of Life – a Romance*, Westminster Communications & Publications, Washington, DC, 1979. 195 pp. (Now only obtainable from the author at PO Box 259, Poolsville, MD 20837, USA.)

19 The project team must team up

Time and again as we have gone through our case studies we have seen the crucial role that is played by the project team. We have seen that a project team must be motivated, that it must have freedom of action, or independence. We have also seen that there must be a common spirit, a united objective, and scope for initiative. Above all, the team must have a leader, the project manager, who is able to inspire and communicate with his team.

Our very first case study came from Japan and that country is currently set forth by management experts as an example to the rest of the world. The success of industry in that country, with its products appearing in volume almost everywhere in the world, including all the industrialised countries, gives rise to the obvious question: what is the secret of their success? Perhaps it is as well to realise that not everyone nor every company in Japan is successful. Japan has its bankruptcies, companies that are not getting on too well and projects that were failures for one reason or another. Perhaps if we look at that aspect for a moment, we might learn a little more about that road to success.

Honda is a Japanese company known worldwide, first for its motorbikes and more recently for its cars. But it was not always so. The company has risen to its position of dominance over the years. Many articles have been written on the rise of Honda and the reasons. Attention was drawn to the lavish spending on research and development and the role that technological advancement was playing in the company's success.(1,2) But the president of the company, whilst admitting that Honda was indeed technically in advance of its rivals, and an affluent company, maintained that capital investment alone is not enough to bring success. Far more important, in his view, were quality and productivity – factors which depend both on the performance of the workers and the quality of the management. It seems that the rigid organisational structure present in a great many companies is not conducive to success. We have already mentioned the fact that in Japan it is a fairly usual policy to reward by merit, rather than by seniority, with the result that members of a team may on occasion earn more than the one leading them. There is no clearcut organisation or company structure chart for Honda, but it *does* use the project team concept.

We see the same in the most successful of the companies elsewhere, particularly in the United States, where a rigid management structure is most prevalent. Just to illustrate the motivation that can exist in a properly inspired and led workforce, the story is told of the Honda worker who, returning home from work each evening, never failed to straighten up the windshield wipers of every Honda car that he passed. With such strong feelings of loyalty, the workers will inevitably be continually striving for quality. How to instil such loyalty and devotion to duty is another matter. So important is motivation within the Honda management concept that when they built their first US plant, back in 1982, at Marysville, Ohio, one feature was that each new employee was asked to plant a tree.(3) It was felt that this gesture would foster loyalty to the company and mitigate against the prevailing American outlook that only money matters. People matter, and the singular success of the Japanese is due, not to complex management systems, but to their attaching proper importance to their most vital resource: those actually working on the project.

The project manager

We have already had a lot to say about the leader of the project team – the project manager. Back in Chapter 4 we asserted that his qualities were crucial to success and in the case studies through which we have worked since then we have seen it all work out in practice. The project manager is, of course, the key figure in any construction company and the major construction companies have a very large number of project managers at their disposal. For instance, Bechtel, one of the worldwide majors, often the first and always in the first five companies listed in the survey *Top 400 Contractors* in the USA published annually by the magazine *Engineering News Record*, is said to have some three hundred and fifty project managers of various categories in its service. From time to time the sayings and doings of this company's project managers are publicised and their comments on their work can be most helpful. The project manager responsible for the world's largest LNG (Liquid Natural Gas) project is quoted as saying:(4)

> The role of a project manager is essentially to keep an objective view of the whole project – its trends, problems and activities – from an informed viewpoint. It's important that the project manager does not become, for example, the engineering manager or construction manager on the project, but stands back and ensures that engineering and construction are performed and properly managed.

This particular project manager was an Englishman, and turning to consider projects overseas, he says:

> In handling projects overseas there is a constant need to bear in mind how the environment, the society, and its religion and customs will impact on the working of the project. For example, while many people speak English, it's not their mother tongue, and there's a need to use mutually understood vocabulary and avoid idioms.

Another senior project manager, responsible for a project that will involve more than 11 000 workers, lays emphasis on the importance of strict adherence to the project schedule. However, simply getting a large project started is probably a project manager's most difficult assignment, in his view. But once started, it is the team spirit that is all-important. He says:(4)

> The most satisfying part of my job is being able to work alongside a group of competent engineers and construction people who perform day-to-day tasks. In my job, I get to participate as a team member with a group of highly experienced, qualified individuals who all have the same objectives and goals and who are all doing their utmost to bring off a successful project.

So now we are back with the project team and its attributes once again.

Yet another project manager, with more than thirty years of experience behind him, describes himself as a firm believer in 'cooperative management'. That is an aspect of project management that we have dwelt on at length: the Japanese have developed cooperative management to a fine art and now all the world seeks to imitate them. This project manager goes on to say:(4)

Generally, people are interested in performing well and cooperating if they are treated like human beings and not criticised unnecessarily . . . You've got to . . . compliment people on their good efforts and performance, you've got to work with them, put forth the effort to help them work with one another. If you're going to get the job done well, it will be through team work and cooperation, not through fighting with one another.

Notice that the same lessons emerge time and again: it is a simple message, but it needs to be listened to and then brought into constant practice. Let us take one last lesson from this man with long experience. He recognises that people want to feel that they are part of a team, that they are producing and achieving something. How do you do this?

You have to be a good listener and respect the thoughts and ideas of the project team members. Then you have to be able to evaluate this input and provide appropriate direction. You have to be able to recognise capability in individuals and give them every opportunity to use their initiative. The younger people of today are going to be the managers of the future and we must help them gain experience. Technical training is essential, but I don't think you can be highly technical or theoretical and be a good project manager on that basis.

He goes on to say that 'if you manage too much, you'll stifle initiative. If you give good people a free rein, you're stimulating their initiative. I learned these lessons from the best people in the business'.

Here we have a variety of recurrent themes, all of which have come before us time and again as we have followed the history of the various successful projects we have been studying. Words and phrases like 'learning', 'initiative', 'experience', 'being a good listener', 'team work', 'cooperation'. The team members all have the same objectives and goals and are continually striving together that success might result.

The client-contractor relationship

So far we have been looking at the project team as an entity, but its purpose derives from its client. In the specific cases we have just been citing, the client is an 'outsider', but whether the project team is set up by a construction contractor to serve a client or whether the project team is set up within a company to perform a specific task – and we have looked at both situations – the client-contractor relationship is still there. And it is very important. Once again, communication seems to be the key. The client must know what is going on. Our project managers have something of significance to say about this as well. To quote yet once more:(4)

> I believe in direct and frequent communication with the client. We tell them exactly what we see in the job. We listen to their suggestions and recommendations and respond honestly . . . I try to work with the client as though I were a part of the client organisation.

We see that listening comes to the fore and communication is seen as the key. We ourselves would also like to lay a great deal of stress on that word 'honestly'. There is a proverb to the effect that 'honesty is the best policy' and this is very true in project management. Confidence and trust between the various parties involved is crucial to success. Each group – owner, managing contractor and subcontractors – have their role to play, and there should be no conflict. Guess, in his analysis of a major public utility project, declares that 'success depends on the degree of trust and communication between *guardians* and spenders'.(5) Notice his choice of words. This study also made an interesting comparison between project execution and a multi-course dinner: all the dishes have to be served at the same sitting, so that the preparation of each must begin at a different time. A delightfully simple illustration of the planning effort.

Project team organisation

However much of a 'team' all those working on a project may be, they still need to have structure and organisation. A great many different organigrams have been published in this context: Figure 19.1 presents but one possibility in relation to a construction site. It is not our intention to go into detail at this point: that has been done elsewhere.(6) The point we really wish to make is that the organisation, to be effective, has to be straightforward and simple. The most complex projects should still have a simple organisation and this is achieved by breaking down a major project into a series of smaller ones. We have seen examples of this in our case studies.

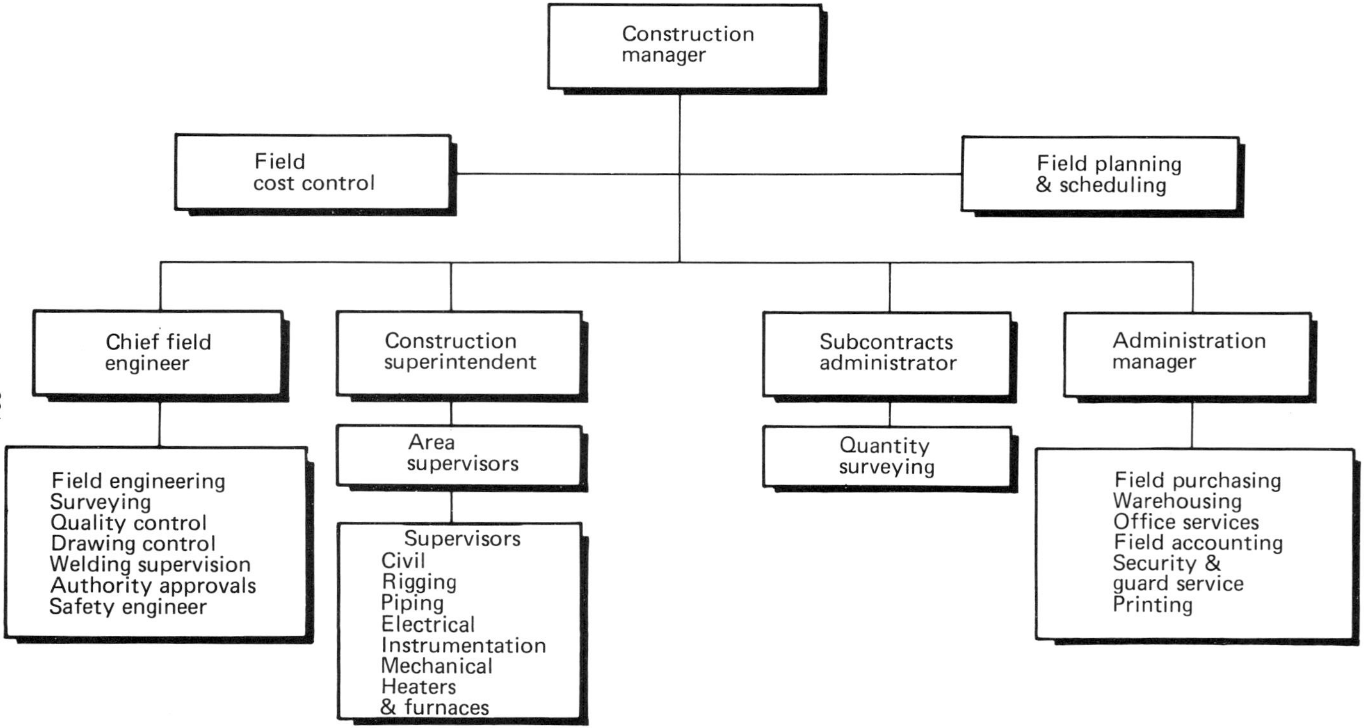

Figure 19.1 Typical construction site organisation
The number of personnel covered by this organigram will vary according to the size and complexity of the project.

Even with major, very complex projects in the North Sea, for example – when the project is often managed by the owner, or the 'senior partner' when a consortium is involved – the organisation remains simple and straightforward. This came out very clearly in a paper presented at a seminar on 'cost engineering offshore' which laid down the principles on which effective cost control is based within the BP project management teams.(7) The organigram is much the same as the one before you in Figure 19.1, except that there is an additional branch devoted to the managing contractor. The sections in the paper dealing with project development, project strategy, the coordination procedure, cost codes and the control estimate follow familiar paths. Commitment control, changes in scope and variation orders also follow a familiar pattern – and we would have been disappointed had it been otherwise. Emphasis is laid on the need to develop complete procedures for project coordination, along with the control estimate and a cost coding system at an early stage. We are told that if the procedures are correctly prepared and sensibly operated a smoother running project will result.

What we wish to emphasise is that simplicity should be the keynote in project management. However complex a project may be in terms of its engineering, bursting with high technology of one sort or another, this does not mean that the project management needs to be any different at all. Certain special requirements, such as 'clean conditions', may require special attention, but the fundamentals of project management should be kept simple. The analysis of a project achieved by breaking it down into areas or sub-projects, combined with the breakdown by cost code, is always sufficient, nor should the cost code be too elaborate.

Keep it simple

We are not the only ones to advocate simplicity in management by any means. One down-to-earth book on this subject identifies three foundation blocks for good management:(8)

 1 Back-to-basics management
 2 Interpersonal relations
 3 Effective communication

Yes, we have heard it all before and we think that this theme, central to successful management, is well summed up in the acronym we quote so often: KISS – Keep It Simple, Stupid! This acronym has been at the heart of all our writing on project management and we still seek to keep it there, so convinced are we of the merits of simplicity. It is a well-established fact, little though we may like to hear it, that humans are not good at processing large streams of new data – this being the only area, apart from speed, where the computer has the edge over the human. It has also been established that the most that we can hold in our short-term memory, immediately accessible without further thinking, or forgetting something, is some six or seven items of data. Thus, if we wish for success, we really do have to 'keep it simple'.

This applies to the project team not only in its organisation but in its constitution. A team should bring together all the qualities required for success: qualities which any one individual will never possess. One expert has identified eight key team roles said to be essential to effectiveness, each of them being associated with a particular personality.(9) These are:

1 *Leader* Calm, confident, controlled
2 *Office worker* Conservative, dutiful, predictable
3 *Completer* Painstaking, orderly, conscientious, anxious
4 *Monitor* Sober, unemotional, prudent
5 *Designer* Individualistic, orderly, conscientious
6 *Searcher* Extroverted, enthusiastic, curious
7 *Shaper* Highly strung, outgoing, dynamic
8 *Operator* Socially oriented, mild, sensitive

Obviously the 'leader' will be the project manager, whilst the 'monitor' type could make a good quality-control man. And so we could go on. How accurate this analysis is, we wonder; but it remains true that with an optimum mix of personalities a team can achieve far more than the individuals in that team, operating singly, could ever accomplish. This is called *synergy*: literally, their combined effort exceeds the sum of their individual efforts. This comes from good interpersonal relations, one of the foundation blocks for good management mentioned a little earlier.

Getting the best out of people

Teams *have* to have a leader and we have already looked at the project manager and the view he takes of his job. But it seems, when we come to analyse the wide range of requirements, that the successful project manager is something out of the ordinary. He is called upon to be highly intelligent, but not too clever. He must be forceful, but still remain sensitive to people's feelings. He must be dynamic, the driving force on the project, yet he has to exercise much patience. A fluent communicator, yet a good listener. What a man! Yet we can find them scattered all over the world, despite the fact that some of the requirements we have just listed seem to be mutually exclusive. In addition, as we have just seen, he must have the right team working with him: a team which he will have a large share in both selecting and building together. They will be what *he* makes them. Individuals *can* grow in their jobs, assume ever greater responsibility, and thrive, if they are working in a contented, collaborative, team-oriented climate. One writer on this aspect of our subject puts it thus:(10)

> The task is not to change people. People are perfectly alright the way they are. The task is not to motivate people. People are inherently self-starting. The task is to remove those things that demotivate them, to get them out of their way. Or, more precisely, to create those kinds of organisational structures that allow workers to get at problems and act in some independent ways so they can develop their skills solving problems related to their own jobs.

Thus the full potential of the project team will be realised and success follows. We are emphasising once again the importance of the individual. He must be allowed to get on with his job and this is true all the way, from the project manager downwards. This introduces us to another fundamental principle of management that should never be forgotten.

The principle of delegation

The project manager is accountable to his senior management for the successful management of his project, and through them he is accountable to his client. An obligation is thereby placed on him, above all, to bring that project to a successful conclusion. But it often happens that whilst the project manager is held accountable, he is not given the appropriate responsibility or authority to discharge his obligation to his management effectively. Once he has been made accountable he should have both the right and the obligation to make those decisions and to take those actions which he judges to be necessary within the scope of his responsibility, without having to seek the approval of others. This is called the 'principle of delegation'. He may well consult with others, including his superiors, but his should be the decision. How else *can* he be held accountable? Once a decision he has made, or would have made, is made by another, it is *that* person who is both responsible and accountable, not the project manager.

All too often there is a certain reluctance in this respect, with senior management seeking to keep major decisions in their own hands. Whilst it true that limits of authority have to be, indeed *must* be set, they should be carefully laid down. Only decisions involving matters outside the scope and direct knowledge of the project manager should be left outside his power. A common instance in this context relates to money. Limits may well be placed on the project manager to spend discrete sums of money, but care should be taken to see that these limits on his authority do not inhibit him from discharging his responsibilities. Experience is once again the best teacher, but we would recommend that the guidelines in this context should always be drawn up well in advance. Each position of responsibility should have a 'job description'. This should be a written document, a brief but positive statement of the basic objectives of the position, and some detail of the specific activities involved. But not only the individual job, but the project as a whole should also be defined in this way.

When is a team really a team?

There is no reason at all why a group of individuals, brought together to act as a team, should automatically function effectively, however excellent they may be, each one, as individuals. For a team to work together as a team it is necessary not only that the attributes of the individual and the tasks which he is given should be properly matched, but that the several tasks within the team should be properly correlated. The team concept has been challenged, particularly in relation to the running of companies, it being said that the 'team concept' challenges the effectiveness of the role of chief executive.(11) In our parlance that is the project manager most of the time and whilst we would agree that the project manager should lead and decide, yet he should work with and through his project team. There should be both cooperation and consultation between the various team members, both inside and outside the formal meetings, each bringing his own specialised view to the problems that arise. The qualities that should and *must* be seen in an effective team can be listed thus:

THE PROJECT TEAM MUST TEAM UP

- people must trust each other
- feelings can be expressed freely
- commitment to the project is high
- objectives are common to all
- listening is high
- conflict is worked through
- decisions are by concensus
- people are open with each other

It is hardly necessary to elaborate on this list of team qualities. They should all be present and to the extent that they are not seen, the team effort and ultimately the project will suffer. It is said that, particularly in company management, in the Western world at least, natural social reticence thrives on understatement, innuendo, speaking in code and that to break out of this mode of working requires enormous effort on the part of any management group and its leader. Maybe, but when we come to the project team that *must* happen. Politics – company politics – have no place on the project. People *must* say what they mean, express their feelings openly, trust their colleagues and speak their mind.

One study on team building comes up with the conclusion that the need to share, to work as a team, is directly related to the degree of uncertainty in the task they have to perform.(12) If everything is going well, according to plan, there is nothing to share: each individual just gets on with his allotted task. This brings us to the principle of 'management by exception': it is the exceptions that need to be highlighted, studied, for action to be determined and taken to resolve the problem disclosed. This is where the team comes together to work as a team and with every project problems will arise continuously that need to be studied and resolved *by the team*. The team acts on 'information received', and this brings us to the next significant aspect of team work.

Management information and reports

The project specification will define the project in terms of nature, cost and time taken. Plans will have been laid – that, after all, was where we began (Chapter 1). From then on, all that the project team really need to discuss are deviations from the agreed plan. This calls for a system of management information, so that management may know the deviations of the plan once it has been agreed. But notice that it is only the deviations and the departures from the plan that should be the subject of detailed reporting and analysis. This leads to decisions defining the action to be taken to bring the project back to the plan. This means that in all such reports there is continuous comparison between the initial agreed plan (or any subsequent agreed revision) and the current expectations.

The level that such reports reach in management should depend upon their significance and magnitude in relation to the project as a whole. Once again we have to respect the limited ability of the human mind to assimilate data, and ensure that only the relevant information is provided. Indeed, good project management will ensure that only essential information is incorporated in such reports. This means that a lot of thought has to be given to the content of reports and the level to which any particular report should go. This means that reports should be condensed, factual, complete and up-to-date. Above all, reports at one level should not include detailed data which is properly the concern of subordinates at a lower level. Whilst senior executives are entitled to ask for and get any specific information they may feel they require, excessive demands in this direction tend to undermine the concept of delegation and makes those responsible for the particular aspect being investigated feel that they are not trusted to do their job properly.

The spirit of cooperation

In any and every project we have the owner, or client, and contractors, sometimes led by a managing contractor. The owner may himself be the leader of a consortium, whilst the managing contractor on major projects may be the result of a consortium as well, a number of distinct construction companies, to some extent competitors, pooling their skills and experience. We have seen a number of examples of these various alternatives and combinations of interest that have worked very well indeed: the spirit of cooperation has indeed been there.

Looking at what is happening in a little detail, we see a number of project teams, who not only have to work as teams within themselves, but have to cooperate with one another. The several teams should remain individual and distinct teams, each with their own role to play in relation to the successful completion of the project, but there should be good cooperation between these several groups. How shall we know when that occurs? What should we watch for? What should we see? The essentials are very much the same as we listed above for effective team work, but there are significant differences. Cooperation between the various project teams – between owner, contractor and subcontractors – will be successful when:

- people are working together at all levels
- commitment is high
- people are negotiating freely
- information passes on a need-to-know basis
- conflict is accommodated
- politics are contained
- people cooperate to get the job done
- personal feelings are subjugated to the work
- trust and openness are present, even if measured

If our two lists are compared, it will be seen that when we consider cooperation between teams coming from different backgrounds, but required to work together to achieve a common objective – the completion of a project – we have to recognise that they can have a different viewpoint. It is this that brings politics and its consequences into play. This factor has to be recognised and it cannot be avoided, but the project will go well if it is kept in place and not allowed to dominate. That is why we suggest that cooperation is effective only if personal feelings (which are often 'company' feelings) are subjugated to the common objective and there is trust and openness between the several parties.

A case in point

Perhaps this is best illustrated by example. Lummus Canada received a contract from Esso Chemical Canada and during construction in the field the two companies developed what was considered to be a unique integration of their field staffs.(13) The Esso personnel on site constituted some 30 per cent of the total site administration, Lummus personnel the other 70 per cent. But they *all* reported to the Lummus Canada Construction Manager. This integration was not the result of some grand design but evolved from a series of *small* steps taken at site.

Now that it is all over, Esso are on record as saying that this integration, with single (not dual) reporting to management, saved some eighteen man-years, or about 15 per cent of the total supervisory and technical manpower that had been estimated to be required for the project. The integration, it seems, was brought about largely by pressure of circumstances. Whilst it brought better site relations and speeded completion, it was originally necessitated by a shortage of technical manpower. There were initial problems, largely psychological and ego-related. But once the staff had traded their respective 'hard hats' (Esso wore blue and Lummus white), uniting in their common objective of completing the project on time and within budget, these hurdles were crossed and success ensued. We are told that everyone on site, irrespective of the hat they wore, had the same basic attitudes and objectives. As a result of the good personal relations between the two groups, having different basic loyalties, now merged into one, the work progressed smoothly and was completed successfully. Yet, in spite of the success achieved on this occasion, an Esso executive warns:

> . . . integration can be implemented only on an individual project basis, and it requires total owner and contractor commitment to the concept.

This comment makes it very clear that whilst one united team is seen to be very desirable, political and personal attitudes can well present problems when it comes to integration. In this one case political feelings *were* contained and personal feelings *were* subjugated to the work to the degree necessary to allow a group to work for someone whom they would normally regard as 'lesser' than themselves – the contractor's manager – but apparently it took some doing. It remains an outstanding example of owner/contractor cooperation and something to be emulated, not forgotten.

The above example from Canada demonstrates the knitting together of personnel from two very different companies to build a team. A parallel problem is the creation of team identity *within* a company. We have seen the way in which that can be done: we saw, in the case of the General Motors *Fiero* project (Chapter 10) the members of the team taken away to a separate building well away from their normal place of work. Another very interesting technique came to our notice, which could be adapted in some form when physical separation of the team is not possible. To speed construction and maintain control on a building project for the University of California a contractor broke up the wall pouring crews into three squads, one for each of three construction areas and outfitted them in T-shirts of different colours – red, green and blue, corresponding to a colour code given to each area.(14) This not only developed a team spirit, but allowed the job superintendents to monitor operations very closely.

Summary

We have seen that the putting together of a properly integrated project team, or teams, led by a project manager with the appropriate experience, is an essential preliminary to a successful project. We have also seen some of the qualities that should be present in such teams as they work together: commitment, trust, openness, and a spirit of cooperation, with all on the project working together towards a common objective. Every project has its problems and these are best dealt with by teamwork: by a team whose project manager is prepared and able to lead his team in the difficult task ahead of them. As a team they have the best chance of success.

References

1 Article: 'Honda thrives on unrestricted R&D', *Industrial Week*, 180, 21 January 1974, pp.28-9.
2 Wax, A.J., 'Technology – Honda's new moneymaker', *Commercial & Financial Chronicle*, 218, 5 November 1973, p.1361.
3 Cieply, M., 'Meanwhile, back in Marysville', *Forbes*, 133, 12 March 1984, p.127.
4 Article: 'Bechtel's project managers', *Bechtel Briefs*, October 1979, pp.4-13. (*Bechtel Briefs* is published for employees and friends by Bechtel, San Francisco.)
5 Guess, G.M., 'Role conflict in capital project implementation – the case study of Dady County metrorail', *Public Administration Review*, 45, Sept/Oct. 1985, pp.576-85. (Professor Guess is responsible for the Institute of Public Administration, Georgia State University, Atlanta, USA.)
6 Stallworthy, E.A. and Kharbanda, O.P., *Total Project Management*, Gower, Aldershot, 1983, 329pp.
7 Plumb, D., 'Client project execution', *Cost Engineer*, Vol.23, No.4, July 1985, pp.4-8. (One of a series of papers presented at a seminar on the theme 'Cost Engineering Offshore'.)
8 Culligan, M.J., Deakins S., and Young, A.H., *Back to basics management – the lost craft of leadership*, Gower, 1983, 161pp.
9 Belbin, R.M., *Management Teams – Why They Succeed or Fail*, Heinemann, 1981, 179pp.
10 Bennett, D., *Successful Team Building through TA*, Amacom, New York, 1975.

11 Casey, D., 'When is a team not a team?', *Personnel Management*, January 1985, pp.26-29.
12 Critchley, B. and Casey, D., 'Second thoughts on team building', *Management Education and Development*, Vol.15, Pt 2, 1984.
13 Article: 'Esso Chemical projects set new high in client/contractor relations', *Canadian Update*, Spring 1984, pp.12-13. *Canadian Update* is a house magazine published by Lummus Crest Inc., Bloomfield, New Jersey, 07003 USA.
14 Article: 'Teamwork spells success at UCLA', *Engineering News Record*, 211, 12 January 1984, pp.54-5.

20 Prevention is better than cure

Some fifteen years ago Britain and Northern Ireland, which together make up the United Kingdom were importing all the oil they needed at around US$2.20 a barrel. Today, whilst they may still import oil to get the right mix of crudes for refinery purposes, they have actually been self-sufficient for a number of years. Over the same period the cost of oil has risen to some US$30 a barrel and the efficient use of energy has been one of the touchstones to success, not only in the UK but worldwide. One result of this has been an intensive effort to economise on energy consumption, together with a switch from oil to coal burning in a number of power stations. This trend is illustrated in Figure 20.1, where we see the movement from decade to decade since 1950. The situation changed dramatically in 1984, due to the coal strike, (1) but the trend has now reasserted itself. The Coal Board have an ambitious investment programme and it could be that towards the end of this century, if that programme is successful, the gas industry might be using coal to make substitute natural gas (synfuel in the USA) as the gas from the North Sea begins to fail. In our review of

	1950		1960		1970		1980	
	Fuel use	(%)	Fuel use	(%)	Fuel use	(%)	Fuel use	(%)
Coal	204.3	(89.6)	198.6	(73.7)	156.9	(46.6)	121.9	(37.0)
Oil	22.9	(10.0)	68.1	(25.3)	150.0	(44.6)	121.0	(36.7)
Natural gas	—	(—)	0.1	(—)	17.9	(5.3)	71.1	(21.6)
Nuclear	—	(—)	0.9	(0.4)	9.5	(2.8)	13.3	(4.0)
Hydro	0.9	(0.4)	1.7	(0.6)	2.3	(0.7)	2.1	(0.7)
TOTAL	228.1	(100)	269.4	(100)	336.6	(100)	329.4	(100)

Figure 20.1 Consumption of primary fuels in the UK
This table presents the consumption of primary fuels for energy use in million tonnes of coal or coal equivalent, that comparison may be made. The impact of the depression can be seen, illustrated by lack of growth between 1970 and 1980, but there had also been substantial economies. *(Source: Department of Energy, UK)*

successful projects we have looked at projects in all these different fields of endeavour. That is almost inevitable, since this is an area where major investment is still taking place worldwide. The development of gas and oil fields in the North Sea has presented a major challenge to the construction industry, but it is a challenge that has been met and overcome. Continuing technological development over the years has made projects that were unthinkable ten years ago but routine today. And this process of development does not stop. No doubt in ten years time they will be doing other things which are equally unthinkable today. Development – sound development – plays a significant role in every successful project.

The road to success

The early seventies saw the first major projects in the North Sea, and very ambitious forecasts were then made, as illustrated in Figure 20.2. These early forecasts have not been met for a variety of reasons: development delays, reservoir problems, accidents and investment uncertainty created by an ever-changing tax regime. If we go back to those days, and assess what was happening, we see projects being built that called for substantial design development, the use of high technology, that in addition had very special environmental hazards to overcome. But did that justify the gross underestimating that occurred, underestimating that caused one writer to describe what was going on as 'a Wagnerian financial opera'?(2) He said:

> It is a recognised problem of operators that accurately forecasting the final cost of a project is very difficult and creates a problem of investment analysis and in deciding the correct economic indicators. It is a well-known fact that many of the North Sea fields which have been developed were *grossly* underestimated.

So serious was the situation at that time that in a review of the situation we said, to quote, that:(3)

> 20% of North Sea fields were up to 200% overrun
> 30% of North Sea fields were up to 100% overrun
> 50% of North Sea fields were up to 50% overrun

But no longer. The successful projects in the North Sea that we reviewed in Chapter 17 are not alone: most projects there these days are completed on schedule and within budget. But why? What has happened? The basic reason, we feel, is growing experience: learning the lessons. We learn from experience and we learn most from our own mistakes. He is a wise man indeed who can learn not only from his own mistakes but from the mistakes of others – there are not so many people like that about. These North Sea projects were all development projects and they still are: that

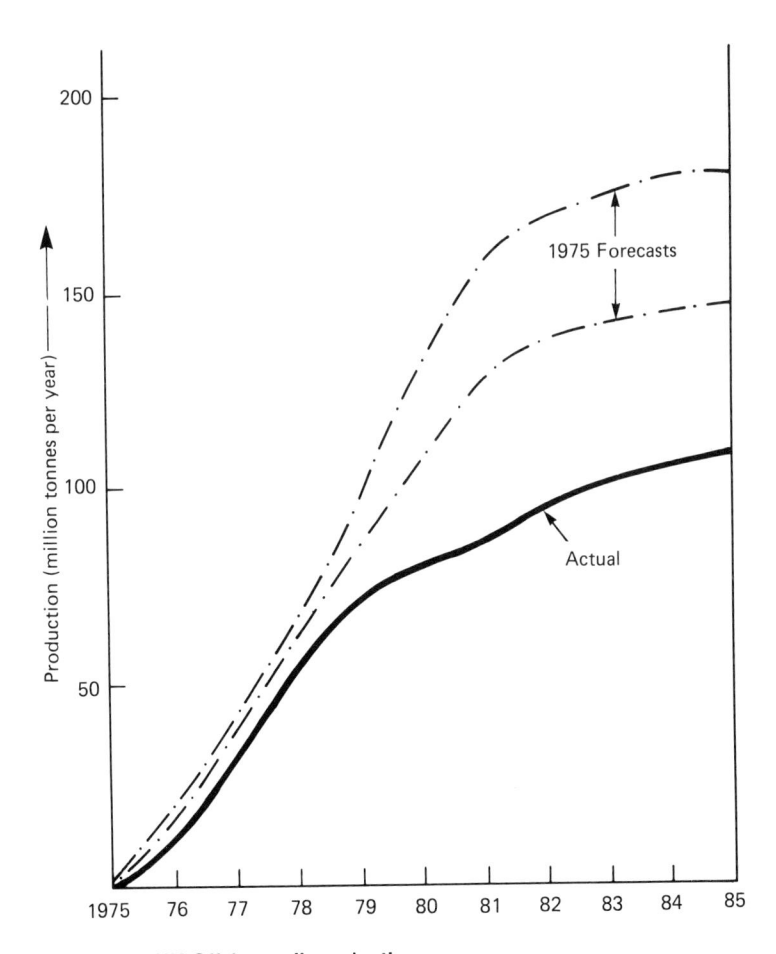

Figure 20.2 UK Offshore oil production
Comparison is made by these graphs between the early forecasts and the latest projections, almost exclusively in the North Sea at this stage, although other offshore areas are now being explored.

factor – the development factor – always needs to be assessed and allowed for. The learning began to bear fruit after some ten years. Conoco, to take but one example, began the planning of their Murchison Project in the North Sea by taking stock of the problems that confronted them. In order to learn from the mistakes of others and so, hopefully, not repeat them, a complete study of the earlier projects was undertaken and the data applied. This was, in effect, a 'book of errors'. The actual title was: *'Application of North Sea Experience to Murchison Project Planning'*.(4) Then, despite the usual catalogue of mishaps, including a strike and the collapse of a giant crane, the project was successfully completed. Thus, if we are to talk about prevention being better than cure, then the best road to prevention is via experience. If you have not got the experience, then look for those who have.

Continuing innovation

One of our case studies in Chapter 17 was what we might call 'The Statfjord Story', one special feature being that the support structure for the production platform was built of concrete. There were in all three such structures, each somewhat different in that they had to be tailor-made to suit their specific locations. This arises because of the differing water depths and soil conditions that inevitably occur from location to location. Norwegian Contractors, using the tradename Condeep, secured their first contracts, both in the UK North Sea sector, in 1974 and have gone on from strength to strength. But as the waters in which such structures have to be placed get ever deeper, the complexities of design grow. To meet the need, this company have been developing what they call the Condeep T300 deepwater platform. To give the appropriate strength, the support structure has to have a much larger base, calling for inclined legs. Now a major breakthrough in concrete construction techniques has been achieved by Norwegian Constructors. Called conical inclined slipforming, this new procedure aims to boost the load-carrying capacity during tow-out by giving each of its tripod legs a conical configuration. A large-scale test structure was built, perhaps one third the size of any potential structure for use, in order to demonstrate the feasibility of the new construction method. The test structure is illustrated in Figure 20.3. Called 'The Leaning Tower of Stavanger', it actually leans much more than the famous tower of Pisa, 16° instead of 5°, whilst it is nearly the same height. Built purely for test purposes, it has cost in all some US$3 million. To illustrate the complexities of the research, Figure 20.4 illustrates some of the elaborate calculations that had to be made to define the geometry of the structure and to analyse the test results. Our purpose in citing this example is to give some small idea as to the extent and depth of research that lies behind the completion of such projects, contributing much to their ultimate success. Here we have an instance of careful, applied research, and the use of the knowledge gained will result in the project where this development is used being a success. It was the setting up of optimistic cost budgets based on incomplete or limited technical definition that contributed significantly to the substantial cost overruns on those earlier projects in the North Sea, to which we referred above.

It is interesting to hear that, whereas when the tower was first put in hand the intention was to demolish it again, it is now being used for cement storage – Norway's largest store! At the top of the tower there is a pavilion with a presentation room. The view from here is quite fantastic.

Take the time

When we start to look for the basic reasons for success in the various projects that we have been looking at, it does not seem to have come via sophisticated project management. The project itself may be full of high technology, may demand a high level of technical skill in design, but the *management* of the project remains straightforward, even simple. The basic rules of project management which we outlined in Part 1 ('The management concept') remain valid however large or however complex the project. May we repeat yet once again our acronym as being very sound advice in this context: KISS – Keep It Simple, Stupid!

It does appear, however, that the planning and particularly the pre-planning, is one very important ingredient in success. The proper time must be taken in planning the project before it is set on the road and by this we mean not only the project itself, but also the project administration in all its detail. We have looked at projects involving consortia, we have looked at projects built in remote corners of the earth and those engaged on these projects have always laid great emphasis on the value of detailed scheduling and careful assessment of all the logistics. But much also rests with the subcontractors that are employed. Competent subcontractors also contribute much to the success of a project and competence is very largely the result of experience. This may be summed up in two simple rules:

1 Take the time to make a sound assessment of project cost and duration *before* you start;
2 Always ask yourself to what extent this project is a 'develop-

Figure 20.3 Concrete innovation
Here we see 'The leaning tower of Stavanger', total height 50 metres, with a diameter varying between 16 and 23 metres. (Thanks are due to Norwegian Contractors, of Stabekk, Norway, for permission to publish this photograph.)

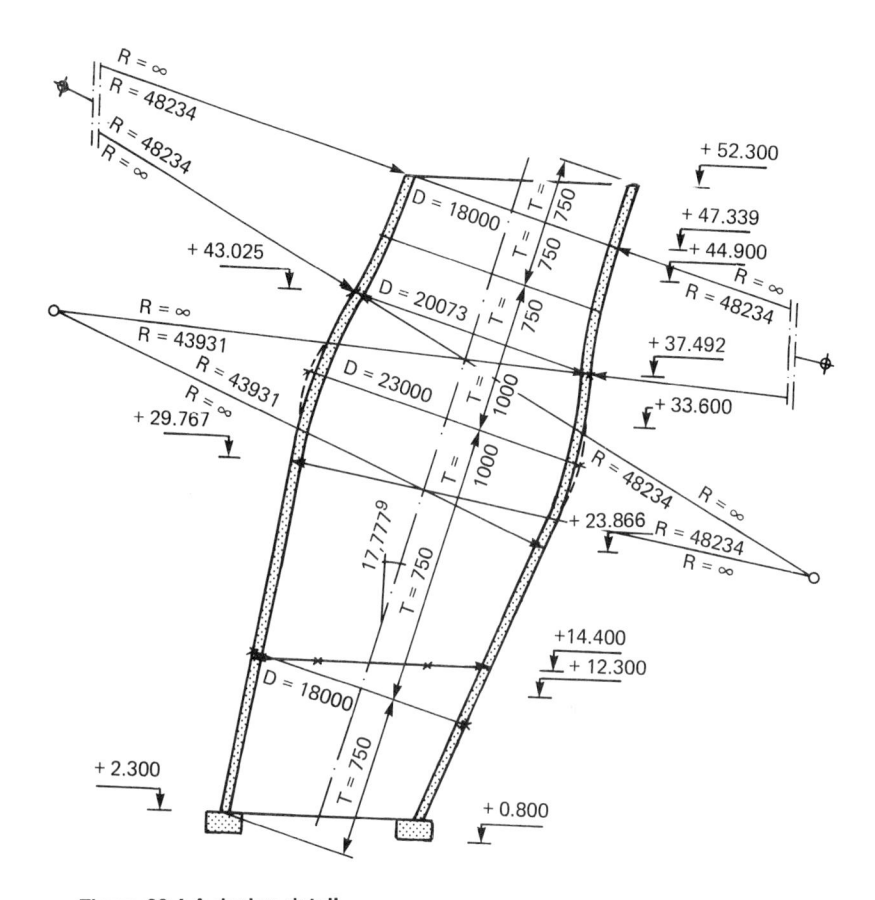

Figure 20.4 A design detail
The complex shape of the test structure (see Figure 20.3) necessitated extensive use of computer programs to define the intended geometry, and to analyse the results. (Data from Norwegian Contractors, Stabekk, Norway.)

ment' project, and then try to make the appropriate allowances for that fact.

This demands a substantial degree of engineering development *before* the decision is taken to proceed. It is quite probable that between 3 and 5 per cent of the total project cost may have been spent before enough data is available to establish meaningful estimates of cost and time, and to set out a detailed project schedule. Whilst such expenditure would be abortive should the decision be taken not to proceed, nevertheless this money should be spent. Most major companies approach their larger projects this way, releasing sufficient funds to allow the project to proceed to the point when the project plan can be firmed up, before finally authorising detailed engineering and construction. Sometimes, long delivery items will be authorised for purchase pending final definition whilst the project in total is not approved and could be aborted. This involves a degree of financial risk, but it could be a risk worth taking, because the project will be completed that much earlier.

Scope changes

Change costs dear and everyone with any experience of project work knows this very well indeed, yet changes will still come. With the best will in the world to freeze the scope of a project and so inhibit change, it never works in practice. So the administrative procedures must take full account of the possibility and legislate for it. There are in essence two different types of change, one coming from a definite change in scope, the other resulting from the detailed development of the project. The important thing is that however the change arises, it must be properly registered and authorised. We strongly recommend that the project procedures incorporate the rule: no change without proper evaluation and formal authorisation. But it is equally important that the project manager ensures that the rule is not only written down but adhered to.

The human condition

Whilst we have had much to say about management techniques and have seen that sound management is at the heart of every successful project – sound *simple* management – we also have had to realise that both the managers and the managed are people: individuals with weaknesses, frailties, ambitions, longings and desires. A new book on making money that has become a cult with US investors contains nuggets of Swiss wisdom that are very relevant in this context.(5) For instance, we have stressed the importance of sound planning, but always in what we might fairly call a short-term context, even although many projects can take five years or more from concept to completion. The distilled wisdom here declares:

> Long-range plans engender the dangerous belief that the future is under control.

A related comment:

> Human behaviour cannot be predicted. Distrust anyone who claims to know the future, however dimly.

These comments incorporate a very important principle which should never be lost sight of. The future is uncertain and, as Robert Burns once remarked: 'the best-laid plans of mice and men gang aft agley'.

Another very human failing is a reluctance to recognise the inevitable. The comment here is:

> When the ship starts to sink, don't pray. Jump.

We have devoted a chapter to demonstrating the desirability of cancelling a project when the situation demands it. One paper, dealing with the way in which cost overruns and completion delays should be tackled has a section headed: 'abandon if necessary'.(6) We are told that when a new project overruns its budget, managers should seek causes before remedies. One is warned against indiscriminate cost cutting and advised rather to recost the entire project. If, following such a review, the project is not viable, then it should be abandoned. The comment is made that the number of bad projects that reach the operational stage serve as proof that their supporters often balk at this decision. There are a number of reasons for what amounts to irrational behaviour when such a crisis occurs and it is a brave project manager indeed who dares to recommend abandonment once a project is well on the way. But it should be done when the situation demands it. Once again, we come up against very human traits: the desire to save a reputation, the fear that one's career will be wrecked. The solution lies in good management, yet once again. The good manager will seek to create an environment that rewards honesty and courage, not punishes it. The good project manager will face up to the decisions he has to make and make them, however unpleasant the results may be.

Ever learning

If there is one theme that has predominated throughout this book it is the vital role played by experience, and experience only comes through learning. This is a subject that has been formalised in many different ways. When we come to construction, particularly repetitive construction such as is to be met in an aircraft factory, one speaks of a 'learning curve'. We have also seen that there can be a learning curve in relation to major construction projects. We consider all the work that has gone on and is still going on in the North Sea, as described in Chapter 17, an outstanding example of that. But even when we look at what we might call 'one off' projects, such as those built in the remote areas of the world, the learning factor is still there. The companies employed on such projects were chosen because they had learnt a great deal over the years and were able to apply their accumulated experience to the project and so achieve success.

But there is another problem. Both companies and projects can suffer if that experience is dissipated, or goes elsewhere and this is something that can happen all too easily. That pipeline project in Nigeria (Chapter 7) was a good example of that. Reactivated after a period, the company that was given the project got the contract because those engineers who had previously worked on the project were still with the company. Thus the relevant experience was

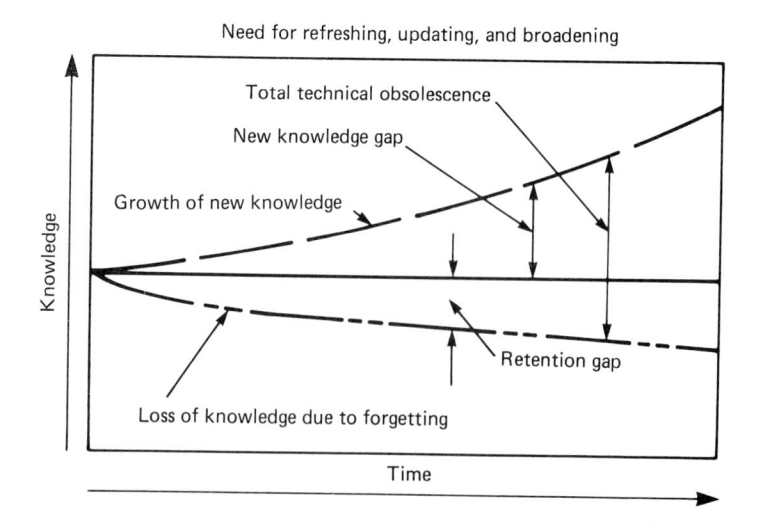

Figure 20.5 A diagram to think about
To quote: 'a diagram for the promotion of continuing education and professional development. I leave you to ponder its meaning.' (Author unknown.)

already available. Those engineers had acquired their knowledge – had learnt – from their previous experience in Nigeria.

But it is also true that we forget things very easily. We once saw a very illuminating diagram over the title 'A picture to think about'. We cannot trace its source, but we believe that it was first developed to encourage continuing education and continuing professional development, an exercise that we have seen the Japanese do much to foster and which we believe has contributed much to their national success. This diagram, which we reproduce as Figure 20.5, could well be called the 'forgetting curve'. The implications of the graph are quite clear, and it carries a great lesson to management. It is still true, despite the evidence to the contrary in the success stories we have been surveying, that a great many projects are approached by owner and contractor alike almost as if they had never built such a project before. Part of this is perhaps due to a law said to have been discovered by students of human behaviour, that the solution of one set of problems only leads to another set. Experience undoubtedly shows this is true: life – and projects – are always one long string of problems. But they can be solved and are solved, one by one.

When considering the implications of 'forgetting', Peter Drucker suggests that there are some things that are better forgotten.(7) We have said much about innovation and emphasised that it is a policy which should be systematically followed for success. Peter Drucker says that there should also be 'systematic abandonment'. Everything we do should get a regular 'live-or-die' scrutiny. This automatically demands innovation, since the gaps left by discontinued procedures or products would have to be filled. This analytical approach would encourage the habits of flexibility and continuous learning, with the result that change would be accepted as normal and providing opportunity. So we reiterate: you are never too old to learn and learning should be a continuing process.

The last point we wish to make in this context is that since 'learning' should be a continuous process, it should – nay, *must* be going on throughout each and every project, whether that project is a success or a disaster. What is more, the several parties to the contract – owner and contractor alike – should not only be learning, but sharing their newly acquired knowledge. We learn most from the mistakes that are made as a project goes forward and this means that those who observe those mistakes should be *constructive* in their criticism, not destructive. If this is true then those who make mistakes will not be so likely to conceal them whenever that is possible. We should not be embarrassed by the mistakes we make or the weaknesses that may be exposed. Far better to see them in full view, so that the reasons for failure may be established. Then we will do better next time. It is still true, as it has always been true, that 'the man who never made a mistake never made anything'. Every good project manager knows this very well indeed − he has made a good many himself!

References

1. Kharbanda, O.P. and Stallworthy, E.A., *Management Disasters and How to Prevent Them*, Gower, Aldershot, 1986, 230pp. (See Chapter 9, 'The anatomy of a coal strike'.)
2. Sinclair, M., 'The economic problems of North Sea projects − a Wagnerian financial opera', *Cost Engineer* (UK), Vol. 19, No.1, 1980, p.22.
3. Kharbanda, O.P. and Stallworthy, E.A., *How to Learn from Project Disasters*, Gower, Aldershot, 1983, 273pp.
4. Article: 'Murchison Field Platform', a 4-page supplement in the *Financial Times*, 17 September 1979.
5. Gunther, M., *The Zurich Axioms*, Souvenir Press Ltd, 1985.
6. David, D.M., 'New projects: beware of false economies', *Harvard Business Review*, March-April 1985, pp.95-101.
7. Wilson, J.W., review of *Innovation and Entrepreneurship*, by Peter F. Drucker, Harper & Row, 1985, in *Business Week*, 10 June 1985, pp.7-8.

Index

Italic numerals refer to figures

Abbott, K.W., 48
Accidents
 frequency rate at Ok Tedi, 200
Advanced Project Management (Harrison F.L. 1981), 18
Ajaokuta steel mill, 90
Alcoa, 155
Aldikacti, Hulki
 and the Fiero, 117
American Motors Corporation
 stake in China, 162
Amey Roadstone Construction Limited
 consortium member, 191
Argenti, J., 4, 18
 The Argenti System, 4
Arkansas Power & Light Company (US), 43
Art of Corporate Success – The Story of Schlumberger (Auletta 1984), 135
Asahan Development Authority, 155-6
Asahan project (Indonesia), 153
Asimov, Isaac
 and robots, 65
Association of Cost Engineers
 Estimating Check List, 213
AT&T
 compared to Schlumberger, 127
Atomic Safety and License Board (The), 109
Auditor
 role of, 43
 the pre-emptive audit, 43
Auletta, K., 135
 and Schlumberger, 126
Aureville, Pondicherry, 141
Avonmouth (UK)
 port of shipment, 193

Babani, A., 65, 70
Back to basics management (Culligan et al 1983), 243

Baker, A.
 Vice-president General Electric (US), 67
Baldwin, P.L., 160
Battelle Institute
 leading research, 63
Batten, R., 213
Bechtel, 13, 52, 101
Bechtel Civil & Minerals Inc.
 consortium member, 197
Bechtel/MKI
 construction consortium, 199
Beijing Jeep Corporation (China), 162
Belbin, R.M., 124, 243
Belle Chasse Training Centre
 used by Schlumberger, 129
Bennett, D., 123, 124, 243
Berger, M.A., 48
Best Company Book (The), STC, 55
Bid analysis form, *80*
Blue Ribbon Medal
 Japanese industrial award, 69
Boeing, 101
BP, Magnus Field Production Platform, *183*
Brazil
 and the Itaipu dam, 222
Brooks, F., 99
Burck, C.G., 124
Burke, James E. (Chairman of Johnson & Johnson)
 and Tylenol, 218
Business of Winning – How to Succeed in Business by Really Trying (Heller 1981), 58
Byrne, J.
 broadcast re Tylenol, 218
Byrne, J.A., 70
Byron Plant
 successfully completed, 107

257

258 INDEX

Cable and Wireless
  and satellite link, 194
Calcutta
  floods, 143
Canada
  example in team building, 242
Canadian Met-Chem Consultants
  (MET-CHEM), 141
Cape Town (South Africa)
  used as ferry terminal, 193
Car industry
  Also see General Motors
  small cars, 113
  the electric car project, 116
  the Fiero, 117
Casey, D., 244
Cerveza
  offshore platform, 203
CF Industries Donaldsonville,
    Louisiana, US
  production records, 153
Channel Tunnel
  project in prospect, 87
Chen Jin-Hua
  China's minister of the petrochemical
    industry, 167
Cherokee
  type of Jeep, 162
Chicago
  and Tylenol, 218
China
  and joint ventures, 161-70
  and the construction industry, 50
  the social scene, 168
China National Technical Corporation
    (CNTIC)
  joint venture companies, 167
China Petro-Chemical International
    Company (SINOPEC), 167
Chongqing (China)
  world's largest city, 162
Cieply, M., 243
Client, *see* Owner
Clifford, C., 94
Collier, D.C.
  energy task force, 113
Collins, D.
  and Tylenol, 219
Colmaco (Australia)
  and aluminium smelting project in
    New Zealand, 155
Combustion Engineering Inc., 94
Commitments
  commitment control, 27-8
*Communicate – Parkinson's formula for
    business survival (Parkinson &
    Rowe 1972)*, 58
Communication
  importance of, 233
Communications
  role of, 56-8
Company failure, 36
Computers
  and IBM, 97
  role in project management, 236
Computing Scale Company of
    America, 97
Concem, purpose built barge, 210
Consensus in Japan, 62
Condeep
  concrete structures for the North
    Sea, 209
Condeep T300
  deepwater platform, 248
Conoco
  learning from experience, 248
Consolidated Edison
  and nuclear power, 107-8
Consortium
  between Japan and Indonesia, 156
  for Mount Pleasant Airport project,
    191
  use in Japan, 63
Construction
  live site working, 178
  management, 50
  use of cranes, 184
*Construction – A Way of Life, a
    Romance (Halmos 1979)*, 135, 228
Construction industry
  Japanese, 49
  Korean, 49
  Mexican, 49
  Turkish, 49
*Construction Management (Kavanagh
    Muller & O'Brien 1978)*, 58
Consultant, definition, 11
Contingency
  Also see Estimating
  use of, 23-4
Contracts
  contractual provisions, 141
  negotiation with Chinese, 165
  choice of, 33
*Control of Investment in New
    Manufacturing Facilities
    (Stallworthy 1973)*, 35
Cook County Medical Examiner (USA)
  and Tylenol, 218
Cook, J., 70, 111
Cooperation
  in project teams, 240
Copper
  fall in price of, 201
Corfield, Sir Kenneth, 55-6
*Corporate Failure (Kharbanda &
    Stallworthy 1985)*, 48, 58, 94
*Corporate Planning – Theory and
    Practice (Hussey 1984)*, 18
Corrie, R.K., 18

INDEX

Cost coding
  a management tool, 25
Cost control
  and planning, 30
  early warning signals, 42
  effective project cost control, 20
  potential, 40
  role of the estimate, 21
  the 'point of no return', 86
Coventry (UK)
  twinned with Jinan (China), 163
CPM, 8
Cranes in construction work, 184
Crawford, M., 94
Critchley, B., 244
Criticism
  role of, 255-6
CTR (Computer-Tabulator-
    Recording), 97
Culligan, M.J., 243

Dairy
  on the permafrost, 190
Davey, Lynda, 227
David, D.M., 256
Davis, D., 85, 94
Davy Ashmore (UK)
  management contractor, 78
Davy McKee, 14
  and fertiliser plant project, 224
Deakins, S., 243
Decision making
  importance of, 195
  need for, 218
Delegation
  principle of, 237
Development factor
  need for assessment, 248
Dingle, J., 50, 58
Dinsmore, P.C., 58
Diversification
  importance of, 131
Dorn, R.
  and the Fiero, 119
Dowell
  acquisition by Schlumberger, 132
Downsizing
  in US car market, 114
Dresser Industries Atlas Oilfield
    Services Group
  competitor to Schlumberger, 130
Drucker, P., 45, 48, 57, 256
  and 'forgetting', 255
Dudinka
  transhipment port, 191
Dutch
  and sea transport, 176

Earl & Wright (US)
  and Nigerian contract, 91

Early warning signals
  see Cost control
East Breaks Field (Gulf of Mexico)
  offshore platforms, 203
East Cove (Falkland Islands), 191
Eates, P.
  GM vice-president, 114
Economic Decision-making for
    Engineers and Managers (Lu
    1969), 58
Edid, M., 124
Eiffel Tower
  possibility of transport, 180
Ekofisk
  waterflood platform project, 182
Electrical Machinery Law (Japan), 63
Electricité de France (EDF)
  and nuclear power, 110
Elf
  partner in Statoil, 208
Energy
  problem in US, 113
Engelberger, J.F., 70
England, motor vessel used as 'ferry',
    193
Entrepose (France)
  awarded pipeline contract, 91
Entrepreneur
  definition, 118
Entrepreneurial spirit
  in project leadership, 194
Environment
  impact of, 187
Escalation
  assessment of, 24-5
Esso
  partner in Statoil, 208
Esso Chemical Canada
  example in team building, 241
Estimating capital cost
  use of contingency, 21
Estimating Check List for Offshore
    Projects
  use of, 207
Expatriate
  role of, 223
  in Saudi Arabia, 225
Expenditure
  relation to value of work done, 28
  use of record, 34
Export-Import Bank of Japan, 156
Exxon
  compared to Schlumberger, 127

Fairchild Camera and Instrument
    Corporation
  acquisition by Schlumberger, 132
  subsidiary of Schlumberger, 128
Falkland Islands, 187
  Mount Pleasant Airport project, 191

Fanuc, 66
FBI, relation to Tylenol recall, 219
Fiero sports car project, 117, 119-20, *121*
Finland
  and trade with Soviet Union, 187
Finn-Stroi Limited
  construction company, 187
Fisher, A.R., 124
Flint, C., 97
Fluor Corporation, 13, 101
  Sasol plants, 72
Fly River and Ok Tedi project, 197
Food & Drug Administration (US)
  reaction to Tylenol recall, 219
Ford Motor Company, 64
Forex Neptune
  subsidiary of Schlumberger, 128
Foulkes, F.K., 70
France
  and nuclear power, 105
Freehlich, L., 70
Frigg Field
  and Norwegian Trench, 208
  special features, 204
Fularji Heavy Machinery Works
  coal gasification facility, 168

Gantt charts, 8
GEC Telecommunications
  contracts in China, 163
  telephone exchanges in China, 166
General Electric, 67
General Motors, 64, 66, 134
  market share, 112
  new car development, 113-24
Government of Indonesia
  see Indonesia
Government of Iran
  see Iran
Government of Papua New Guinea
  and Ok Tedi project, 200
Graphoanalysis
  see Handwriting
Great Plains Coal Gasification Project, 88-9
Gregory, Jenny, 213
Gribben, R., 58
Guess, G.M., 243
  key to success, 233
Gulf of Mexico
  first offshore platforms, 203
Gunther, M., 256

Halmos, E.E., 135, 228
Handwriting
  use for personnel selection, 45
Harris, C.L., 104
Harris, M., 104
Harrison, F.L., 18

Hatch Associates Ltd. (Toronto), 77
Hayes, R.H., 18
Heller, R., 58
Helsinki, 187
  port of shipment, 191
Henty, C.J., 160
Hindustan Steelworks Construction Ltd. (HSCL), 141
Hirsch, J.L., 70
Hitachi Zosen (Innoshima)
  shipyard in Japan, 176
Hollerith Tabulating Machine Co., 97
Honda (Japan)
  example in innovation, 229
How to Learn from Project Disasters (Kharbanda & Stallworthy 1983), 18, 103, 160, 213, 227, 256
Howe (India), 142
HSCL (Hindustan Steelworks Construction Ltd.), 140
Hudson, P.D., 18
Huettentechnik GmbH., 147
Hussey, D.E., 4, 18

IBM
  and competing designs, 121
  and project, 97-103
  compared to Schlumberger, 127
IBM – Colossus in Transition (Sobel 1984), 97, 103
ICL, 56
Ilmenite smelting process, 77
Imeg (London)
  and Nigerian contract, 91
IMI Titanium Limited, (UK), 84
In Search of Excellence, (Peters & Waterman 1982), 58, 103, 124, 135
India
  and the construction industry, 50
  example of team selection, 223
Indian Government
  and Kudremukh project, 139
Indiana Public Service Company
  and nuclear power, 107
Indonesia
  agreement with KIOCL (India), 148
  technology transfer, 150
  use of foreign labour, 150
Indonesian Asahan Aluminium, 156
Industrial Development Corporation (IDC)
  and minerals mining, 75-6
Inflation
  and escalation, 24
Initiative
  need for scope, 232
Innovation
  and Honda, 229
  at Ok Tedi, 198
  displayed in workforce, 195

example of Schlumberger, 129
 in concrete platform design, 248
 Also see Technological innovation
Innovation and Entrepreneurship (Drucker 1985), 256
Institution of Professional Engineers (New Zealand), 50
Integration
 of management structures, 242
Intelsat
 satellite link, 194
International Construction (Stallworthy & Kharbanda 1985), 18, 110, 160, 186, 213
International Time Recording Co., 97
Intrapreneur
 need for independence, 120
Intrapreneuring – Why you don't have to leave a Corporation to become an Entrepreneur (Pinchot 1985), 124
Intrapreneurship
 definition, 118
Investment
 in North Sea oilfields, 203
Iran
 and Kudremukh project, 140
Ireland, E.T., 58
 presidential address, 50
Isaacson Steel Company (Seattle)
 plant for China, 166
Itaipu Dam project, 222

Japan
 and Asahan project, 153
 and Kudremukh project, 140
 and teamwork, 116
 example in team building, 229
 example in team formation, 102
 example of recovery, 61
 productivity, 61
Japan as Number One – Lessons for America (Vogel 1979), 103
Japanese Industrial Robot Association (JIRA), 64
Japanese International Cooperation Agency, 156
John Laing Construction Limited
 consortium member, 191
Johnson & Johnson
 and Tylenol, 218
Johnson, W.G., 70
Joint venture
 for Mount Pleasant Airport project, 192
 in China, 161-170
 making them work, 221

Kacho (team leader or section head in Japan), 102

Kaiser, 155
Karanatka Power Corporation, 141
Kavanagh, T.C., 58
Kawasaki
 and robots, 65
Kellogg
 and Indonesia, 151
 in China, 164-5
 joint ventures in China, 167
Kellogg Sriwidjaja (KELSRI), 151
Khanna, K.C., 141
Kharbanda, O.P., 18, 35, 48, 58, 83, 84, 94, 103, 110, 111, 135, 160, 186, 213, 227, 243, 256
Kibler, B.E., 135
Kiunga, 197
Koren, Y., 70
Kostomuksha
 location, 188
 new town/mining project, 189
Kuantan, East Malaysia
 power station under construction, 177
Kudremukh Iron Ore Co. Ltd. (KIOCL), 141
Kuhn, D.C., 227
Kujang (Indonesia), 151
Kyoto Ceramics (Japan)
 a rapidly growing company, 129

Laing-Mowlem-ARC (LMA),
 consortium for Mount Pleasant Airport project, 192
Lake Toba, 154
Lakhya Dam (The)
 crisis situation, 143
Lambrines, J., 70
Lattin, Clark P. Jr., 171
Lawson, J., 94
Learning
 learning curve, 254
 need for, 254
 the 'forgetting' curve, 254-5
Learning curve
 significance of in construction, 209-10
Lehr, Lew
 a notable intrapreneur, 122
Limber, T.P., 58, 227
Listening
 importance of, 232, 233
Lock, D., 35
Lockheed, 40
Lovins, Amory
 and nuclear power, 105
Lu, F.P.S., 54-8
Luddites
 typical mentality, 67
Lummus Canada
 example in team building, 241
Lummus Crest, 89

Lurgi Chemie, 147
Lynch, B., 48
M.W. Kellogg Company
  see Kellogg
Madras High Court, 144
Magnus Field Production Platform, 183
Mammoet Mail
  house magazine, 186
Mammoet Transport B.V.
  (Amsterdam), 186
  role in transport of heavy loads, 177
Management
  and innovation, 129
  assessing the human factor, 252
  by consensus, 62
  comments of Peter Drucker, 45
  construction management, 50
  developing motivation, 129
  feasibility study, 54
  go back to basics, 235
  importance of, 217-27
  importance of team, 98
  importance of training, 129
  Japan as example, 62
  Japanese, characteristics of, 68
  layered, 45-6
  lessons from Japan, 68
  management information, 239
  management reports, see Reports
  money management, 51
  of projects, 38
  reports, 81
  striving for perfection, 125, 135
  the role of research, 128
  the secret of success, 133
  use of feasibility study, 87
Management Disasters (Kharbanda & Stallworthy 1985), 94, 111, 227, 256
Management Teams – Why They Succeed or Fail (Belbin 1981), 124, 243
Managing Capital Budget Projects (Pomeranz 1984), 48
Managing contractor
  definition, 11
  role, 12
Mangalore
  and Kudremukh project, 142
Marble Hill, Indiana Power Plant
  abandonment, 107
Matthew Hall Engineering Ltd.
  and Magnus Field Production Platform, 183
Matthew Hall PLC
  annual turnover, *14*
  example of success, 15
McDermott Inc. (New Orleans)
  offshore platforms, 203
McDermott International
  their *Derrick Barge 102*, 180
McNeil Consumer Products
  manufacturers of Tylenol, 219
MECON (Metallurgical & Engineering
  Consultants (India) Ltd.), 140
Mehta, D., 57, 58
Merchant Providence
  used as jetty head, 193
Mexico City
  compared to Chonqing (China), 162
Milk products
  in Soviet Union at Norilsk, 191
Miller, W.B., 48
MIM (Management Information
  Meeting, STC), 55
Mining
  gold and copper, 195
  iron ore, 189
  of nickel and copper, 190
Mining Deposits Ltd. (Brisbane), 77
Ministry of International Trade and
  Industry (MITI), 62-3
Mirchandani, H.V., 148
Mistakes
  learning from, 221
Mitsui Engineering and Shipbuilding
  Company Ltd.
  and Derrick Barges, 181
Mitsui, Yoshiki
  President Mitsui High-tec, 69
Mobil Exploration Norway Inc.
  and Statfjord project, 210
Modular transporter
  use on projects, 177
Modules
  use of, 175
Money
  an engineering material, 50
  management of, 51
Montrose
  North Sea oilfield, 203
Moore, S., 213
Moore, T., 227
Morgan Equipment (San Francisco)
  construction equipment company, 184
Morgan, D., 213
Morgan, H.
  founder of Morgan Equipment Co., 186
Morrison-Knudsen International
  consortium member, 197
Motivation
  see Management
Mount Pleasant Airfield
  in service, 193
Mount Pleasant Airport
  project on Falkland Islands, 191
Mowlem International Limited
  consortium member, 191

INDEX

Muller, F., 58
Murchison Project
  developed by Conoco, 248
Murmansk, 191
Murphy, T.P., 227
My years with General Motors (Sloan 1972), 124

Nader, R.
  and nuclear power, 105
NASA
  and the project centre concept, 114
National Coal Development Corporation (China)
  and Morgan Equipment Co., 185
New Mangalore Port, 147
New Mangalore Port Trust, 141
New Zealand
  and aluminium smelting, 155
Nigeria
  pipeline contract, 90
Nigerian Government
  industrial development programme, 90
Nigerian National Petroleum Corporation (NNPC)
  and pipeline, 90
Nippon Asahan Aluminium, 156
Norilsk Dairy Project, 190
Norsk Hydro
  partner in Statoil, 208
North Sea
  and offshore oilfields, 203
  challenge to construction industry, 246
  early projects had overruns, 246
Norway
  its energy situation, 208
Norwegian Contractors
  and Condeep structures, 209
  and Statfjord 'B', 210
  concrete structure design, 248
Norwegian Trench
  problems of, 208
Nuclear energy
  see Nuclear power plants
Nuclear power plants
  financing problems, 109
Nuclear power plants, development, 105-10
Nuclear Regulatory Commission (The), 109

O'Brien, J.J., 58
Oben (Nigeria), 90
Obianyor, D.F., 94
  and Nigerian pipeline contract, 91
Offshore projects
  see Projects
Ohne, M., 70

Ok Tedi – Evolution of a Third World Mining Project (Pintz 1984), 202
Ok Tedi Gold and Copper Project
  outline, 196-8
  scope of, 195
Ok Tedi Mining Ltd.
  consortium of mining interests, 197
Oman
  working in, 223
Overseas Economic Cooperation Fund (The), 156
Owner
  relationship with contractor, 232

P.T. Pupuk Sriwidjaja (PUSRI), 151
Palembang (South Sumatra), 151
Papua New Guinea, 187
  location Ok Tedi project, 197
Paraguay
  and the Itaipu dam, 222
Parana River
  location of Itaipu Dam project, 222
Parkinson, C.N., 58
People's Republic of China
  see China
Performance Analysis Services Ltd, 48
Pernis refinery
  project involving specialised transport, 178
Personnel
  selection of, 45
PERT, 8
Pertamina (Indonesia)
  cooperation with TOTAL, 151
Peters, T.H., 135
Peters, T.J., 58, 103, 122, 124, 128
Peterson, A., 202
Petrofina
  and handwriting tests, 46
Phillips
  contract with McDermott, 182
Pinchot, Gifford III, 122, 124
Pintz, Dr. W.S., 202
  author of *Ok Tedi*, 195
  views on Ok Tedi project, 200
Pisa
  leaning tower of, 248
Planning, 3
  advance planning, 140
  and cost control, 30
  assessment of resources, 17
  constraints, 16
  crucial to success, 249
  role of pre-emptive audit, 44
Plumb, D., 243
Plumb, R., 213
Pomeranz, F., 48
Pontiac (a GM division)
  and the Fiero, 117

Port Moresby
  entry port, Ok Tedi project, 197
Potter, R., 70
Power Gas, *See* Davy McKee
Practical Corporate Planning, (Argenti 1980), 18
Pre-resourcing (partnership with key vendors)
  importance of, 120
Prediction
  of company failure, 36-7
Pre-emptive audit, 44-6
Prefabrication
  use of, 191
Prevention
  keeping within time and cost, 245-56
Prince Andrew (His Royal Highness)
  opens airport on Falkland Islands, 191
Productivity
  in Japan, 61
Project centre concept
  see Projects
Project cost control
  at Richards Bay Minerals, 79
Project Cost Control in Action (Kharbanda, Stallworthy & Williams 1980), 35, 48, 84
Project management
  Also see Management
  and cost control, 93
  and North Sea projects, 204
  assessing development factor, 248
  at Consolidated Edison, 108
  coping with crisis, 217
  decision making, 218
  keep it simple, 235
  principle of delegation, 237
  public relations, 110
  role of computer, 236
  role of experience, 226
  role of project manager, 39
  team selection, 223
  the job description, 238
  the language problem, 226
Project Management Handbook (Lock (ed.) 1986), 35
Project manager
  and overseas projects, 231
  as team builder, 230
  as team leader, 236
  cooperative management, 231
Project planning
  for Kudremukh project, 139
  Kostomuksha project, 190
Project specification
  role of, 239
Project team
  and the Fiero, 118
  appropriate size, 102
  cooperation between teams, 241
  essential qualities, 239
  example of Japan, 102, 229
  in 3M, 103
  need for cooperation, 240
  organisation, 233
  role of, 229-43
  role of members, 236
Projects
  administrative procedures, 26
  and project management, 38-9
  cancellation, 86
  control of commitments, 27
  cost coding, 25
  cost control, 30
  cost overruns, reasons for, 32
  development phases, *47*
  execution in North Sea, 208
  financing, 89
  form of contract, 33
  government intervention, 89
  importance of transport, 175
  in the North Sea, 205-6
  Kostomuksha project in Soviet Union, 189
  need to cancel when appropriate, 253
  Norilsk dairy project, 190
  offshore, 203-13
  organisation, 233
  phases, 5-6
  project cost control, 20
  project definition, 4
  project organisation, 11
  role of feasibility study, 87
  significance of environment, 187
  the Asahan project, 153
  the Chevette Project Centre, 114
  the cultural gap, 223
  the downsizing project, 115
  the Fiero project, 117
  the Kudremukh iron ore project, 139-48
  the project centre concept, 114
  the project plan, 8-9
  the project team, its strength, 116
  the project team concept in IBM, 101
  the Statfjord gas gathering project, 208
  value of work done, 28
Promoter
  definition, 11
  Also see Owner
Property Services Agency (PSA)
  Department of Environment office, 191
Public relations
  need for openness, 219
Pullman Kellogg
  see Kellogg

INDEX 265

Qatar
 location of fertiliser plant project, 225
Quality
 control of, 52
Quebec Iron and Titanium Corporation, 76, 77
 its smelting technology, 75

Railways Construction Agency, 143
Reed. D., 70
Reeve, Ron, 70
Reports
 need for, 239
 reporting levels, 240
Rheingold, E.M., 170
Riboud, J.
 as chief executive, 126-9
Richard Bay Minerals Project
 typical joint venture, 221
Richards Bay Iron and Titanium, 76
Richards Bay Minerals
 and mining, 75
Richmond Refinery (Chevron),
 construction by Bechtel, 184
Robot Institute of America (The), 63
Robotics, *see* Robots
Robotics for Engineers (Koren 1985), 70
Robotics in Practice (Engelberger 1980), 70
Robots
 definition of, 63
 development of, 63-6
 numbers worldwide, 65
 types of, 64
Rogers, J., 84
Rolls Royce, 40
Romanian government
 and Kudremukh ore, 147
Rowe, N., 58

Saga
 partner in Statoil, 208
SAIL (Steel Authority of India Ltd.), 140
Santana
 VW car for Chinese market, 162
Sasol
 synfuels plants, 72
Saturn
 new car project at GM, 122
Scheuerle (West Germany)
 constructor of hydraulic platform trailers, 177
Schlumberger, 55
 company profile, 126
 growth, 131
 management policy, 128
 the brothers Conrad and Marcel, 127

Schlumberger Adventure (Schlumberger 1984), 135
Schlumberger, A.G., 135
Schumacher, E.F., 112, 124
Scope changes, 23
 importance of, 252
Sedco
 acquisition by Schlumberger, 132
Seo, Keijiro, 160
Shanghai Automobile and Tractor Industry Corporation (SATIC), 162
Shanghai Communique
 negotiated by Nixon, 163
Shanghai Steel Structure Factory
 new steel plant, 166
Sharjah
 working in, 223
Shaw, G., 149
Sheets, K.R., 94
Shell
 and Brent 'B' field, 209
 partner in Statoil, 208
 report on North Sea projects, 205
Shell Nederland Raffinaderij
 Pernis refinery, 178
Shenkar, O., 70
Sichuan
 Chinese province, 166
Sichuan Telecommunications Exchange Equipment Factory
 joint venture, 166
Silgarde, M.B.
 and Kudremukh project, 140
Simplicimus, J., 83
Sinclair, M., 256
Sloan, A.P. Jr., 124, 134
 on General Motors, 115
Small is Beautiful (Schumacher 1973), 124
Smith, R.
 chairman, General Motors, 66
Sobel, R., 103
Soeharto (President of Indonesia), 153
Soehoed, A.R.
 leader Indonesian team, 155
Somare, Michael
 Prime Minister, Papua New Guinea, 201
Sono, Ayako, 70
South Africa
 and synfuel plants, 88
South African Coal, Oil and Gas Company
 see Sasol
South Korea
 example in efficiency, 225
Soviet Union
 and trade with Finland, 187
Spafford, R., 202

266 INDEX

Staats, E.B., 48
Staats, Elmer
 former Comptroller General of the United States, 43
Stallworthy, E.A., 18, 35, 48, 58, 83, 84, 94, 103, 110, 111, 135, 160, 186, 213, 227, 243, 256
Standard Telephones and Cables (STC), 55
Stanley (Falkland Islands), 191
Statfjord field
 its concrete platforms, 209
Statoil (Norway)
 partner in Statoil, 208
Statpipe Project
 and pipelaying at depth, 204
 partners, 208
Stavanger
 Leaning Tower of, 248, 250
Strategic planning
 see Corporate planning
Success
 how to ensure, 246
 the road to, 54-5
Successful Team Building through TA (Bennett 1975), 243
Sumitomo Chemical
 and project in New Zealand, 155
Surbiton (suburb of London)
 location of project office, 193
Switzerland
 Swiss wisdom, 253
Synfuels
 manufacture at Sasol, 72
Synthetic Fuels Corporation, 88
Synthol Process, 88
System 360
 developed by IBM, 99-103

Team members, see Personnel
Teamwork
 role of, 45
Technological innovation
 on North Sea projects, 205
Technology
 continuing development for North Sea projects, 207
 proper use of, 246
 transfer, 75, 150, 152
 and the Itaipu Dam project, 222
Telephones
 potential in China, 163
Tennessee Valley Authority (TVA)
 and nuclear power, 106
Thomas, K., 171
Thomas, K.O., 18
Titanium manufacture, 75
Total
 partner in Statoil, 208
 refinery at Flushing, 177

Total Indonesie, 151
Total Oil Marine
 their MCP-01 platform, 204
Total Project Management, (Stallworthy & Kharbanda 1983), 48 58, 83, 135, 243
Trade with China, 164
Training
 importance of, 129
Transport
 importance to project, 175-80
 modular transporter, 177
 types of vessel available, 176
Tylenol
 coping with the problem, 219
 manufactured by Johnson & Johnson, 218

Unimation, and robots, 64
Union Corporation Limited
 engineering services, 74
 role in joint venture, 221
United States
 and nuclear power, 105
 cooperation with China, 163
University of California
 project gives example in team building, 242
University of Canterbury (New Zealand), 54
Upper Zakum
 world's biggest pipeline project, 208

Value of work done
 assessment of, 28-30
Van Gend & Loos, transportation company, 180
Vendors
 and pre-resourcing, 120
Vitner, G., 70
Vogel, E., 103
Volkswagen
 cooperation in China, 162

Washington Public Power Supply System
 and nuclear power, 107
Waterman, H. Jr.,, 135
Waterman, R.H., 58, 103, 122, 124, 128
Watson, T., 97
Watson, Thomas Jr., 99
Wax, A.J., 243
Weiss, A., 70
West Germany
 cooperation with China, 162
Western Electric (US), 68
Wijsmuller (towing company), 210
Williams, L.F., 35, 48, 84
Willis, W.F., 110
Wilson, J.W., 256

Wimpey
  projects worldwide, 183
Wireline logging technique
  and Schlumberger, 127

Yamazaki Machinery Works
  and robots, 66
Yang Taifang

Posts and Telephones minister
  (China), 163
Yoshioka, H., 70
Young, A.H., 243
Yrkesfjorden
  and Statfjord 'C' platform, 209

Zurich Axioms (Gunther 1985), 256